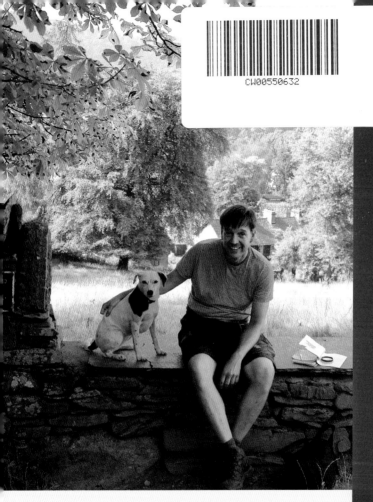

Born in Chatham, Kent, **HENRY STEDMAN** has been writing guidebooks for almost 20 years now and is the author or co-author of over half a dozen Trailblazer titles including *Kilimanjaro*, *Hadrian's Wall Path*, *Coast to Coast Path* and all three books in the *South-West Coast Path* series. When not travelling or writing, Henry lives in Battle, maintaining his Kilimanjaro website and arranging climbs on the mountain through his company, Climb Mount Kilimanjaro.

DAISY is Henry's dog, though any assumption that ownership equates with control can be dismissed in this instance. An experienced walker, Daisy has already completed the Hadrian's Wall Path, Coast to Coast, Offa's Dyke and the entire South-West Coast Path with Henry. In fact, given the amount of running around she does, for every ten miles that Henry completes, Daisy does about thirty. Daisy's ambition is to walk all 15 National Trails. Her owner hasn't the heart to tell her that the Dales Way (like the Coast to Coast Path) is not actually a National Trail.

Author

Dales Way
First edition: **2016**

Publisher Trailblazer Publications
The Old Manse, Tower Rd, Hindhead, Surrey, GU26 6SU, UK
info@trailblazer-guides.com, www.trailblazer-guides.com

British Library Cataloguing in Publication Data
A catalogue record for this book is available from the British Library

ISBN 978-1-905864-78-2

© **Trailblazer** 2016: Text and maps

Series Editor: Anna Jacomb-Hood
Editor: Clare Weldon
Layout: Anna Jacomb-Hood
Cartography: Nick Hill **Proof-reading**: Jane Thomas **Illustrations**: © Nick Hill (p68)
Photographs (flora): C1 top right © Henry Stedman; all other flora © Bryn Thomas
All other photographs: © Henry Stedman unless otherwise indicated
Index: Anna Jacomb-Hood

The maps in this guide were prepared from out-of-Crown-
copyright Ordnance Survey maps amended and updated by Trailblazer.

Acknowledgements

Thanks to Joel for all the driving, conversation – and modelling duties! Thanks also to the
people I met along the trail for tips and advice but in particular, Pete Rafferty, landlord at
the Globe Inn in Kendal, for the help he extended to two knackered trekkers and their dog
when they turned up at his pub one night bedraggled, homeless and hungry. He made sure
that by the time we left his premises we'd both been comfortably housed and well fed.

At Trailblazer, thanks to Clare Weldon for editing, Nick Hill for cartography, Anna
Jacomb-Hood for layout and the index and Jane Thomas for proof-reading.

A request

The author and publisher have tried to ensure that this guide is as accurate and up to date
as possible. Nevertheless, things change. If you notice any changes or omissions, please
write to Trailblazer (address above) or email us at 🖳 info@trailblazer-guides.com. A free
copy of the next edition will be sent to persons making a significant contribution.

Warning: hill walking can be dangerous

Please read the notes on when to go (pp13-15) and safety (pp55-8). Every effort has been
made by the author and publisher to ensure that the information contained herein is as accurate and up to date as possible. However, they are unable to accept responsibility for any
inconvenience, loss or injury sustained by anyone as a result of the advice and information
given in this guide.

PHOTOS – Front cover and **this page**: The path winds past the ruins of Bolton Abbey
and the Priory Church.
Previous page: The bench that acts as the finishing line for the Dales Way.
Overleaf: The viaduct at Ribblesdale, still conveying trains across the valley.

Updated information will be available on: 🖳 **www.trailblazer-guides.com**

Printed in China; print production by D'Print (☎ +65-6581 3832), Singapore

Dales Way

38 large-scale maps & guides to 23 towns and villages
PLANNING – PLACES TO STAY – PLACES TO EAT
ILKLEY TO BOWNESS-ON-WINDERMERE

HENRY STEDMAN

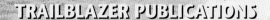

TRAILBLAZER PUBLICATIONS

INTRODUCTION

Dales Way

PART 1: PLANNING YOUR WALK

Practical information for the walker

Budgeting

Itineraries

What to take

Getting to and from the Dales Way

PART 2: MINIMUM IMPACT & OUTDOOR SAFETY

Minimum-impact walking

Outdoor safety

PART 3: THE ENVIRONMENT & NATURE

Conserving the Dales Way

Flora and fauna

Contents

Contents

ABOUT THIS BOOK

This guidebook contains all the information you need. The hard work has been done for you so you can plan your trip from home without the usual pile of books, maps and guides.

When you're all packed and ready to go, there's comprehensive public transport information to get you to and from the trail and 39 detailed maps (1:20,000) together with 6 town and village plans to help you find your way along it.

The guide includes:

● All standards of accommodation with reviews of campsites, bunk-houses, hostels, B&Bs, guesthouses and hotels
● Walking companies if you want an organised or self-guided tour and baggage-carrying services if you just want your luggage carried
● Itineraries for all levels of walkers
● Answers to all your questions: when to go, degree of difficulty, what to pack, and the approximate cost of the whole walking holiday
● Walking times in both directions
● Cafés, pubs, tearooms, takeaways, restaurants and shops for buying supplies
● Rail, bus and taxi information for all villages and towns along the path
● Street plans of Ilkley, Grassington, Kettlewell, Sedbergh, Kendal, and Bowness-on-Windermere
● Historical, cultural and geographical background information
● GPS waypoints

❏ **MINIMUM IMPACT FOR MAXIMUM INSIGHT**

We do not inherit the earth from our ancestors: we borrow it from our children. **Native American proverb**

By their very nature, walkers tend to be both interested in and concerned about the natural environment. This book seeks to reinforce that interest and concern. There are sections devoted to minimum-impact walking and conservation, with ideas on how to broaden that ethos, as well as a detailed, illustrated chapter on wildlife.

There can be few activities as 'environmentally friendly' as walking. By developing a deeper ecological awareness through a better understanding of nature, and by supporting rural economies, sensitive forms of transport and low-impact methods of farming and land use, we can all do our bit to ensure that the environment remains in safe hands for generations to come.

(Opposite): Braving the stepping stones across the Wharfe to Bolton Abbey. There is a much easier footbridge you can take nearby!

INTRODUCTION

The Dales Way stretches for approximately 81 miles (130km) between the towns of Ilkley, at the southern end of the Yorkshire Dales National Park, and Bowness-on-Windermere, the most popular tourist destination in the Lake District National Park.

The walk is often described as one of the easiest of the long-distance paths in Britain, and it's

The Dales Way is often described as one of the easiest of the long-distance path in Britain ... but it's not entirely without gradients

true that most of the first half of the trail is largely level as it follows the meandering River Wharfe. The Dales Way is not entirely without gradients, of course, and there are steep sections, particularly as the path approaches the source of the Wharfe and the watershed, and

The old bridge at Ilkley marks the beginning of the Dales Way.

again on the approach to the Lakes. It's likely that you'll also have to complete a couple of long days on the trail, too, as the path passes through countryside where facilities and accommodation are scarce. Nevertheless, the fact remains that the Dales Way is one of the UK's shortest and most straightforward long-distance trails. Finding and sticking to the trail is also particularly easy, thanks to the wealth of signposts along the way and the superb maintenance of the trail itself.

No surprise, then, that we consider this to be a path that can be tackled by everyone, regardless of their age: I've seen babies conveyed along the trail in prams and on the backs of their parents, while the most fashionable hair colour on the Dales Way amongst both sexes is what can most kindly be described as a distinguished silvery-grey. And it is a great trail for those who've never

Though it's only just over 80 miles in length, the Dales Way manages to pack an awful lot of interest into its relatively short span

attempted a long-distance path before and want to dip their toes in the water and see whether hiking is for them, before moving on to tackle some of the more challeng-

ing long-distance trails such as the Coast to Coast Path, or the Pennine Way.

But the delights of this trail aren't confined to novices. For though it may be only just over 80 miles in length, the Dales Way manages to pack an awful lot of interest into its relatively short span. The charming, lively Victorian spa town of Ilkley; the old cotton mill centre of Addingham and the mining town of Kettlewell; the majestic ruins of Bolton Abbey and the busy tourist hub at

The end. A rare scene of tranquillity in busy Bowness-on-Windermere, the most popular destination in the Lake District.

Grassington; and the picture-perfect settlements at Appletreewick, Burnsall, Grassington, Kettlewell, Starbotton, Hebden and Buckden – all are encountered on or just off the trail, and all before you've even completed the first half of the walk too! The Wharfe itself is splendid too. Where it's placid and becalmed, anglers wade in to fish for trout and weary hikers sit, paddle in the shallows and cool their overheated feet, while kingfishers and dippers flit across the surface. But in certain places the Wharfe is frothing and furious, most famously at the raging Strid, the final resting place of more than one foolhardy traveller down the centuries.

Nor does the scenery lose any of its grandeur as you wave farewell to the Wharfe in favour of neighbouring Dentdale. Here the delights of the natural landscape are supplemented by several magnificent viaducts and bridges, built during the railway boom of the 19th century, which you pass by, alongside and under on your way to the smooth-

There are **link routes** to Ilkley so you can join the Dales Way from Harrogate, Bradford or Leeds – see pp69-74. The Harrogate link route takes you past Swinsty Reservoir (above).

topped Howgills, a delightfully hilly corner of the Yorkshire Dales. And then at the end of the trail (and having passed under a couple more breathtaking viaducts), you are rewarded for all your efforts over the previous days with magnificent views of some of England's mightiest peaks as you move into the Lake District – and your second national park on the trail.

I could spend pages eulogising about the beauty and diversity of this path. But as anyone who's walked a long-distance trail before knows, the things you see on the way are only part of the enjoyment. For walking is just as much about the people you meet and the food you eat, the things you stop to do and the things that happen to you along the way. It is of such things that memories are made.

❏ **Just how long is the Dales Way?**
One would have thought, for such an easy-to-follow and well signposted trail, that there wouldn't be much dispute about the total length of the trail. But you'd be wrong because, for some reason, none of the authorities seems to be able to agree on the exact distance the Dales Way walker covers. The sign at the start says 82 miles, though the official website states that the distance from Ilkley to Bowness-on-Windermere is *about* 80 miles. Another guidebook records the distance as 78 miles, as does The Long Distance Walkers Association. The two baggage-carrying companies operating on the Dales Way, Sherpa and Brigantes, state that it's 82 miles and 'about 80 miles' respectively, while Wikipedia says it's 84 miles.

For the record, my measurements (taken from my trusty GPS) measured the Dales Way to be 81 miles, or 81¾ miles if taking the Alternative (High Level) Route (see p126), which is neatly exactly halfway between the two most extreme estimates given above. But while my figure may indeed be a decent estimate of the length of the trail itself, I am not saying that this is the total number of miles you will cover on your trip, for it does not account for all that walking to the pub or B&Bs off the track, going the wrong way and even, as some Pythagorians like to consider, the fact that walking up and down hills technically covers more ground than if the terrain was flat!

INTRODUCTION

❑ Yorkshire Dales National Park and Nidderdale AONB

The term 'Dale' is an old Norse word meaning 'valley'. The Dales are a series of valleys in Northern England, mainly in the county of Yorkshire, that have been enlarged and shaped by glaciers, mainly in the most recent Ice Age around 100,000 years ago. The **Yorkshire Dales National Park** encompasses most of the major dales – Swaledale, Wensleydale, Wharfedale and others – with umpteen other smaller dales, including Dentdale and Lunedale that feature on the Dales Way, that run like filigree between them. Established in 1954 to protect the Dales' unique landscape and environment, it covers a total area of 680 square miles (1769 sq km) but will be enlarged in 2016 (see p50). The park lies on both sides of the Pennines and spills over the Cumbrian border to encompass the Howgills, the little-known region of smooth-topped hills on the western side of the Dales.

The original boundaries of the park pretty much described the limits of the **Askrigg Block**, an enormous slab of granite deep underground. Down the millennia on top of this slab of granite has been laid carboniferous limestone which gives rise to the unique topography, the terraces and pavements, that are such a distinctive characteristic of the area. On the Dales Way you actually walk over the **Dent Fault System** (see p140), which in essence means you are stepping off the Askrigg Block; in doing so you then enter the Howgills, now also part of the national park, whose geology is defined by the Ordovician and Silurian slates and gritstones, which were laid down about 100 million years before the Dales' limestone.

But the national park is not just about the geology and nature, as splendid as it is. Farmers have worked and shaped this terrain for many, many centuries and the landscape is now predominantly a man-made one. The Yorkshire Dales are also home to the **Victoria Caves** where evidence has been found of the hippo, rhino, hyena and mammoth which would have lived here around 130,000 years ago. More recently, following the last Ice Age the cave was used for hibernating by brown bear and amongst the bones was an 11,000-year-old harpoon point – the first evidence of human habitation in the Dales.

On the eastern side of the Dales the park boundary abuts **Nidderdale AONB** (Area of Outstanding Natural Beauty), which is often included as part of the actual national park but it is in fact separate to it. Subtract Nidderdale from your map of the Dales National Park and you'll see that the Dales Way bisects the park from south-east to north-west. Thus, apart from Swaledale, the most northerly dale, the Dales Way does a very good job of providing walkers with the opportunity of seeing as much of the park as possible. And if you take the Harrogate Link Route, described on pp72-3, then you cross right through Nidderdale, too.

Most of the Dales area is given over to fields of livestock and pasture, each separated from the next by **drystone walls**; indeed, so ubiquitous are these that there are estimated to be 12,000-15,000 miles of stone walls in the Yorkshire Dales National Park alone, with every metre of wall built from about one metric tonne of stone.

History

Managing to construct such a lovely and relatively level trail through some of England's bumpiest landscapes takes a certain sort of genius, and the person in possession of that genius was **Colin Speakman**, who together with his friend Tom Wilcock and Colin's wife Fleur developed the trail, beginning back in the late '60s. The actual trail has been changed and improved several times down the years as access to new land and routes has become available; though these days the alterations are far less frequent, and far less dramatic too as the path become more established and recognised. And with the change to the national park boundaries in 2016 (see p50), who knows, it may change again so that people walking the Dales Way need never leave a national park throughout the walk's entire length!

Coming down from Cam Fell to Ribblesdale and its impressive viaduct.

Though Tom is sadly no longer with us, Colin Speakman continues to play an active part in the life of the trail and is the chair of the **Dales Way Association**, whose website (💻 www.dales way.org) is the best place to get updates on the state of the trail and any temporary diversions that have been put in place.

How difficult is the Dales Way?

In all honesty, it's not. Sure, there are a few steepish ascents that will have you blowing hard, and your knees might complain during some of the longer descents too. But overall the

Overall the Dales Way is short, fairly level and well signposted

INTRODUCTION

The bouncy suspension bridge near Hebden –
hold on!

Dales Way is short, fairly level, well signposted, with plenty of towns and villages en route should you need to buy provisions or seek help. With civilisation never far away your chances of losing your way, or suffering from hypothermia or heatstroke are slender; indeed, the biggest danger along the whole path is being squashed by a car on the busy B6255 before Bolton Abbey. Nevertheless, it would be foolish to take the Dales Way too lightly. Like any long-distance trail, it deserves respect.

Most importantly, perhaps, you should read up about each stage of the trail beforehand and prepare properly for it, for there are a couple of stages where shops, cafés and accommodation are pretty much non-existent, so you need to plan your day sensibly, maybe by preparing a packed lunch before you set off and taking plenty of water.

You should also read the section on trail safety (pp55-8).

How long do you need?

Most people take about a week to complete the Dales Way. It can be done much more quickly and if you feel the need, by all means do it in four days or fewer. Just don't bore me in the pub with tales of your exploits. If, on the other hand, you prefer to take 6-8 days or more on the trail, taking the time to drink in the magnificent scenery, while pausing here and there to smell the flowers or gaze at otters frolicking in a stream, then I believe you're walking the Dales Way as it's meant to be walked. And in this case you can bore me in the pub all you want about the marvels that you've seen. Because I love otters. Especially ones that frolic.

Most people take about a week to complete the Dales Way

Time for tea at Burnsall, a perfect stop on a sunny day. There's no shortage of pubs and tea rooms along the Way.

❏ **Flood damage to the Dales Way**
Parts of the Way were damaged by recent winter storms. Most sections have now been repaired but you should check the **Dales Way website** (🖥 www.dalesway.org) for the latest information about the diversions around River Mint footbridge and Sprint Mill footbridge near Burneside which were still in place in mid 2016.

When to go

SEASONS

Britain is a notoriously wet country and the Yorkshire Dales and Lake District are two of the wettest parts of it. With the Dales Way taking less than a week, it is possible to walk the entire route without experiencing even a drop of rain. But you'd be lucky. That said, with 150 wet days per annum in the Yorkshire Dales, you'd be even unluckier to have wet weather every day of your trek.

The main trekking season in the Dales runs from Easter to when the clocks change at the end of October. You can walk outside of this season, of course, but the shorter days, the lack of fellow trekkers and inclement weather mean that it's a trickier undertaking – and if there's snow about it's also considerably more dangerous. Furthermore, you may also find that many of the B&Bs and other amenities may be closed for the season, particularly in rural areas.

Spring

A beautiful spring day is one of the true, unfettered joys of living in Britain. With birds singing, flowers budding and lambs gambolling, it's just wonderful. However, spring also happens to be one of the wettest times of year, so be prepared for the worst and bring your rain gear; this will improve your chances of not being rained upon no end. Aside from Easter, you should find the trail to be very quiet – allowing you to enjoy the delights of the season undisturbed.

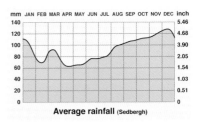

Average rainfall (Sedbergh)

Summer

The main disadvantage with summer is that it can get a little too busy in the Dales and the Lake District. But arrive outside of the main school summer holidays and

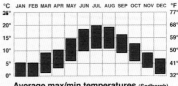

Average max/min temperatures (Sedbergh)

❏ FESTIVALS AND ANNUAL EVENTS

January to March

● **Kendal Food Festival** (🖥 www.kendalfestivaloffood.co.uk) takes place over two days in mid March. At its heart is the North Country Food and Drink Market, held right in the town centre, though surrounding it are cookery demonstrations, talks and tastings.

April to June

● **Dentdale Music & Beer Festival** (🖥 www.dentmusicandbeer.com) A 3-day free festival held in mid to late June – one of the most picturesque places to get hammered to the strains of street musicians. Originally founded in response to the foot-and-mouth crisis in the early 2000s, all profits are still ploughed back into community projects, such as the primary school or the restoration of Dent's church bells.

● **Sedbergh Music Festival** (🖥 www.sedbergh.org.uk/musicfestival) A biennial music festival, due to be held next over a fortnight in June 2018.

● **Grassington Festival** (🖥 www.grassington-festival.org.uk) Started in 1981 and taking place every year over 15 days in late June and early July, Grassington plays host to some fine live music, dance, theatre, comedy, film, visual art displays, masterclasses, workshops – and much, much more. One of the founders was Colin Speakman (see p11).

July to September

● **Buckden Village Festival** (🖥 www.buckdenvillagefestival.co.uk) brings together Buckden and the surrounding villages over a weekend in July. A fête is the centrepiece of the fun, usually augmented with a parade and other events; all proceeds go towards the village hall and grounds.

● **Bowness-on-Windermere Festival of Fun** (🖥 www.facebook.com/Windermere festival) takes place over the August weekends at The Glebe. A child-oriented festival, events vary from year to year but can include mini-Olympics and a Teddy's Got Talent Show.

● **Sedbergh Sheep Fest** (🖥 www.facebook.com/sedberghsheepfest) occurs over nine days in September every year, with most shop windows adorned with a sheep (not a real one) in fancy dress sitting in the window. Parades, street entertainers, concerts, photo competitions and other fun events abound.

● **Ilkley Summer Festival** (🖥 summerfestival.ilkley.org) Live music every weekend throughout August.

October to December

● **Ilkley Literature Festival** (🖥 www.ilkleyliteraturefestival.org.uk) Annual festival of literature and the arts usually taking place over around 17 days in early October.

● **Kendal Mountain Festival** (🖥 www.mountainfest.co.uk) takes place over a weekend in November every year – a rather odd time, seeing as it bills itself as the UK's foremost festival for 'outdoor enthusiasts'. A very social gathering, the festival includes a film competition and plenty of guest speakers.

● **Grassington Dickensian Festival** (🖥 www.grassington.uk.com/dickensian-festival) The town may have little to do with the revered Victorian novelist – there's no evidence that he ever visited – but that doesn't stop the locals dressing up in their finest 19th-century dress to parade around town for three days in December. Given how pretty the town is at any time of year, it does make for a very photogenic festival. Musicians, dancers and street entertainers all add to the jollity.

it shouldn't be too bad. Other than this, there are no negatives to trekking in summer. The weather is usually better (though bring your waterproofs nevertheless – remember, it does rain for 150 days a year in the Dales, and some of those have to be in summer!), the days are at their longest and all the campsites, cafés and other facilities will be open. Furthermore, if you're in need of company you won't be short of trekking companions on the Dales

Lune Viaduct, now disused, was built in 1860.

Way – which could be useful if you're far from civilisation and need help. Remember to book your accommodation in advance if trekking in this season, particularly if staying in B&Bs.

Autumn

September and early October are lovely times to walk. The relative 'chaos' of the summer months have abated to be replaced by a more tranquil, sedate scene. The shops, B&Bs and pubs should all still be open, as should the campsites, and I find that their owners are more relaxed and friendly, presumably because they've survived and thrived in the main trekking season, and thus can afford to take their foot off the gas and relax a little. The weather is usually pretty settled at this time, though do follow the forecasts closely as there are the occasional storms at this time. By the time mid October rolls around the days are getting rather short and the weather may well be getting wilder – time for most trekkers to hang up their trekking gear for another year.

Winter

Happen upon one of those clear, crisp winter days when the wind is becalmed and the sun is shining and you're in for a treat – and if there's snow on the ground it can feel like you're walking in the middle of a Christmas card. That said, those days can be few and far between. What's more, most of the accommodation outside of the larger towns will be closed and many of the pubs, shops and cafés operate reduced opening hours. It is also, of course, more dangerous to be out on the fells at this time – and given the record of flooding in the region over the past few years, it's not particularly sensible to be walking by the riverside all day – which pretty much rules out all of the Dales Way.

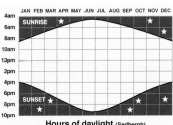

Hours of daylight (Sedbergh)

PLANNING YOUR WALK

1

Practical information for the walker

ROUTE FINDING

The presence of signposts and waymarking is good along the Dales Way and finding the correct trail shouldn't be a problem. Even in the

remotest sections, such as the crossing from Cam Houses into Dentdale (see p121), where landmarks are few and the mist often rolls in, there seems to be little problem in staying on the correct trail, with the path fairly clearly scored into the ground and signposts frequent. Sure, there may be occasions on the trail when you have to pause, scratch your head and study the maps in this book closely – you may even initially choose the wrong path – but it usually becomes obvious pretty quickly that you've made a mistake and need to head back to rejoin the correct trail.

As well as looking out for signposts, do try to keep at least one eye on the maps in the Route Guide section of this book to make sure you're not unwittingly straying too far off course – though don't spend all your time with your head buried in this book, or you'll be losing sight of why you came here in the first place.

GPS

GPS technology is an inexpensive, well-established if non-essential, navigational aid. Within a minute of being turned on and with a clear view of the sky, **GPS receivers** will establish your position and elevation anywhere on earth to an accuracy of within a few metres. Most **smartphones** also have a GPS receiver built in and mapping software available to run on it (see box p39).

Don't treat a GPS as a replacement for maps, a compass and common sense. Every electronic device is susceptible to battery failure or some electronic malfunction that might leave you in the dark. GPS should be used merely as a backup to more traditional route-finding techniques and is best used in conjunction with a paper map.

(Opposite): Admiring the view from near Scot Gate Lane above Consitone.

Using GPS with this book – waypoints

Though a GPS system is not essential on the Dales Way, for those who have one I have provided GPS waypoints for the route. **Waypoints** are single points like cairns. This book identifies key waypoints on the route maps. The book's waypoints correlate to the list on p101 which gives the grid reference and a description. You can download the complete list as a GPS-readable .gpx file of grid references (but with no descriptions) from 🖳 www.trailblazer-guides.com. It's anticipated that you won't tramp along day after day, ticking off the book's waypoints, transfixed by the screen on your GPS or smartphone; the route description and maps should be more than adequate most of the time.

It's worth repeating that 98% of people who've ever walked the Dales Way did so without GPS so there's no need to rush out and buy one – or a new GPS-enabled smartphone for that matter. Your spending priorities ought to be on good waterproofs and above all, footwear. However, correctly using this book's GPS data could get you back on track and dozing in front of the pub fireplace all the sooner.

ACCOMMODATION

The route guide (Part 5) lists a fairly comprehensive selection of places to stay along the trail. The two main options are: camping, staying in hostels/bunkhouses, or using B&Bs/pubs/hotels. Few people stick to just one of these the whole way, preferring, for example, to camp most of the time, stay in a hostel where possible but splash out on a B&B or hotel every once in a while.

The table on p32 provides a snapshot of what type of accommodation and services are available in each of the towns and villages, while the tables in the box on p31 provide some suggested itineraries. The following is a brief introduction as to what to expect from each type of accommodation.

Camping

Campers are fairly well served on the Dales Way and it's possible to devise an itinerary that allows you to camp every night that you're on the trail. There are a couple of big advantages with camping. It's more economical for a start, with most campsites charging somewhere between £4 and £8. Secondly, and best of all, there's **rarely any need to book**, except possibly in the very high season, and even then you'd be highly unlucky not to find somewhere. This, of course, gives you greater flexibility, allowing you to alter your itinerary at the last moment – something that's far more complicated, if not impossible, to do if you're staying in B&Bs.

The campsites vary and you get what you pay for: some are just a farmer's spare field with a toilet and a tap; others are full-blown caravan sites with sparkling ablutions blocks, laundry facilities, wi-fi, shops, coffee shops and fire pit hire. Showers are usually available, occasionally for a fee, though more often than not for free.

Note that some of the bigger towns along the way – including Ilkley, Grassington and Sedbergh – do not have recognised campsites within two miles of them. Note, too, that there are a couple of big sections, from Buckden to Dent and Sedbergh to Burneside, where there are no shops, so if you're planning on cooking your own food while camping you'll need to plan accordingly and carry your food with you.

Wild camping (ie camping not in a regular campsite; see p53) is also possible along the route but please don't do so in a field without first gaining permission from the landowner.

Remember that camping, be it wild or 'tame', is not an easy option, especially for a solo walker. Walked continuously, the route is wearying enough without carrying

the means to sleep and cook with you. Should you decide to camp at campsites, consider employing one of the baggage-carrying companies mentioned on p27, though this does mean the loss of spontaneity which is the whole point of camping – and, of course, they can't deliver to any wild camping locations!

Bunkhouses/bunk barns

Bunkhouses/bunk barns are agreeable places with fluffed-up bedding, bathrooms you'd be happy to show to your parents and even kitchen and lounge areas. The description 'bunkhouse' is often used in place of 'small hostel' or 'independent hostel' to distinguish a private enterprise from lodgings under the YHA banner (see below) which can sometimes be huge properties with scores of beds, hyperactive school groups and, depending on your age, unhappy memories of a long-gone institutional past.

Along the Dales Way those who want to stay in bunkhouses/bunk barns are poorly served. It's not that there aren't many – I counted seven in total, so you should in theory be able to stay in one for every night on the trail – but unfortunately, all but one of them accepts group bookings only and individuals aren't allowed to stay unless they book the entire place for themselves (which costs several hundred pounds a night). If they're not busy they may allow individual trekkers to stay (the excellent Swarthghyll Farm near Oughtershaw is one that seems happy to do this) but it does mean that you can't book your spot more than a day or two in advance and many bunkhouses wouldn't even contemplate this arrangement, wanting group bookings only.

Hostels

There are three hostels on (or just off) the Dales Way. Only one of them (at Kettlewell) is owned by the **Youth Hostels Association of England and Wales** (YHA). Despite the name, anyone of any age can join the YHA. This can be done at any hostel, or by contacting the YHA (☎ 01629 592700 or ☎ 0800 019 1700, 🖥 www.yha.org.uk). The cost of a year's membership is £20 for an adult (£15 if you pay by direct debit), £10/5 for anyone under 26. Anyone who is a member of Hostelling International (HI) is automatically a member of the YHA. Having secured your membership, YHA hostels are easy to book, either online or by phone through the contact details on p19. Since non-members have to pay around £3 more per night, it is worth joining if you expect to stay in a YHA hostel for more than six nights in a year; in other words, it's not really worth joining them for the Dales Way alone, but if you think you might use them elsewhere within the year it may be worth investigating, particularly as members also get discounts at various stores (the camping outlet Millets being one).

The hostels along the Dales Way, whether privately owned or part of the YHA, come equipped with a whole range of facilities including a laundry service and drying rooms, lounges with television, free wi-fi, and fully equipped kitchens. Breakfast and/or dinner (of varying quality) are offered, as is a packed lunch. They are also great places to meet fellow walkers, swap stories and compare blisters. Weighed against these advantages is the fact that you may have to share your night with a heavy snorer sleeping in the same dorm. Some rooms now have en suite facilities but in others you have to share a shower room, though there are usually enough showers so that the waiting time is minimal.

If you're travelling out of the main season (particularly between November and February) you may find some hostels are shut to walkers during the week, or completely. Even in high season some are not staffed during the day and walkers may have to wait until 5pm before checking in, though you may be able to access the kitchen and leave luggage in a secure room before 5pm. And finally, the cost of staying in a hostel, once breakfast has been added on, is in many instances not that much cheaper than staying in a B&B, especially if you're walking with someone with whom you can share a room.

Bed and breakfasts

Bed and breakfasts (B&Bs) are a great British institution and many of those along the Dales are absolutely charming, with buildings often three or four hundred years old. Older owners often treat you as surrogates for their long-departed offspring and enjoy nothing more than looking after you.

As the name suggests, they provide you with a bed in a private room, and breakfast – a hearty, British-style cooked one unless you specify otherwise

---

❑ Airbnb

The rise and rise of Airbnb (⌨ www.airbnb.co.uk) has seen private homes opened up to overnight travellers on an informal basis. While accommodation is primarily based in cities, the concept is spreading to more rural areas, but do check thoroughly what you are getting and the precise location. At its best, this is a great way to meet local people in a relatively unstructured environment, but be aware that these places are not registered B&Bs, so standards may vary, yet prices may not necessarily be any lower than the norm.

As for the Dales Way, a quick look at the site tells us that there are half a dozen places currently advertised in Ilkley – which, given the paucity of 'regular' B&B accommodation there, could prove a lifesaver. There are further options all the way along the path. Note, however, that in this book we haven't listed specific properties that can be found on the Airbnb website as they tend to change quite frequently. Don't forget that you'll still need to sort out where you're going to eat, so while that cottage in the middle of nowhere may look perfect, you'll need to have somewhere nearby that serves food or else bring some supplies along (and make sure the place you're staying has cooking facilities!).

beforehand – though they range in style enormously. Most B&Bs on the route have **en suite rooms** – which means a room with bath or shower facilities is attached to the bed room. Where a room is advertised as having **private facilities**, it means that the bathroom is not directly connected to the room though there is a bathroom elsewhere that is reserved solely for the use of the room's occupants. Finally, **shared facilities** mean that you share a bathroom with the occupants of at least one other room. With private/shared facilities there may be a bath, which is what most walkers prefer at the end of a long day, and the bathroom is seldom more than a few feet away from your room.

These rooms usually contain either a double bed (known as a double room), or two single beds (known as a twin room). Some places have rooms which sleep up to three/four people. Solo trekkers should take note: single rooms are not so easy to find so you'll often end up occupying a double/twin room, for which you'll have to pay a single occupancy supplement (see p30).

Some B&Bs provide an evening meal (almost always you need to book this in advance); if not, there's often a pub or sometimes a restaurant nearby or, if it's far, the owner may give you a lift to and from the nearest place with food. Packed lunches (where available) should also be requested in advance. For details of likely costs see p30.

Booking Most B&Bs have their own website and may offer online/email booking but for some you will need to phone. Most places ask for a **deposit** (about 50%) which is generally non-refundable if you cancel at short notice. Some places may charge 100% if the booking is for one night only. Always let

---

❏ **Should you book your accommodation in advance?**
Accommodation along certain sections of the Dales Way is patchy at best, particularly the 22-mile stretch between Buckden and Dent and the 16-mile haul from Sedbergh to Burneside (two sections which together total about half the walk!). In the high season of **June to August**, therefore, unless camping, it's essential you have your night's accommodation secured. How soon you start booking is up to you but doing so the night before is no longer dependable. If you start booking **up to six months** in advance you'll have a good chance of getting precisely the accommodation you want. Booking so early does leave you vulnerable to changing circumstances of course, but with enough notice it's likely your deposit will be returned as they can easily fill your bed; ask on booking. Outside the high season and away from weekends, as long as you're **flexible**, you might get away with booking just a couple of weeks, days or even just hours in advance. Having said that, some establishments I've spoken to told us that May and September were in fact their busiest months. However, **weekends** are busy everywhere, especially in **the Lakes**.

If you've left it too late and can only get accommodation for parts of the walk but are set on a certain period, **consider camping** to fill in the gaps. If using a baggage service, they can cart the gear from door to door at no extra effort to yourself. Campers, whatever time of year, should always be able to find somewhere to pitch their tent, though ringing in advance will at least confirm that the campsite is still open. There are also a few **hostels** and a **bunkhouse** if you're willing to 'slum it' for a night. Do be careful when travelling out of high season, however, as many hostels close during the week and shut altogether in winter. Once again, it's worth booking in advance.

the owner know as soon as possible if you have to cancel your booking so they can offer the bed to someone else. Larger places take credit or debit cards. Most smaller B&Bs accept only cheques by post or payments by bank transfer for the deposit; the balance can be settled with cash or a cheque.

Guesthouses, hotels, pubs/inns

A guesthouse offers bed and breakfast but should have a better class of décor and more facilities, such as a lounge for guests; they are also likely to offer an evening meal. All of which makes guesthouses sound very much like hotels except, unlike a hotel, they are unlikely to offer room service.

Pubs/inns may also offer B&B accommodation and tariffs are no more than in a regular B&B. However, you need to be prepared for a noisier environment, especially if your room is above the bar.

Hotels do usually cost more, however, and some might be a little displeased by a bunch of muddy trekkers turning up. That said, most places on the walk, particularly in the quieter towns and villages, are used to seeing trekkers, make a good living from them and welcome them warmly.

As for B&Bs (see p21), you may have to pay a deposit. See Budgeting, p30.

FOOD AND DRINK

Breakfast

Stay in a B&B/guesthouse/hotel and you'll be filled to the gills each morning with a cooked English breakfast. This generally consists of a bowl of cereal followed by a plateful of eggs, bacon, sausages, mushrooms, tomatoes, and possibly baked beans or black pudding, with toast and butter, and all washed down with coffee, tea and/or fruit juice. Enormously satisfying the first time you try it, by the fourth or fifth morning you may start to prefer the lighter continental breakfast or porridge, which most establishments now also offer.

Alternatively, and especially if you're planning an early start, you might like to request a packed lunch instead of this filling breakfast and just have a cup of coffee before you leave.

Lunch

Your B&B host, or hostel, can usually provide a packed lunch at an additional cost and if requested in advance, though there's nothing to stop you preparing your own. There are some fantastic locally made cheeses and pickles that can be picked up along the way, as well as some wonderful bakers still making bread in the traditional manner. Alternatively, stop in a pub or café.

Remember, too, to plan ahead: at least four of the stages in this book are devoid of eateries or shops so read ahead about the next day's walk to make sure you never go hungry.

Elevenses/afternoon teas

Never miss a chance to avail yourself of the treats on offer in the tearooms and cafés of Cumbria and Yorkshire. Nothing relaxes and revives like a decent pot of tea and the opportunity to accompany it with a scone served with jam and cream, or a cake or two, is one that should not be passed up.

Evening meals

Pubs are as much a feature of this walk as the viaducts and vistas that you enjoy along the way, and in one or two cases (the Craven Arms at Appletreewick springs to mind, and the busy Red Lion at Burnsall) the pub is as much a tourist attraction as the finest ruined abbey. Most of them have become highly attuned to the needs of walkers and offer both lunch and evening meals (with often a few regional dishes and usually a couple of vegetarian options), some locally brewed beers, a garden to relax in on hot days and a roaring fire to huddle around on cold ones. The standard of the food varies widely, though portions are usually large, which is often just about all walkers care about at the end of a long day.

In bigger towns that other great British culinary tradition, the **fish 'n' chip shop**, can usually be found (Grassington, Sedbergh, Burneside, Kendal,

---

❏ Local food and drink

Yorkshire isn't renowned for the subtlety of its local delicacies but the **food** does tend to be hearty and tasty – which is all most trekkers care about. The most famous local delicacy is Yorkshire pudding, a side dish usually accompanying a roast dinner (especially roast beef) and made of eggs, flour and milk or water. Though I describe it as a side dish, often in Yorkshire it actually acts as the dish itself, with the rest of the main course – the meat, veg and gravy – placed inside one giant Yorkshire pudding!

Another curious local custom – and one that seriously disturbed my walking companion – is the habit of putting hot food, such as roast beef, inside a baguette and then serving it with gravy. My friend could never quite work out the best way of tackling it and whether cutlery should be involved, but to be fair these strange hot baguettes were quite more-ish.

As for the local **drinks**, well it won't surprise you to find that beer production is thriving in the Dales. At Ilkley there's **Wharfedale Brewery** (🖥 www.wharfedale-brewery.com), which is based at the back of the Flying Duck near the town centre and is where the Dales Way Association often meets, and **Ilkley Brewery** (🖥 www.ilkleybrewery.co.uk). **Goose Eye Brewery** (🖥 www.goose-eye- brewery.co.uk) is based in Keighley; in nearby Skipton there are a couple more breweries with fine reputations, including the **Copper Dragon** (🖥 www.copperdragon .uk.com) and the **Dark Horse** (🖥 www.darkhorsebrewery.co.uk).

The largest brewery on the trail, however, is at the other end of the trail at Staveley where the shiny glass and metallic **Hawkshead Brewery & Beer Hall** (also a restaurant) is not what one imagines a traditional brewery to look like, though you can't fault the beers they produce. As befits its location, the brewery's beers come with names like Lakeland Gold (4.4%) and Windermere Pale (3.5%). But away from the population centres you'll still find creditable breweries such as **Dent Brewery** (🖥 www.dentbrewery.co.uk) which supplies several pubs including The George and Dragon in Dent itself. If you like a dark beer, Dent Porter (3.8%) is one of the nicest I've tasted.

There are several superb pubs where you can sample some of the finest local beers including the Blue Bell Inn at Kettlewell, The Buck Inn at Buckden, The Red Lion at Burnsall and both the Craven Arms and The New Inn at Appletreewick.

Staveley and Bowness all have one); most of these towns have some sort of Chinese and/or Indian **takeaway too**. These provide a welcome change from too much pub food and are usually the only places serving food late in the evenings, staying open until at least 11pm.

Catering for yourself

There are several stores along the path and as long as you plan ahead and aren't too fussy you should be able to find something to cook for yourself. Once again, the sections from Buckden to Dent and Sedbergh to Burneside provide the self-

---

❏ Information for foreign visitors

● **Currency** The British pound (£) comes in notes of £50, £20, £10 and £5, and coins of £2 and £1. The pound is divided into 100 pence (usually referred to as 'p', pronounced 'pee') which come in 'silver' coins of 50p, 20p, 10p and 5p, and 'copper' coins of 2p and 1p. Up-to-date currency **exchange rates** can be found on 🖳 www .xe.com/ucc, at some post offices, and at most banks and travel agents.

● **Business hours** Most **village shops** are open Monday to Friday 9am-5pm and Saturday 9am-12.30pm. Many choose longer hours and some open on Sundays as well. Occasionally you'll come across a local shop that closes at lunchtime on one day during the week, usually a Wednesday or Thursday; this is a throwback to the days when all towns and villages had an 'early closing day'. **Supermarkets** are open Monday to Saturday 8am-8pm (sometimes up to 15 hours a day) and on Sunday from about 9am to 5 or 6pm, though main branches of supermarkets generally open 10am-4pm or 11am-5pm.

Main **post offices** generally open Monday to Friday 9am-5pm and Saturday 9am-12.30pm; **banks** typically open at 9.30/10am Monday to Friday and close at 3.30/4pm, though in some places both post offices and banks may open only two or three days a week and/or in the morning, or limited hours, only. **ATMs** (**cash machines**) located outside a bank, shop, post office or petrol station are open all the time, but any that are inside will be accessible only when that place is open.

Pub hours are less predictable; although many open daily 11am-11pm, opening hours in rural areas and during quieter periods (early weekdays, or in the winter months) are often more limited: typically Monday to Saturday 11am-3pm & 5 or 6-11pm, and Sunday 11am/noon-3pm & 7-10.30pm. The last entry time to most **museums and galleries** is usually half an hour, or an hour, before the official closing time.

● **Public (bank) holidays** Most businesses are shut on 1 January, Good Friday (March/April), Easter Monday (March/April), the first and last Monday in May, the last Monday in August, 25 December and 26 December.

● **School holidays** School holiday periods in England are generally: a one-week break late October, two weeks around Christmas/New Year, a week in mid February, two weeks around Easter, a week in late May/early June (to coincide with the bank holiday on the last Monday in May), and six weeks from late July to early September.

● **Documents** If you are a member of a National Trust organisation in your country bring your membership card as you should be entitled to free entry to National Trust properties and sites in the UK. English Heritage also have a membership card allowing free access to their sites. That said, there are none of either actually on or very close to on the Dales Way so don't take out membership specifically for the walk!

● **Travel/medical insurance** The **European Health Insurance Card** (EHIC) entitles EU nationals (on production of the EHIC card) to necessary medical treatment under the UK's National Health Service while on a temporary visit here. However,

catering trekker with the most problems, as there are no shops anywhere on these sections. Part 5 goes into greater detail about what can be found where, while for a quick glance at what's available do look at the Town & Village Facilities Table on p32.

Drinking water

There may be plenty of ways of perishing on the Dales Way but, given the amount of time you spend walking by a river, thirst won't be one of them. That said, it's not advisable to drink directly from these rivers: you won't ever truly

---

this is not a substitute for proper medical cover on your travel insurance for unforeseen bills and for getting you home should that be necessary. Also consider cover for loss or theft of personal belongings, especially if you're camping or staying in hostels, as there will be times when you'll have to leave your luggage unattended.

● **Weights and measures** Following a European Commission directive, milk in Britain can still be sold in pints (1 pint = 568ml), as can beer in pubs, though most other **liquids** including petrol (gasoline) and diesel are now sold in litres. Road **distances** can also continue to be given in miles (1 mile = 1.6km) rather than kilometres, and yards (1yd = 0.9m) rather than metres.

The population remains divided between those who still use inches (1 inch = 2.5cm) and feet (1ft = 0.3m) and those who are happy with centimetres and millimetres; you'll often be told that 'it's only a hundred yards or so' to somewhere, rather than a hundred metres or so. Most **food** is sold in metric weights (g and kg) but the imperial weights of pounds (lb: 1lb = 453g) and ounces (oz: 1oz = 28g) are often displayed too. The **weather** – a frequent topic of conversation – is also an issue: while most forecasts predict temperatures in °C, many people continue to think in terms of °F (see temperature chart on p13 for conversions).

● **Time** During the winter the whole of Britain is on Greenwich Meantime (GMT). The clocks move one hour forward on the last Sunday in March, remaining on British Summer Time (BST) until the last Sunday in October.

● **Smoking** Smoking in enclosed public places is banned. The ban relates not only to pubs and restaurants, but also to B&Bs, hostels and hotels. These latter have the right to designate one or more bedrooms where the occupants can smoke, but the ban is in force in all enclosed areas open to the public – even in a private home such as a B&B. Should you be foolhardy enough to light up in a no-smoking area, which includes pretty well any indoor public place, you could be fined £50, but it's the owners of the premises who suffer most if they fail to stop you, with a potential fine of £2500.

● **Telephones** The international access code for Britain is ☎ 44, followed by the area code minus the first 0, and then the number you require. Within the UK, to call a number with the same code as the landline phone you are calling from, the code can be omitted: dial the number only. It is cheaper to ring at weekends (from midnight on Friday till midnight on Sunday), and after 7pm and before 7am on weekdays. **Mobile phone reception** is not bad though you'll find a big black spot with no reception stretching from Kettlewell to Dent. If you're using a mobile phone that is registered overseas, consider buying a local SIM card to keep costs down; also remember to bring a universal adaptor so you can charge your phone. See also p26 for details about using a public phone.

● **Internet access** See p26.

● **Emergency services** For police, ambulance, fire and mountain rescue dial ☎ 999, or the EU standard number ☎ 112.

know what's recently defecated or died in them further upstream, and the run-off from the neighbouring fields could contain pesticides and other nasty chemicals. Instead, always get your water from a tap where you know the water is safe to drink, and maybe carry some purifying tablets just in case you run out along the trail and need to collect some from nature. In hot weather aim to drink **three or four litres** per day, supplemented by rehydration tablets.

MONEY

You'll find **banks** – or at least **ATMs** (cashpoints) – along the Dales Way, at places such as Ilkley, Grassington, Sedbergh, Burneside (£1.99 charge for withdrawal), Kendal, Staveley (£1 charge) and Bowness. The section you need to watch out for is from Grassington to Dent/Sedbergh, where there aren't any. But there are also not many places where you can spend money on this stretch, unless you fancy a cream tea at Half Island House in Beck Foot, or your B&B and pub/restaurant accepts payment in cash only, or if you have any mishap or change your plans – so make sure you have enough cash to cover these outgoings. However, the village stores at Kettlewell and Dent offer a **cashback** system; if you pay for goods by debit card they will advance cash against the card. You'll usually have to spend a minimum of £5 with them first. Many of the pubs along the way will also be happy to do this, particularly if there's no cashpoint nearby.

    Post offices also provide a very useful service whereby you can get cash (by debit card) for free if you bank with most British banks or building societies (for a full list see 🖳 www.postoffice.co.uk/branch-banking-services).

    Though most places now accept **debit/credit cards**, there's usually a minimum spend so it's a good idea to carry at least £50-100 with you in cash, just in case. The almost obsolete **chequebook** could also prove useful as a back-up.

INTERNET ACCESS

Most places to stay offer **wi-fi** free to visitors. If you're camping, you may find the pubs are your best bet for a good connection, though note that the Sportsman's Inn at Cowgill has no internet service and elsewhere in Dentdale it's a little slow.

OTHER SERVICES

Most small villages have a **post office** that doubles as the local store and bank (see Money, above). Nearby you'll usually find a **phone box**, though be warned, to combat vandalism some only accept cards, taking a £1 connection fee which is charged whether you get an answer or not. Otherwise 60p is the minimum fee to make a cash call; no change is given.

    There are **outdoor equipment shops** and **pharmacies** in the larger towns of Ilkley, Grassington, Sedbergh, Kendal and Bowness, and **tourist information centres** at the same places.

WALKING COMPANIES

It's possible to turn up with your boots and backpack at Ilkley and just start walking without planning much other than your accommodation (about which, see the box on p21). The following companies, however, are in the business of making your holiday as stress-free and enjoyable as possible.

Baggage carriers

At the time of research two baggage-carrying companies serve the Dales Way; Sherpa Van also provides **accommodation booking**. With both these services you can usually book up to around 8pm the previous evening, though it can be cheaper if you book in advance.

● **Brigantes Walking Holidays and Baggage Couriers** (☎ 01756 770402, 💻 www.brigantesenglishwalks.com; Nr Skipton, N Yorks; see also below) run a family operated baggage-courier service with locally based drivers covering the whole of the north of England. For baggage transfer they charge from £8 per person per day, operating from 1st April to 1st October, though they do specify a two-person minimum booking with a maximum weight of 17kg per bag.

● **Sherpa Van** (baggage service ☎ 01748 826917, 💻 www.sherpavan.com; Richmond, N Yorks) is a national organisation that runs a baggage-delivery service from March to mid October for many of Britain's walking and cycling trails including the Dales Way. They stipulate a maximum weight per bag of around 20kg and charge £8.50 per bag. Bookings less than £25 will be subject to a £5 admin fee. The service runs east to west, from Ilkley to Bowness, and one passenger may accompany each bag if ill or injured.

See their website, or call them (☎ 01609 883731), for details of their accommodation-booking service.

Self-guided holidays

Self-guided means that the company will organise accommodation, baggage transfer (some contract out the work to other companies), transport to and from the walk and various maps and advice, but leave you on your own to actually walk the path and cover the cost of lunch and dinner.

● **Absolute Escapes** (☎ 0131 240 1210, 💻 www.absoluteescapes.com; Edinburgh)
● **Alpine Exploratory** (☎ 0131 247 6702, 💻 www.alpineexploratory.com; Edinburgh)
● **Brigantes Walking Holidays and Baggage Couriers** (see above)
● **Celtic Trails** (☎ 01291 689774, 💻 www.celtictrailswalkingholidays.co.uk; Chepstow)
● **Contours** (☎ 01629 821900, 💻 www.contours.co.uk; Matlock)
● **Discovery Travel** (☎ 01904 632 226, 💻 www.discoverytravel.co.uk; York)
● **Footpath Holidays** (☎ 01985 840049, 💻 www.footpath-holidays.com; Nr Warminster, Wilts)
● **Freedom Walking Holidays** (☎ 07733 885390, 💻 www.freedomwalking holidays.co.uk; Goring-on-Thames)

PLANNING YOUR WALK

● **Let's Go Walking** (☎ 01837 880075, or ☎ 020 7193 1252, 🖳 www.letsgo walking.com; Devon)
● **Macs Adventure** (☎ 0141 530 8886, 🖳 www.macsadventure.com; Glasgow)
● **Mickledore** (☎ 017687 72335, 🖳 www.mickledore.co.uk; Keswick, Cumbria)
● **Nearwater Walking Holidays** (☎ 01326 279278, 🖳 www.nearwaterwalking holidays.co.uk; Cornwall)
● **NorthWestWalks** (☎ 01257 424889, 🖳 www.northwestwalks.co.uk; Wigan)
● **Responsible Travel** (☎ 01273 823700, 🖳 www.responsibletravel.com; Brighton)
● **Sherpa Expeditions** (☎ 020 8875 5070, 🖳 www.sherpaexpeditions.com; London)
● **The Walking Holiday Company** (☎ 01600 713008, 🖳 www.thewalking holidaycompany.co.uk; Monmouth)
● **Walk The Trail** (☎ 01326 567252, 🖳 www.walkthetrail.co.uk; Cornwall)
● **Where2Walk** (☎ 07824 304060, 🖳 where2walk.co.uk)

Group/guided walking tours

If you don't trust your navigational skills or simply prefer the company of other walkers as well as an experienced guide, one of HF Holidays guided walks may be of interest. Packages generally include all meals, accommodation, transport arrangements, minibus back-up and baggage transfer.

● **HF Holidays** (☎ 0345 470 8559; 🖳 www.hfholidays.co.uk; Herts) Offer a walk along the entire route based at their country house Newfield Hall, Airton; they also offer guided walks from Sedbergh (their base for those is Thorns Hall)

WALKING WITH A DOG

The Dales Way is a dog-friendly path, though it's extremely important that dog owners behave in a responsible manner. Dogs should always be kept on leads while on the footpath to avoid disturbing wildlife, livestock and other walkers. Dog excrement should be cleaned up and not left to decorate the boots of others; take a pooper scooper or plastic bag if you're walking with a dog.

It's particularly important to **keep your dog on a lead** when crossing fields with livestock in them, especially around calving or lambing time which can be as early as February or as late as the end of May. Most farmers would prefer it if you did not bring your dog at all at this time.

For general information about long-distance walking with a dog see pp170-1.

DISABLED ACCESS

Many areas of the trail are inaccessible to the majority of wheelchair and users, but access has been provided in a few sections, such as from the Red Lion pub in Burnsall to Loup Scar, now extended to the suspension bridge at Hebden.

For more on countryside access for the disabled, contact Disabled Ramblers (🖳 www.disabledramblers.co.uk).

Budgeting

England is not a cheap place to go travelling and, while the north may be one of the less expensive regions, the towns and villages in the national parks get all the business they can handle and charge accordingly.

There's nothing wrong with planning a budget trek, for example by camping every night and cooking your own food, but don't be too 'fundamentalist' on this matter, for there's no point scrimping and saving if it just means you'll have a miserable time. In particular, if the weather's unceasingly soggy don't persevere with camping night after night; there are few things more depressing on any trek than carrying a heavy, saturated tent, especially if the overnight rain also meant that you got little sleep. So if it looks as if it's going to rain again, and you're already feeling exhausted, bite the bullet and pay the extra to get a proper roof over your head. That way at least you can dry out your luggage (many places have a drying room), get a good night's sleep and recharge your batteries (both literally and metaphorically).

If the only expenses of this walk were accommodation and food, budgeting would be a piece of cake. Unfortunately, in addition to these there are all the little **extras** that push up the cost of your trip: for example beer, cream teas, buses or taxis, baggage carriers, laundry and souvenirs. It's surprising how much these add up! None of these is absolutely essential to helping you complete the trek, but each could make your trek a lot more straightforward – and a great deal more enjoyable too.

CAMPING

You can survive on less than £10-15 per person (pp) per day if you use the cheapest campsites, don't visit a pub, avoid all museums and other tourist attractions, forage for and cook all your own food from staple ingredients ... and generally have a pretty miserable time of it.

Even then, unforeseen expenses will probably nudge your daily budget up. Include the occasional pint, and perhaps a pub meal every now and then, and the figure will be nearer £20-30pp per day.

HOSTELS AND BUNKHOUSES

The charge for staying in a **hostel** is £16.50-22 per night, and it's £12.50 to stay in the only **bunkhouse**, the Station Inn at Ribblehead, that allows individual trekkers to stay. Whack on another £6 for breakfast and £10 for lunch in a café, and £10-15 for an evening meal (though you can use their self-catering facilities for both), and overall, it will cost £30-40 per day, or £50-60 to live in a little more comfort, enjoy the odd beer and go out for the occasional meal.

B&Bs , PUBS, GUESTHOUSES AND HOTELS

B&B prices start at £21pp per night based on two sharing a room at the Sun Inn at Dent, though this is very much an exception and a price of £30-40pp (based on two sharing) is more normal, though for the most luxurious en suite places in a popular tourist haunt such as Grassington expect to pay £75pp. Add on the cost of food for lunch and dinner – a packed lunch from a B&B may be around £6 and an evening meal £15-20 – and you should reckon on about £60pp minimum per day. Staying in a guesthouse or hotel will cost more.

If walking on your own remember that there is often a supplement of £10-20 for single occupancy of a double or twin room; you may even have to pay the full price of the room.

Itineraries

Part 5 of this book has been written from east to west (or, more accurately, from south-east to north-west), but there is of course nothing to stop you from tackling it in the opposite direction (see below).

To help plan your walk look at the **planning maps** (see opposite inside back cover) and the **table of town & village facilities** (on p32), which gives a rundown on the essential information you'll need regarding accommodation possibilities and services at the time of writing.

You could follow one of the **suggested itineraries** (see box opposite) which are based on preferred type of accommodation and walking speed. There's also a list of **day and weekend walks** on pp33-5 which cover the best of the path, most of these are well served by public transport; in addition, see box p34 for an itinerary for doing the walk in day trips. The bus services table is on pp48-9 (see box p45/46 for rail/coach services) and **public transport map** on p47.

Once you have an idea of your approach turn to Part 5 for detailed information on accommodation, places to eat and other services in each village and town on the route. Also in Part 5 you will find summaries of the route to accompany the detailed trail maps.

WHICH DIRECTION?

To be honest, it doesn't really matter. Most people trek from south-east to north-west. So, if you are walking alone but wouldn't mind some company now and again you'll find that most of the other Dales Way walkers are heading in your direction.

But it could be argued that by heading in the other direction the prevailing (west) winds will, more often than not, be behind you. Then again, if you do walk north-west to south-east you could end up squinting more as the sun will be in your face for much of the day (assuming that you see it, of course). However, there is also something to be said for finishing your walk in the Lake

District, from where you can continue your adventure by scaling a few of England's highest peaks.

SUGGESTED ITINERARIES

The suggested itineraries (see box below) are based on two different accommodation types: camping and bunkhouses/hostels; and B&Bs. Each is then divided into three alternatives depending on your walking speed (relaxed, medium and fast). They are only suggestions so feel free to adapt them.

Don't forget to **add your travelling time** before and after the walk to get a better idea of how many days you'll need in total.

CAMPING (AND BUNKHOUSES/HOSTELS)

Night	Relaxed pace Place	Approx Distance miles / km	Medium pace Place	Approx Distance miles / km	Fast pace Place	Approx Distance miles / km
0	Ilkley		Ilkley		Ilkley	
1	Appletreewick	12 / 19.6	Appletreewick	12 / 19.6	Appletreewick	12 / 19.6
2	Kettlewell	11½ / 18.5	Buckden	16⅛ / 25.5	Buckden	16⅛ / 25.5
3	Nethergill	11½ / 18.5	Cowgill	17⅛ / 27.3	Cowgill	17⅛ / 27.3
4	Station Inn, Ribblehead	7 / 11.4	Bramaskew Farm	15 / 24.3	Bramaskew Farm	15 / 24.3
5	Dent	11⅝ / 18.7	Burneside	11½ / 18.5	Bowness	21 / 33.8
6	Bramaskew Farm	9⅝ / 15.5	Bowness	9½ / 15.4		
7	Burneside	11½ / 18.5				
8	Bowness	9½ / 15.4				

Notes: It is possible to camp everywhere (see p19); in addition there is a YHA hostel at Kettlewell, bunkhouse at Ribblehead and hostel at Bowness.

STAYING IN B&Bs

Night	Relaxed pace Place	Approx Distance miles / km	Medium pace Place	Approx Distance miles / km	Fast pace Place	Approx Distance miles / km
0	Ilkley		Ilkley		Ilkley	
1	Stangs Lane	11 / 17.9	Burnsall	13¼ / 21.5	Grassington	16¾ / 27.2
2	Kettlewell	12½ / 20	Buckden	14⅞ / 23.6	Swarthghyll	19¾ / 30.3
3	Swarthghyll	12½ / 20	Station Inn, Ribblehead	14⅛ / 22.6	Dent	15⅝ / 25.3
4	Cowgill	10 / 16	Dent	11⅝ / 18.7	Burneside	21⅛ / 34
5	Dent	5⅝ / 9.2	Burneside	21⅛ / 34	Bowness	9½ / 15.4
6	Sedbergh	5⅝ / 9.2	Bowness	9½ / 15.4		
7	Patton Bridge	13¼ / 21.5				
8	Staveley	8 / 12.9				
9	Bowness	6¼ / 10				

PLANNING YOUR WALK

TOWN AND VILLAGE FACILITIES

PLACE*	DISTANCE* MILES / KM	BANK* (ATM)	POST OFFICE*	TOURIST INFO*	EATING PLACE*	FOOD SHOP*	CAMP-SITE	BUNK/ HOSTEL*	B&B*
Ilkley		✓	✓	TIC	✓✓	✓			✓✓
(Addingham) 2½ / 4.1					✓	✓			✓
(¼ mile / 400m off path)									
Bolton Abbey 3½ / 5.7			✓		✓	✓	✓		
Barden Bridge 3½ / 5.7				✓ (1/1.6)				(G)	
Stangs Lane 1½ / 2.3						✓			✓
Appletreewick 1 / 1.6					✓	✓			✓
Burnsall 1¼ / 2					✓✓	✓			✓✓
(Hebden) 1½ / 2.4					✓	✓			✓✓
(½ mile / 800m off path)									
Grassington 2 / 3.4		✓	✓	NPC/HUB	✓✓	✓		(G)	✓✓
(Conistone) 2½ / 4.1					✓				✓
(1mile / 1.6km off path)									
Kettlewell 4¼ / 6.6		#	✓		✓✓	✓	✓	YHA	✓✓
(Starbotton) 2¼ / 3.5					✓	✓			✓
(⅛ mile / 200m off path)									
(Buckden) 2¼ / 3.5					✓✓	✓		(G)	✓
(⅛ mile / 200m off path)									
Hubberholme 1¼ / 2					✓			(G)	✓
Beckermonds 4 / 6.3						✓			
Nethergill 1¾ / 2.8						✓			
Swarthghyll 1 / 1.6								(G)	✓(SC)
Far Gearstones 4½ / 7.2								(G)	
(Ribblehead) 1½ / 2.4 (road walk)					✓		✓	B	✓
Cowgill 4½ / 7.2					✓		✓		✓
Lea Yeat ¾ / 1.2							✓		✓(SC)
(Dent) 4¾ / 7.6		#	✓		✓✓	✓	✓		✓✓
(⅛ mile / 200m off path)									
(Sedbergh) 5 / 8		ATM	✓	TIC	✓✓	✓		(G)	✓✓
(½ mile/ 800m off path)									
Bramaskew 4½ / 7.2							✓		✓
Lowgill 3 / 4.8					✓				
Lambrigg 2¼ / 3.5									✓
Grayrigg Foot 1½ / 2.4							✓		
(Patton Bridge) 1 / 1.6							(✓ ON TRAIL)		✓
(½ mile/ 800m off path)									
Burneside 3¾ / 6		✓(£1.99)	✓		✓	✓	✓		✓
(Kendal) (train)		✓	✓	TIC	✓✓	✓		H	✓✓
(Staveley) 3½ / 5.7		✓(£1)	✓		✓✓	✓			✓
(¼ mile / 400m off path)									
Bowness 6 / 9.9		✓	✓	TIC	✓✓	✓	✓	H (1 / 1.6)	✓✓

TOTAL 81 MILES (130.2KM)   *see opposite for notes

THE BEST DAY AND WEEKEND WALKS

The following suggested trails are for those who don't want to tackle the entire path in one go, or just want to get a flavour of the challenge before committing themselves. In my opinion they include the best parts of the Dales Way; they are all described in more detail in Part 5.

Day walks bring you back to your starting point, either along other routes not mapped in this book or in some cases by using public transport; however, check the services mentioned still operate before you set off.

Bolton Abbey to Grassington   10¾ miles/17.3km (pp87-101)

A short walk but one that encompasses an awful lot, beginning with the delights of Bolton Abbey and including lovely Strid Wood, ancient Barden Bridge, a gorgeous stretch of easy wandering to the riparian villages of Appletreewick and Burnsall, and an elegant stroll to finish up at Grassington. All flat, all wonderful and it is also possible to take different paths on the eastern side of the Wharfe that will take you back to the starting point, a grand walk that will be about 22¾ miles in total (36.6km). Alternatively, bus No 74/74S (874 on Sunday) can convey you between Bolton Abbey and Grassington.

Grassington to Buckden   11⅜ miles/18.3km (pp101-14)

The first high-level stage of the trail as you leave Wharfedale's main tourist centre to walk through some ancient archaeology on windswept fells. Great views over the valley are a feature of the descent into Kettlewell, whereafter the terrain is flat and easy as you follow the river's course up to Buckden. The 72A & 72B and 874 bus services run between Buckden and Grassington. Can be combined with the route above for a great weekend's walking!

Far Gearstones to Lea Yeat via the Dales Way, returning via Wold Fell on the Alternative (High Level) Route
19¼ miles/31km (pp130-4 & pp126-7)

A huge loop that takes you across the fell and down under the Dent Viaduct to Dentdale on the long road route, then up via England's highest railway station and along Galloway Gate and the Pennine Bridleway to Cam Houses, where you take the official path once more to Cam High Road and the Pennine Way back to Far Gearstones.

PLANNING YOUR WALK

---

* Notes for town and village facilities table

PLACE	Places in brackets (eg Addingham) are a short walk off the route.
DISTANCE	Distances given are between places directly on the Dales Way. Distances in brackets are for places off the route; ⅛ mile = 220 yards
BANK	# = cashback available
TOURIST INFO	TIC = Tourist information centre; NPC = national park visitor centre HUB = Community-run organisation providing tourist and local info
EATING PLACE	✔ = one place, ✔✔ = two, ✔✔✔ = three or more
BUNK/HOSTEL	YHA = YHA hostel, H = independent hostel, (G) = groups only
B&BS	✔ = one place, ✔✔ = two, ✔✔✔ = three or more; (SC) = self-catering

If the distance is too ambitious, a much simpler alternative is to come off the official path on the Dent Road, walk down to Newby Head and pick up the Alternative (High Level) Route via Gavel Gap to Cold Keld Gate – a much more manageable 9-miler.

If you're relying on public transport you'll need to catch a train to Ribblehead – a 1½-mile (2.4km) walk from Far Gearstones – or Dent Station, which is on the trail. There are few facilities en route though The Station Inn (Ribblehead) can provide you with food and accommodation; the Sportsman's Inn at Cowgill can do the same, though the opening times are more limited at the latter.

PLANNING YOUR WALK

❏ **Doing the Dales Way in day trips**

There are some very handy services that enable you to walk for the whole day before catching the bus back again at the day's end, thereby enabling you to complete most of the path in day trips if you so desire. For example, the **74/74S service** (see box pp48-9 for details) runs between Ilkley and Grassington via several places which are on the path. So you can arrive in Ilkley in the morning, set off on the trail, stop when you get tired at any of those villages – and then catch a bus back to Ilkley. Indeed, on Sunday/Bank Holidays the service (now renumbered 874) runs all the way to Buckden. **Note that, whatever day you walk, you need to check and double-check the bus times as they are prone to change – and no service on the Dales Way is frequent; also many operate only in the main season.**

It's not all plain sailing, of course. Buckden to Dentdale is one 'problem' stage where you'll have to travel via Skipton to get between the two (bus from Skipton to Buckden, train back from Dent to Skipton) – a massive detour that few will think worth it. And from Dent/Dent Station onwards, in order make things easier for yourself, it's worth **walking at a weekend**. The **S1 service** operates only on Saturday but travels between Dent Station and Kendal; the W2 operates on a Wednesday but does not go to Dent Village, which is about four miles from Dent Station.

Here's a suggested itinerary for doing the entire way in day trips. As always, do check online for the latest info before setting off on any of these stages.

Day 1: Drive/public transport to Ilkley. Walk Ilkley to Grassington. Take a 74/74S/874 bus (no service on Tue or Thur) back to Ilkley.

Day 2: Drive/bus to Grassington. Walk to Buckden. Take bus 72A/72B (Mon-Sat), or 874 (Sun/Bank hols only), back to Grassington.

Day 3: Drive/public transport to Skipton. Take bus 72/72A/72R (Mon-Sat) to Grassington and then 72A/72B (Mon-Sat), 800 (Tue & Sat only), or 875 (both Sun & Bank hols only) to Buckden. Walk to Dent Station on the Alternative (High Level) Route. Return by train to Skipton.

[NB If you want to take the regular (low level) route you'll have to backtrack to Dent Station where the alternative (high level) route joins the regular route; see Map 21, p133 for where to do this.]

Day 4: Drive/public transport to Dent/Dent Station. Walk to Sedbergh. Take a Western Dales Bus S1 (Sat only) or S2 (Sun only) back to Dent Station.

Day 5: Drive/bus to Sedbergh. Walk Sedbergh to Burneside. Train Burneside to Kendal then, if driving, take a bus back to Sedbergh.

Day 6: Drive/public transport to Burneside. Walk Burneside to Bowness. Take one of the many buses from Bowness to Windermere railway station and, if driving, take a train back to Burneside.

Sedbergh to Lincoln's Inn Bridge circular 6⅝ miles/10.7km (pp140-7)
A simple stroll that takes you around the Howgills. Follow the Dales Way to the
Lune Viaduct, where you should divert off to Howgill Lane then take a right on a
public footpath to climb and traverse the lower slopes of Winder's southern face,
the hill overlooking Sedbergh. Drop down to Howgill Lane to re-enter Sedbergh.

Burneside to Bowness   **9½ miles/15.4km (pp154-68)**
The last stretch of the trail is simple enough, though interesting too as you enter
the Lake District National Park. Staveley provides a convenient place to stop for
elevenses or lunch. There's no real chance to loop back on foot so you'll either
have to retrace your steps or, more sensibly, take the bus from Bowness to
Windermere then the train back to Burneside.

What to take

Taking too much is a mistake made by first-time travellers of all types, an
understandable response to not knowing what to expect and not wanting to be
caught short. But unless you want to end up feeling like an overloaded mule
with a migraine you need to pack carefully. Experienced independent hill walkers trim their gear down to the essentials because they've learned that an unnec-
essarily heavy pack can exacerbate injuries and put excess strain on their
already hard-pressed feet.

   Note that if you need to buy all the gear listed, keep an eye out for the ever-
more frequent online **sales** at outdoor gear shops; time it right and you could get
it all half price.

TRAVELLING LIGHT

Organised tours apart, baggage-forwarding services tempt walkers partially to
miss the point of long-distance walking: the satisfaction of striding away from
one coast knowing that you're carrying everything you need to get to the other.
But if you've chosen to carry it all you must be ruthless in your packing choices.

HOW TO CARRY IT

Today's rucksacks are hi-tech affairs that make load-carrying as tolerable as can
be expected. Don't get hung up on anti-sweat features; unless you use a wheel-
barrow your back will always sweat a bit. It's better to ensure there is thick
padding and a **good range of adjustment**. In addition to hip belts (allied with
some sort of stiff back frame), use an unelasticated **cross-chest strap** to keep
the pack snug; it makes a real difference.

   If camping you'll need a pack of at least 60 or 70 litres' capacity. Staying in
hostels 40 litres should be ample, and for those eating out and staying in B&Bs
a 20- to 30-litre pack should suffice; you could even get away with a daypack.

Few backpacks these days claim to be waterproof; use a waterproof **liner** or the elasticated backpack cover like a shower cap that comes with some packs. It's also handy to **compartmentalise** the contents into smaller bags so you know what is where. Take a few (degradable) **plastic bags** for wet things, rubbish etc; they're always useful. Finally, pack intelligently with the most frequently used things readily accessible.

FOOTWEAR

Boots

Don't be tempted by the Dales Way's reputation as an easy walk to turn up at Ilkley in a pair of flip-flops; a good pair of trekking boots is vital. (If you've a real intolerance for ankle protection, a good pair of trail shoes may just suffice; see the last paragraph of this section.) Scrimp on other gear if you must – you'll only use waterproofs some days but you'll be walking every mile on every day. Expect to spend up to £150 on quality, three-season footwear which is light, breathable and waterproof, and has ankle support as well as flexible but thick **soles** to insulate your own pulverised soles. Don't buy by looks or price and avoid buying online until you've been to a shop and tried on an identical pair (and even this can backfire on you). Go to a big outdoor shop on a quiet weekday and spend an hour trying on everything they have in stock that appeals. Then, with boots safely bought, make sure you try them out beforehand, first round the house or office, and then on a full day's walk or two. Trust me, while your friends are wailing over blister-blighted toes, you'll be skipping through the meadows and rejoicing in your decision to choose your boots with care.

An old and trusted pair of boots can be re-soled and transformed with shock-absorbing after-market **insoles**. Some of these can be thermally moulded to your foot in the shop, but the less expensive examples are also well worth the investment, even if the need for replacement by the end of the walk is likely. Some walkers wisely carry old trusted boots in their luggage in case their new footwear turns on them – though this can be quite a heavy tactic. Blisters are possible even with a much-loved boot if you walk long and hard enough; refer to pp56-7 for blister-avoidance strategies.

Many may consider boots over the top for the Dales Way; much of the walking is on easy paths and some experienced walkers have turned to **trail shoes**. They won't last as long as boots, be as tough or crucially, have the height to keep your socks dry in the bogs and streams; but the rewards of nimbleness and greater comfort can transform your walk, just as bad footwear can cast a shadow over it.

Socks

As with all outdoor gear, the humble sock has not escaped the technological revolution (with prices to match) so invest in two non-cotton pairs designed for walking. Although cushioning is desirable, avoid anything too thick which will reduce stability. As well as the obvious olfactory benefits, frequent washing will maintain the socks' springiness.

CLOTHES

Tops

The proven system of **layering** is a good principle to follow. A quick-drying synthetic (or the less odiferous merino wool) **base layer** transports sweat away from your skin; the mid-layer, typically a **fleece** or woollen jumper, keeps you warm; and when needed, an outer 'shell' or **jacket** protects you from the wind and rain. Maintaining a comfortable temperature in all conditions is the key. This means not **overheating** just as much as it means keeping warm. Both can prematurely tire you and, although tedious, the smart hiker is forever fiddling with zips and managing their layers and headwear to maintain an optimal level of comfort.

Avoid cotton; as well as being slow to dry, when soaked it saps away body heat but not the moisture – and you'll often be wet from sweat if not rain. Take a change of **base layers** (including underwear), a **fleece** suited to the season, and the best **breathable waterproof** you can afford. **Soft shells** are an alternative to walking in rustling nylon waterproofs when it's windy but not raining.

It's useful to have a **spare set of clothing** so you're able to get changed should you arrive chilled at your destination, but choose **quick-drying clothes**. Once indoors your body heat will quickly dry out a synthetic fleece and nylon leggings. However, always make sure you have a **dry base layer** in case you go down with hypothermia, or someone you're with does. This is why a quality waterproof is important.

Leg wear

Your legs are doing all the work and don't generally get cold so your trousers can be light which will also mean quick-drying. Although they lack useful pockets, many walkers find leg-hugging cycling polyester **leggings** very comfortable (eg Ron Hill Tracksters). Poly-cotton or microfibre trousers are excellent. Denim jeans are cotton and a disaster when wet.

If the weather's good, **shorts** are very agreeable to walk in, leaving a light pair of trousers clean for the evenings. It also means your lower legs get muddy and not the trousers. On the other hand **waterproof trousers** would suit people who really feel the cold; others may find them unnecessary and awkward to put on and wear; preferring quick drying or minimal legwear.

For muddy sections **gaiters** are a great idea; they also stop irritating pebbles dropping into your footwear. You don't have to wear them all the time, though.

Headwear and other clothing

Your head is both exposed to the sun and loses most of your body heat so, for warmth, carry a woolly beany that won't blow away and for UV protection a peaked cap, a bandana or microfibre 'buff' makes a good back-up or a sweat band. Between them they'll either conserve body heat or reduce the chances of dehydration. **Gloves** are good in wintry conditions (carry a spare pair in winter).

TOILETRIES

Besides **toothpaste**/brush bring **liquid soap** which can also be used for shaving and washing clothes, though **detergent** is better if you're doing a lot of clothes washing. Carry **toilet paper** and a lightweight **trowel** to bury the results out on the fells (see pp52-3). Other items include **ear plugs**, **sun screen**, **moisturiser**; **insect repellent** if camping, and possibly a means of **water purification**.

FIRST-AID KIT

Apart from aching limbs your most likely ailments will be blisters so a first-aid kit can be minimal. **Ibuprofen** and **paracetamol** help numb pain – although rest, of course, is the only real cure. '**Compeed**' or '**Second Skin**' treat blisters (see also p57). An **elastic knee support** is a good precaution for a weak knee as are walking poles. A tube of **Nuun tablets** can flavour water and restore lost minerals on the march, and a few sachets of **Dioralyte** or **Rehydrat** powders will quickly remedy more serious dehydration. Other items worth considering are: **plasters** for minor cuts; a small selection of different-sized **sterile dressings** for wounds; **porous adhesive tape**; **antiseptic wipes**; **antiseptic cream**; **safety pins**; **tweezers**; and **scissors**.

GENERAL ITEMS

Essential

Carry a **compass**, **whistle**, **mobile phone** (and the charging device for it) as well as at least a one-litre **water bottle** or bag; an LED **headtorch**; **emergency snacks**, a **penknife** and a **watch**.

Useful

If you're not carrying a proper bivvy bag or tent, a compact foil **space blanket** is a good idea in the cooler seasons. Many people take a **camera**, **batteries** and **sunglasses**. A **book** is a good way to pass the evenings, especially in mid-summer wild camps. A **vacuum flask**, for hot drinks or soup, is recommended if walking in a cooler season. Studies have shown that nothing improves a hilltop view on a chilly day like a hot cup of tea or soup.

If committed to the exposure of wild camping you'll need a **tent** you can rely on; light but able to withstand the rain and wind. In campsites you may just get away with a cheap tent. Otherwise, a good one-man tent suited to the wilds can cost under £120 and weigh just 1.5kg, with a sub-2kg two-man example costing around £250. An inflatable **sleeping mat** is worth many times its weight.

As for **cooking**, is it really worth the bother? The extra weight and hassle in buying provisions is only viable when shared by a group of three or more; otherwise get down the pub and help support the local economy.

MONEY

Not everybody accepts **debit** or **credit cards** as payment – though many B&Bs and restaurants now do. A **cheque book** from a British bank could be useful in those places where debit/credit cards are not accepted but you should always carry some **cash** with you, just to be on the safe side. See also p26 and the town and village facilities table on p32.

PLANNING YOUR WALK

MAPS

The hand-drawn maps in this book cover the trail at a scale of just under 1:20,000: $3^1/_8$ inches = one mile (5cm = 1km). At this generous scale, combined with the notes and tips written on the maps, and the waypoints – not to mention the fact that the Dales Way is so well signposted – it's quite difficult to get lost. That said, a supplementary map of the region – ie one with contours – can prove

❏ Digital mapping

There are numerous apps and software packages that provide Ordnance Survey (OS) maps for a PC, smartphone, tablet or GPS. Maps are supplied by direct download over the internet. The maps are then loaded into an application, also available by download, from where you can view them, print them and create routes on them.

Digital maps are normally purchased for an area such as a National Park, but the Dales Way walk is available as a distinct product from some vendors. When compared to the five OS Explorer maps that cover the walk, they are very competitively priced. Once you own the electronic version of the map you can print any section of the map as many times as you like.

The real value of the digital maps though, is the ability to draw a route directly onto the map from your computer or smartphone. The map, or the appropriate sections of it, can then be printed with the route marked on it, so you no longer need the full versions of the OS maps. Additionally, the route can be viewed directly on your smartphone or uploaded to a GPS device, providing you with the whole route in your hand at all times while walking. If your smartphone has a GPS chip, you will be able to see your position overlaid onto the digital map on your phone.

Many websites now have free routes you can download for the more popular digital mapping products. It is important to ensure any digital mapping software on your smartphone uses pre-downloaded maps, stored on your device, and doesn't need to download them on-the-fly, as this will be impossible in the hills.

Taking OS-quality maps with you on the hills has never been so easy. Most modern smartphones have a GPS receiver built in to them and almost every device with built-in GPS functionality now has some mapping software available for it. One of the most popular manufacturers of dedicated handheld GPS devices is Garmin, who have an extensive range of map-on-screen devices; prices vary from around £100 to £600.

Smartphones and GPS devices should complement, not replace, the traditional method of navigation (a map and compass) as any electronic device is susceptible to problems and, if nothing else, battery failure. Remember, too, that battery life will be significantly reduced, compared to normal usage, when you are using the built-in GPS and running the screen for long periods.

● **Anquet** (🖳 www.anquet.com) has the Dales Way for £12.93 using OS 1:25,000 mapping. They also have a range of Harvey maps.

● **Ordnance Survey** (🖳 www.ordnancesurvey.co.uk) will let you download and then use their UK maps (1:25,000 scale) on a mobile or tablet without a data connection for a subscription of £3.99 for one month or £19.99 for a year (on their current offer).

● **Harvey** (🖳 www.harveymaps.co.uk) sell their Dales Way map (1:40,000 scale) as a download for £12.99 for use on any device.

● **Memory Map** (🖳 www.memory-map.co.uk) currently sell OS 1:25,000 mapping covering the whole of the UK for £50.

Stuart Greig (🖳 lonewalker.net)

PLANNING YOUR WALK

invaluable should you need to abandon the path and find the quickest route off high ground in bad weather. They also help you to identify local features and landmarks and devise possible side trips.

The most popular map for the Dales Way is **Harvey Maps** (💻 www.harvey maps.co.uk) *Long Distance Route – Dales Way* (£13.95). Their website makes a lot of the fact that it's durable, waterproof, weighs only 60g and can also be downloaded digitally for your iPhone, iPad or Android device. All of which is great, but undoubtedly the main reason for its popularity is the fact that it's the only one to cover the whole route in one sheet. I should also say that while I took it on the route, I never actually unfolded it the whole time from the beginning of the trail to about day four, when I realised I'd actually lost it.

The alternative is to get the complete set of **Ordnance Survey Explorer maps** (💻 www.ordnancesurvey.co.uk). But to cover the whole route you'd have to purchase five maps and spend about £45. (For those whose trip is being subsidised in some way and thus want to take this route, the relevant maps are: **OL297** Map of Lower Wharfedale & Washburn Valley; **OL2** Map of Yorkshire Dales – Southern & Western Area; **OL30** Map of Yorkshire Dales – Northern & Central Area; **OL19** Map of Howgill Fells and Upper Eden Valley; and **OL7** Map of The Lake District: South-Eastern area.) You can now get tailor-made maps that centre on exactly the area you want – though at £16.99, you don't save any money by going down this route.

While it may be extravagant to buy all of these maps, members of Ramblers (see box p42) can borrow up to 10 maps for free from their library, paying only for return postage.

RECOMMENDED READING, LISTENING AND VIEWING

Most of the books listed below can be found in the tourist information centres; the centres at Grassington and Sedbergh have a particularly good supply of books about the path and the places en route. As well as stocking many of the titles listed below, the tourist offices also have a number of books about the towns and villages en route, usually printed by small, local publishers.

If you're a seasoned long-distance walker, or even new to the game and like what you see, check out the other titles in the Trailblazer series; see p175.

Flora and fauna field guides

Collins *Bird Guide* with its beautiful illustrations of British and European birds continues to be the favourite field guide of both ornithologists and laymen alike. For a guide to the flora you'll encounter on the Dales Way, *The Wild Flower Key* (Warne) by Francis Rose and Clare O'Reilly, is arranged to make it easy to identify unfamiliar flowers. Another in the Collins Gem series, *Wild Flowers*, is more pocket sized and thus more suitable for walkers.

There are also several field guide apps for smart phones and tablets, including those that can aid in identifying birds by their song as well as by their appearance.

DVDs and iplayer/podcast downloads

Clare Balding dedicated a whole series of her Radio 4 *Ramblings* show to the Dales Way, and each week she was joined by a guest including, for one episode, Mr Dales Way himself, Colin Speakman. It's an interesting show though in it she manages to find some kind of magic portal, invisible to the rest of us, that means that she can finish one programme at Beckermonds and then start the next at Dent. Similarly, Episode Five finds her pulling into Sedbergh, while Episode Six has her starting at Staveley, a suspiciously convenient five miles only from the very end of the Bowness. But I'm being mischievous, as her job is of course more about entertaining the listening public, which of course she does admirably, and less about completing the entire walk, which is your job! As I write, the series is still available on BBC iPlayer.

Films about the Dales Way itself are rather thin on the ground but the region itself is no stranger to the camera. *Calendar Girls*, based on the true story of a local Women's Institute that decided to produce a charity calendar of themselves naked (though with cakes, garden implements, musical instruments etc placed strategically to protect their modesty), was filmed, before the action moved to LA, around the Dales Way village of Kettlewell; though the ladies on whom the film was based were actually from the Rylstone Women's Institute, about 6km south-west of Grassington. Helen Mirren and Julie Walters were the stars.

Also filmed at least in part in the Dales, the Hollywood blockbuster *Robin Hood, Prince of Thieves* starred Kevin Costner in the eponymous role. In one memorable scene, filmed at Aysgarth Falls, Robin Hood strips naked to bathe under the powerful Hardraw Force, a waterfall in the heart of the Dales National Park, while Maid Marian spies on him from a nearby rock. Robin Hood bathes alone in the scene, with none of the other Merry Men present, though Maid Marian swears that she saw his Little John.

For many people, their first 'experience' of the Yorkshire Dales was via one of the long-running British **TV series** that seemed to dominate our televisions in the '70s and '80s. If you fancy spending an evening watching an actor with his arm up a cow's backside against a verdant Dales backdrop, the boxset of *All Creatures Great & Small* (Universal Pictures UK) is for you. The programme, which ran for six series, was based on the entertaining books by James Herriot, which were in turn based on his experiences as a young vet in the Dales. It is said that HBO are due to remake the series, making it 'sexier and glossier', so expect the vets to be more rugged, and the cows prettier. For those who find Christopher Timothy, Robert Hardy and Peter Davison handsome enough, thank you very much, the box set of all 87 UK episodes (plus three Christmas specials!) is still available in the shops and repeats can regularly be found on the more obscure channels accessible on your TV remote.

Perhaps the most famous TV series set in Yorkshire, however, and which seems to have its heart in the Dales (though it's actually filmed around Holmfirth, to the south), is *Last of the Summer Wine*. Hilarious to anyone over a certain age (that age being about 75), for the rest of society the merits of this comedy about a group of elderly friends behaving, essentially, like children are simply unfathomable. But this lack of 'youth appeal' didn't stop it from

❑ SOURCES OF FURTHER INFORMATION

Online trail information

🖳 www.dalesway.org The official site of the Dales Way Association and the first place to visit for updates, route changes and other Dales-based news.

🖳 www.thedalesway.co.uk Run by the baggage carriers and accommodation bookers Sherpa Van; they have some useful info on the B&Bs along the way.

🖳 ramblingman.org.uk One of the better blogs, written by prolific promenader Andrew Bowden. Lots of useful advice and information though as it's a one-man band the info can be a little dated.

🖳 www.wharfedale-nats.org.uk Website of the Wharfedale Naturalists Society, including updates and any unusual sightings of some of the UK's rarer creatures.

🖳 www.daelnet.co.uk Another Dales-based website, once again very good on the nature of the Dales but also with a directory of accommodation and services in the Dales region.

Tourist information organisations

● **Tourist information centres (TICs)** TICs are based in most cities and major towns throughout Britain and provide all manner of locally specific information; some also offer an accommodation-booking service. There are TICs at **Ilkley**, **Sedbergh**, **Kendal** and **Bowness-on-Windermere**.

In addition to the above there's a Heritage Centre at **Dent** and a National Park Centre at **Grassington** as well as The Hub, a community-run organisation there which provides information for locals and visitors.

● **Yorkshire Tourist Board** (🖳 www.yorkshire.com) The tourist board oversees all the tourist information centres in the county. It's a good place to find general information about the county as well as on outdoor activities and local events. They can also help with arranging holidays and accommodation.

● **Cumbria Tourist Board** (🖳 www.golakes.co.uk) Performing much the same role as the Yorkshire Tourist Board but, of course, for the county encompassing the Lake District – and thus just the last stage or so of the Way.

Organisations for walkers

● **Backpackers' Club** (🖳 www.backpackersclub.co.uk) A club aimed, according to the website, at those who 'propel themselves across the countryside whether by walking cycling, canoe or even cross country skiing!' They produce a quarterly magazine, provide members with a comprehensive advisory and information service on all aspects of backpacking, organise weekend trips and also publish a farm-pitch directory. Membership is £15/20/8.50 per year for an individual/family/anyone under 18 or over 65.

● **The Long Distance Walkers' Association** (🖳 www.ldwa.org.uk) Membership includes a journal (*Strider*) three times per year with details of challenge events and local group walks as well as articles on the subject. Information on over 600 paths is presented in their *UK Trailwalkers' Handbook*, last published by Cicerone in 2009. Membership is £13/19 individual/family or international member.

● **Ramblers** (🖳 www.ramblers.org.uk) A charity that looks after the interests of walkers throughout Britain and promotes walking for health. Membership costs £34.50/45.50 individual/joint and includes their quarterly *Walk* magazine.

PLANNING YOUR WALK

dominating BBC1's Sunday night schedules for almost four decades, from 1973 to 2010, making it Britain's longest-running TV comedy. There's no box set that includes all the shows – presumably they couldn't find a box big enough – but you can find various series on DVD as well as on the smaller TV networks such as Gold, Yesterday and Pick.

The comedian, musician, former *Young One* and Mr Jennifer Saunders (Adrian Edmondson) produced a 12-part series in 2012, *The Dales* (ITV Studios Home Entertainment), that looks at the lifestyle and characters of those who live and work in the region. The documentary both complements and supplements a previous DVD, *James Herriot's Yorkshire* (Guerrilla Films, 2007), that looks at the scenery of the county in general that featured in the aforementioned TV series based on Herriot's books.

Finally, there are a couple of **DVDs** about walking in the Dales – and one specifically about the trail itself. *The Dales Way with Mark Richards* (Quantum Leap Group, 2010) is one of a series of Great Northern walks, this one presented by a man who used to be a companion of Alfred Wainwright on some of his Lakeland wanderings. The same studio also produced the short but spellbinding 52-minute *Yorkshire Dales – A Landscape Of Longing* (Quantum Leap Group, 2005). The second DVD for those interested in hiking in the Dales is *Great Walks – Yorkshire Dales* (Striding Edge, 2006; 85 mins), part of a three-DVD series that concentrates on popular walking destinations. Included is an 11-mile circular walk in Wharfedale centred around Grassington. Another in the series looks at the *Great Walks – The Howgills* (Striding Edge, 2006; 52 mins).

Getting to and from the Dales Way

You shouldn't have any trouble getting to the start of the Dales Way, no matter where you're coming from, with Leeds – and, to a lesser extent, Bradford and Harrogate – well served by trains and buses and equally well connected by road. From any of these three places, Ilkley is but a frequent bus or train journey away – or a day's walk on one of the three link routes (see pp69-74).

Getting away from the Way at Bowness-on-Windermere is only slightly trickier. Windermere railway station is a two-mile bus journey from Bowness. From the station you can catch the branch line to Oxenholme Lake District, which is on the main London to Glasgow West Coast line. Or you can catch a bus from the centre of Windermere to most of the main destinations in the lakes or even a ferry across to the western side of the 'mere', for those who want to continue with their lakeland explorations.

NATIONAL TRANSPORT

All train **timetable and fare information** can be found at National Rail Enquiries (☎ 08457 484950, 24hrs; 🖵 www.nationalrail.co.uk). Alternatively, and to book tickets, you can contact the train companies (for details see box opposite) concerned. Timetables and tickets are also available on ⌨ www .thetrainline.com and ⌨ www.qjump.co.uk. You are advised to book in advance – it may well save you a small fortune. If your journey involves changes, it's worth checking which train company operates each leg of the journey. You may find you can save money by buying separate tickets for each train company rather than one through ticket for your whole journey.

Virgin Trains provides services between London Euston and Glasgow/ Edinburgh via Oxenholme Lake District and the lakes (the so-called 'West

❑ **Getting to Britain**

● **By air** **Leeds Bradford Airport** (⌨ www.leedsbradfordairport.co.uk) is conven- ient for the start of the trail and has flights from many European destinations. **Manchester Airport** (⌨ www.manchesterairport.co.uk) remains the nearest *major* international airport to the Dales Way. Trans-Pennine Express (see box opposite) operates services from Manchester Airport to Leeds, and Metro/Northern (see box opposite) operates from there to Ilkley, so less than two hours after catching the train at the airport you should be in Ilkley. Trans-Pennine Express also operates services between Oxenholme Lake District and the Airport which would be convenient at the end of your walk. Nevertheless, though the number of services to and from these air- ports increases year on year, for most foreign visitors a London airport – particularly **Heathrow** (⌨ www.heathrow.com) and **Gatwick** (⌨ www.gatwickairport.com), but also **Stansted** (⌨ www.stanstedairport.com) or **Luton** (⌨ www.london-luton.co.uk) – remains the most likely entry point to the country.

Several **budget airlines** (easyJet ⌨ www.easyjet.com; jet2 ⌨ www.jet2.com; and Ryanair ⌨ www.ryanair.com) fly from many of Europe's major cities to Manchester and the London terminals (Stansted, Luton, Gatwick and Heathrow).

● **From Europe by train** **Eurostar** (⌨ www.eurostar.com) operates a high-speed passenger service via the Channel Tunnel between Paris, Brussels (and some other cities) and London St Pancras International. This is convenient for both the Virgin Trains East Coast line from Kings Cross to Leeds and for West Coast services between Euston and Oxenholme Lake District (for the branch line to Windermere); for details see box opposite.

● **From Europe by coach** **Eurolines** (⌨ www.eurolines.com) have a huge net- work of long-distance coach services connecting over 600 cities in 35 European countries (plus Morocco) to London. It's cheap, but once such expenses as food for the journey are taken into consideration, it may not be that much cheaper than taking a flight, particularly when compared to the prices of some of the budget airlines.

● **From Europe by ferry (with or without a car)** Numerous ferry companies operate routes between the major North Sea and Channel ports of mainland Europe and the ports on Britain's eastern and southern coasts as well as from Ireland to ports in both Wales and England. For further information see websites such as Direct Ferries ⌨ www.directferries.com.

● **From Europe by car** **Eurotunnel** (⌨ www.eurotunnel.com) operates the shuttle train service for vehicles via the Channel Tunnel between Calais and Folkestone tak- ing one hour between the motorway in France and the motorway in Britain.

Coast' line), as well as those running between London and Leeds (part of the so-called 'East Coast' line); **Cross Country** provides services to Leeds from a number of towns and cities; **Northern Rail** is the main operator for both the

---

❑ **Rail services and operators**
Note that not all stations are listed.

Cross Country (☎ 0844 811 0124, 🖥 www.crosscountrytrains.co.uk)
● Birmingham New St to Newcastle via Sheffield, Leeds, York & Durham, daily 1/hr

(First) TransPennine Express (☎ 0345 678 6974, 🖥 www.tpexpress.co.uk
● Liverpool Lime St to Scarborough via Manchester Piccadilly, Leeds & York, daily 1/hr
● Liverpool Lime St to Newcastle via Manchester Victoria, Leeds & York, daily 1/hr
● Manchester Airport/Manchester Piccadilly to York via Leeds, daily 1/hr
● Manchester Airport/Manchester Piccadilly to Edinburgh via Preston, Lancaster, Oxenholme Lake District, Penrith North Lakes & Carlisle, daily 6-7/day
● Manchester Airport/Manchester Piccadilly to Glasgow via Preston, Lancaster, Oxenholme Lake District & Carlisle, daily 4-5/day

Northern Rail (☎ 0344 241 3454, gen info ☎ 0800 200 6060, Mon-Sat 8am-8pm, Sun 9am-5pm, 🖥 www.northernrailway.co.uk)
● Leeds to Appleby via Keighley, Skipton, Settle, Horton-in-Ribblesdale, Ribblehead, **Dent**, Garsdale & Kirkby Stephen, Mon-Sat 5-6/day, Sun 3/day, a few additional services don't stop at all stations listed and/or only operate on part of the route. (Note that at the time of writing the line between Appleby and Carlisle was closed as a result of a landslip; replacement bus services are operating while the line is repaired.)
● Preston to **Windermere** via Lancaster, Oxenholme Lake District, Kendal, Burneside & Staveley (Mon-Sat around 17/day, Sun 10/day). Not all services stop at Staveley & Burneside.
● Manchester Victoria to Leeds via Bradford Interchange, Mon-Sat 2/hr, Sun 1/hr

Virgin (**West Coast services**; ☎ 0344 556 5650, daily 8am-10pm; 🖥 www.virgin trains.co.uk)
● London Euston to Glasgow Central via Rugby, Stafford, Crewe, Preston, Lancaster, Oxenholme Lake District, Penrith North Lakes & Carlisle, Mon-Fri 5/day, Sat & Sun 9/day, call at Oxenholme, additional services to other destinations
● London Euston to Glasgow Central/Edinburgh via Birmingham, Stafford, Crewe, Preston, Lancaster, Oxenholme Lake District & Carlisle, Mon-Sat 6-7/day, Sun 4/day

Virgin (**East Coast services**; ☎ 0345 722 5333, daily 7am-10pm; 🖥 www.virgin trainseastcoast.com)
● London King's Cross to Leeds via Peterborough, Mon-Sat 1-2/hr, Sun 1/hr

Metro (☎ 0113 245 767, daily 7am-10pm, 🖥 www.wymetro.com; Wharfedale Line; services operated by Northern on behalf of Metro)
● Leeds to **Ilkley** via Kirkstall Forge, Guiseley, Menston, Burley-in-Wharfedale, Ben Rhydding, daily 1-2/hr
● Bradford (Forster Square) to **Ilkley** via Frizinghall, Shipley, Baildon, Guiseley and then as above to Ilkley, Mon-Sat 1-2/hr, Sun 7/day
● Leeds to Skipton via Shipley, Saltaire, Bingley & Keighley, daily 2/hr
● Bradford to Skipton via Frizinghall and then as for the Leeds service, daily 1-2/hr

❑ **Coach services**
National Express services to Leeds include (not note all stops are listed):
● **060 & 061** Liverpool to Manchester Airport, Manchester & Leeds (6/day)
● **319, 320, 321 & 324** Birmingham to Derby, Sheffield, Leeds & Bradford (6/day)
● **380** Bradford to Leeds, Middlesborough & Newcastle-upon-Tyne (1/day)
● **425** London to Leeds, Durham & Newcastle (3/day)
● **561** London to Leeds, Bradford, Keighley & Skipton (1/day)
● **310 & 537** Leicester to Nottingham, Sheffield, Leeds & Bradford (5/day)
● **563** London to Milton Keynes, Leeds, York & Scarborough (1/day)
● **240** Heathrow Airport to Luton Airport, Sheffield, Leeds & Bradford (5/day)
● **571** London to Birmingham, Lancaster, Carnforth, Kendal, Windermere & Whitehaven (1/day).

Leeds to Ilkley service and the Oxenholme Lake District to Windermere branch line; and **Trans-Pennine Express**, which operates services from Manchester to Glasgow via Oxenholme Lake District.

Coach (long-distance bus) travel is generally cheaper (though with the excellent advance-purchase train fares that is not always true) but takes longer. The principal coach operator in Britain is **National Express** (☎ 08717 81 81 81, 24 hrs, 🖳 www.nationalexpress.com); see box above for service details. **Megabus** (🖳 uk.megabus.com) has a more limited service though may be cheaper.

Getting to Ilkley
● **By train** Ilkley railway station is at one end of the Wharfedale Line and served by regular trains from both Leeds and Bradford. In all probability, it is Leeds where you will change trains, as the station there is the second busiest outside London (Birmingham New Street is busier than Leeds).

Leeds is on several lines so is easy to reach from anywhere in Britain. It is at the end of the Leeds branch of the East Coast Main Line from London; it's also on the CrossCountry network between Scotland, the Midlands and South West England; the TransPennine Express with connections to major northern towns and cities; on Northern Railway's network including the starting point for trains on the scenic Settle to Carlisle line; and it lies at the heart of the Metro network connecting Leeds with places in all directions around the city.

● **Coach/bus** Leeds and Bradford are, once again, the closest places to Ilkley that National Express buses serve. From there trekkers heading to Ilkley can take either a train (see box p45) or, from Leeds, a bus (X84; see box pp48-9).

● **Car** Leeds is on the A1/M1 so the simplest route from most places in the UK is to get onto the M1 and head towards Leeds, leaving it at junction 45 for the A659, then head due west on the A660 and A65 until Ilkley is reached. The various online route finders will, of course, provide you with more specific and detailed routes for wherever you live.

Getting to/from Bowness-on-Windermere
● **Train/bus** Trains to Oxenholme Lake District from London/Glasgow (around 2½-3½hrs / 1¾-2hrs) operate on the West Coast line.   *(continued on p50)*

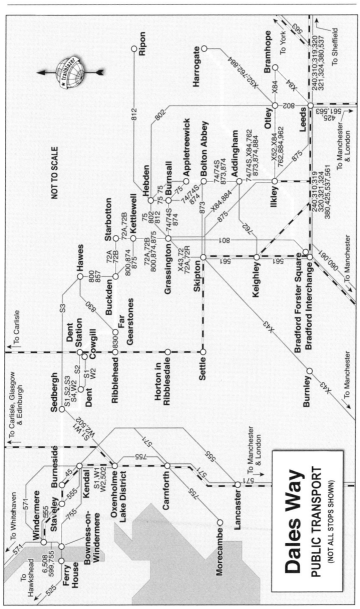

Dales Way
PUBLIC TRANSPORT
(NOT ALL STOPS SHOWN)

PLANNING YOUR WALK

NOT TO SCALE

□ **BUS SERVICES & OPERATORS – DALES WAY**   SEE p47 FOR MAP

Notes

● Service details were as accurate as possible at the time of writing but it is essential to check before travel

● Services on Bank Holiday Mondays are usually the same as Sunday services, not the Monday to Saturday services

● Services generally operate at the same frequency in both directions

● Be aware that where routes are serviced by more than one operator (usually during the peak season), the different operators may not accept each other's tickets

● In rural areas where there are no fixed bus stops it is usually possible to 'hail and ride' a passing bus though it is important to stand where visibility is good and also somewhere where it would be safe for the driver to stop

● Some buses are specifically for schoolchildren with a permit and can't be used by fare-paying passengers; however, these are not listed here

Bus	Route	Frequency	Operator
X43	Manchester to Burnley, Skipton, Threshfield & Grassington	Sun & bank hols 7/day	TBP
X52	Harrogate to Otley & Ilkley	Mon-Sat 9/day	CB
X84	Leeds to Bramhope, Otley, Ilkley, Addingham & Skipton	daily 1-2/hr to Ilkley, Mon-Sat 1/hr to Skipton	First Bus
762	Keighley to Addingham & Ilkley	Mon-Sat 1/hr, Sun approx 1/hr	Keighley
800	Keighley to Addingham, Ilkley, Burley, Otley & Harrogate	Mon-Sat 1/hr	DBus
	Grassington to Threshfield, Kilnsey, Kettlewell, Buckden, Aysgarth, Bainbridge & Hawes	Tue & Sat 1/day	
801	Bradford to Grassington	Tue 1/day	DBus
802	Wakefield to Leeds, Otley, Hebden & Grassington	Sat 1/day	AY
812	Ripon to Hebden & Grassington	Sun & bank hols 2/day	Dales Bus
830	Ingleton to Ribblehead, Far Gearstones, Hawes & Richmond	Sun & bank hols 2/day	TCH/DBus
857	Hawes to Buckden	Sun & bank hols 1/day	DBus
873	Ilkley to Addingham, Bolton Abbey, Strid Wood & Skipton	Sun & bank hols 3/day	DBus
874	Ilkley to Addingham, Bolton Abbey, Strid Wood, Burnsall, Grassington, Kilnsey, Kettlewell & Buckden	Sun & bank hols 2/day (1/day starts in Wakefield)	AY/DBus
875	Wakefield to Leeds, Ilkley, Grassington, Kilnsey, Kettlewell & Buckden	Sun & bank hols 1/day	AY/DBus
884	York to Harrogate, Otley, Ilkley, Addingham, Skipton & Malham	Sun & bank hols 1/day	DBus
962	Otley to Burley station, Ben Rhydding station & Ilkley	Mon-Sat 1/hr	CB (HCT)

Service	Route	Frequency	Operator
72/72A/72R	Skipton to Grassington	Mon-Sat 8-9/day	PD/UWV/NYCC
72A/72B	Grassington to Kettlewell, Starbotton & Buckden (NYCC's 72A service operates to Buckden in term-time only)	Mon-Sat 4-6/day	UWB/NYCC
74/74S	Ilkley to Addingham, Bolton Abbey, Strid, Barden Tower, Burnsall & Grassington	Mon, Wed, Fri 3/day, Sat 4/day	PoftheD
75	Grassington circular route to Hebden, Appletreewick & Burnsall	Mon, Wed, Fri 3-4/day+ 1/day to Bolton Abbey	NYCC
S1	Dent Station to Cowgill, Dent Village, Sedbergh, Oxenholme Station & Kendal	Sat 1/day +2/day Dent Station to Sedbergh +3/day Sedbergh to Kendal	WDCB
S2	Dent Station to Dent & Sedbergh	Sun only 2/day + 2/day Dent to Sedbergh	WDCB
S3	Dent to Sedbergh, Garsdale & Hawes	Tue only 2/day	WDCB
S4	Kirkby Stephen to Ravenstonedale, Dent & Sedbergh	Fri only 1/day	WDCB
W1	Sedbergh to Oxenholme & Kendal	Mon-Fri 2/day	WoS
W2	Cowgill/Lea Yeat to Dent, Millthrop, Sedbergh, Oxenholme & Kendal	Wed 1/day	WoS
6	Barrow to Bowness & Windermere	Mon-Sat 4-5/day, Sun 3/day	S'coach
45	Burneside to Kendal	Mon-Sat 9-11/day	S'coach
502	Kirkby Stephen to Sedbergh, Oxenholme & Kendal, 1/day term-time only		S'coach
508	Penrith to Bowness & Windermere	daily 5/day (Mon-Fri only in term time)	S'coach
525	Ferry House to Hawkshead (see p50 for details of Cross Lakes Shuttle from Bowness to Ferry House)	Mar-Oct 8-10/day	Mountain Goat
555	Lancaster to Kendal to Staveley, Windermere, Grasmere & Keswick	Mon-Sat 1-2/hr till about 4.40pm	S'coach
599	Bowness to Windermere, Ambleside & Grasmere (in the morning services start at Kendal and in the evening they continue to Kendal)	Mon-Sat 2-3/hr	S'coach
755	Morecambe to Carnforth, Kendal, Windermere & Bowness	daily (inc public holidays) 3/day	S'coach

CONTACTS AY (Arriva Yorkshire; ☐ www.arrivabus.co.uk/yorkshire); **CB (HCT)** (Connexions Buses; ☎ 01423 339600, ☐ www.connexionsbuses.com), operated by Harrogate Coach Travel; **DBus** (Dales Bus; ☐ www.dalesbus.org); **First Bus** (☐ www.firstgroup.com/leeds); **Keighley** (☎ 01535 603284, ☐ www.keighleybus.co.uk); **Mountain Goat** (☎ 015394 45161, ☐ www.mountain-goat.co.uk); **NYCC** (North Yorkshire County Council; ☐ www.northyorks.gov.uk); **PoftheD** (Pride of the Dales; ☎ 01756 753123, ☐ www.prideofthedales.co.uk); **S'coach** (Stagecoach; ☐ www.stagecoachbus.com); **TBP** (Transdev Burnley & Pendle; ☎ 0345 60 40 110, ☐ www.lancashirebus.co.uk); **UWV** (Upper Wharfedale Venturer; ☎ 01756 636161, ☐ www.upperwharfedale.com); **WDB** (Western Dales Bus; ☎ 015396 20125, ☐ westerndalesbus.co.uk); **WoS** (Woofs of Sedbergh; ☎ 015396 20414, ☐ woofsofsedbergh.co.uk)

(continued from p46)   Northern services take about 20 minutes to convey you to Windermere Railway Station, from where several buses (Nos 6, 508, 525, 599 and 755) take no more than 10 minutes to Bowness-on-Windermere and the start of the trail (if walking north-west to south-east).

● **Coach/bus**   National Express's No 571 service calls at Kendal and Windermere (see box p46).

● **Boat/bus**   Windermere Lake Cruises (☎ 015394 43360, 🖥 www.windermere-lakecruises.co.uk) operates a Cross Lakes Shuttle service (late Mar to late Oct, daily 10/day) across Windermere which connects with Mountain Goat's bus services to Hawkshead (see box pp48-9) and also other destinations on the western side of the lake. See Windermere Lake Cruises' website for details of cruises they offer on the lake.

LOCAL PUBLIC TRANSPORT SERVICES

Public transport is limited along the Dales Way but most villages have some sort of service. The problem is one of frequency – some of the bus services to the smaller villages operate only on certain days and not necessarily year-round. The important thing, therefore, is to plan meticulously in advance; firstly, by using the summary of services on pp48-9 and the map on p47; then by checking to make sure the service is still operating. To check the current bus timetables, contact **traveline** (☎ 0871 200 2233, 🖥 www.traveline.info); this has public transport information for the whole of the UK and is usually easier than contacting the operator directly as many bus services are run by more than one operator.

The **Cumbria County Council** website (🖥 www.cumbria.gov.uk/buses) has timetables of all their bus services for you to download, while for information about services in **North Yorkshire** visit 🖥 www.dalesbus.org, or 🖥 www .northyorks.gov.uk.

The 2016 boundary changes
In August 2016 the Dales National Park is due to be enlarged by a further 188 sq miles (487 sq km), representing a significant 24% increase on its current size. This expansion will occur largely to the west and north of the existing park. The main purpose of the changes is to finally join the park with the Lake District National Park, England's biggest, with the two meeting along part of the M6 motorway, near junction 38 by Tebay. (The Lake District National Park will also be increasing, incidentally, by a further 3%.) Another major change is that the Howgills are now completely incorporated within the park, as are Mallerstang and Barbon – while Borrowdale will be added to the Lake District (in addition to the Borrowdale that's already part of the Lakes, of course!).

The Dales Way will actually be little affected by the changes. Only the short stretch between the Crook of Lune Bridge and the Lowgill Viaduct will now fall within this new enlarged national park. Nevertheless, the changes are of course to be welcomed as they bring the nation's highest level of protection to some of England's finest landscapes.

MINIMUM IMPACT & OUTDOOR SAFETY

2

Minimum impact walking

In this world in which people live their lives at an increasingly fre-
netic pace, many of us living in overcrowded cities and working in
jobs that offer little free time, the great outdoors is becoming an
essential means of escape. Walking in the countryside is a wonderful
means of relaxation and gives people the time to think. However, as
the popularity of the countryside increases so do the problems that
this pressure brings. It is important for visitors to remember that the
countryside is the home and workplace of many others.

By following a few simple guidelines while walking the Dales
Way you can have a positive impact, not just on your own well-being
but also on local communities and the environment, thereby becoming part of the solution.

ENVIRONMENTAL IMPACT

A walking holiday in itself is an environmentally friendly approach
to tourism. The following are some ideas on how you can go a few
steps further in helping to minimise your impact on the environment
while walking the Dales Way path.

Use public transport whenever possible
Public transport along the Dales Way is not bad (though it can be a
little infrequent at times), with just about everywhere served by at
least one bus or train a day. Public transport is always preferable to
using private cars as it benefits everyone: visitors, locals and the
environment.

Never leave litter
'Pack it in, pack it out'. Leaving litter is antisocial so carry a degradable plastic bag for all your rubbish, organic or otherwise, and even
other people's too, and pop it in a bin in the next village. Or better
still, reduce the amount of litter you take with you by getting rid of
packaging in advance.
● **Is it OK if it's biodegradable?** Not really. Apple cores, banana
skins, orange peel and the like are unsightly, encourage flies, ants
and wasps, and ruin a picnic spot for others; they can also take
months to decompose.

Buy local

Look and ask for local produce to buy and eat. Not only does this cut down on the amount of pollution and congestion that the transportation of food creates, so-called 'food miles', it also ensures that you are supporting local farmers and producers.

Support local traders!

Erosion

● **Stay on the main trail** The effect of your footsteps may seem minuscule but when they're multiplied by several thousand walkers each year they become rather more significant. Avoid taking shortcuts, widening the trail or taking more than one path, especially across hay meadows and ploughed fields.

● **Consider walking out of season** Maximum disturbance by walkers coincides with the time of year when nature wants to do most of its growth and repair. In high-use areas the trail is often prevented from recovering.

Walking at less busy times eases this pressure while also generating year-round income for the local economy. Not only that, but it may make the walk a more relaxing experience with fewer people on the path and less competition for accommodation.

Respect all flora and fauna

Care for all wildlife you come across along the path; it has as much right to be there as you. Tempting as it may be to pick wild flowers, leave them so the next people who pass can enjoy them too. Don't break branches off trees.

If you come across wildlife keep your distance and don't watch for too long. Your presence can cause considerable stress, particularly if the adults are with young, or in winter when the weather is harsh and food is scarce. Young animals are rarely abandoned. If you come across young birds keep away so that their mother can return.

The code of the outdoor loo

For all but a couple of stages, you really shouldn't get caught short and can wait for a toilet until the next town or village. But between Swarthghyll and Dentdale, and from Sedbergh to Burneside facilities are, admittedly, rather scarce (actually, they're non-existent) and for those sections the following advice should be heeded if you need to do something more than just wee. 'Going' in the outdoors is a lost art worth reclaiming, for your sake and everyone else's. As more and more people discover the joys of the outdoors this is becoming an important issue. In some parts of the world where visitor pressure is higher than in Britain, walkers and climbers are required to pack out their excrement. This might one day be necessary here. Human excrement is not only offensive to our senses but, more importantly, can infect water sources.

● **Where to go** If you do have to go outdoors, avoid ruins which can otherwise be welcome shelter for other walkers, as well as sites of historic or archaeological interest, and choose a place that is at least **30 metres away from running**

water. Use a stick or trowel to **dig a small hole** about 15cm (6") deep to bury your excrement. It decomposes quicker when in contact with the top layer of soil or leaf mould. Stirring loose soil into your deposit speeds up decomposition. Do not squash it under rocks as this slows down the composting process. If you have to use rocks to cover it make sure they are not in contact with your faeces.

● **Toilet paper and tampons** Toilet paper takes a long time to decompose whether buried or not. It is easily dug up by animals and may then blow into water sources or onto the path.

The best method for dealing with it is to **pack it out**. Put the used paper inside a paper bag which you then place inside a plastic bag. Then simply empty the contents of the paper bag at the next toilet you come across and throw the bag away. Pack out **tampons** and **sanitary towels**; they take years to decompose and may also be dug up and scattered about by animals.

Wild camping

Wild camping is not encouraged within the national parks which make up the majority of the walk. This is a shame since wild camping is much more fulfilling than camping on a designated site. Living in the outdoors without any facilities provides a valuable lesson in simple, sustainable living where the results of all your actions, from going to the loo to washing your plates, can be seen.

If you do wild camp always ask the landowner for permission. In most cases this is, of course, completely impractical so don't camp on farmland at all, but out on the uncultivated moors or in forests, and stick by the following:

● **Be discreet** Camp alone or in small groups, spend only one night in each place, pitch your tent late and leave early.

● **Never light a fire** Accidental fire is a great fear for farmers and foresters. Never make a camp fire; take matches and cigarette butts out with you to dispose of safely. The deep burn caused by camp fires, no matter how small, damages turf which can take years to recover. Cook on a camp stove instead.

● **Don't use soap or detergent** There is no need to use soap; even biodegradable soaps and detergents pollute streams. You won't be away from a shower for more than a couple of days. Wash up without detergent; use a plastic or metal scourer, or failing that, a handful of fine pebbles or some bracken or grass.

● **Leave no trace** Endeavour to leave no sign of having been there: no moved boulders, ripped up vegetation or dug drainage ditches. Make a final check of your campsite before departing; pick up any litter leaving the place in the same state you found it in, or better.

ACCESS

Britain is a crowded island with few places where you can wander as you please. Most of the land is a patchwork of fields and agricultural land and the terrain through which the Dales Way marches is no different. However, there are countless public rights of way, in addition to the official path, that criss-cross the land. This is fine, but what happens if you feel a little more adventurous and want to explore the moorland, woodland and hills that are near the walk?

MINIMUM IMPACT & OUTDOOR SAFETY

Right to roam

The Countryside & Rights of Way Act 2000 (CRoW), or 'Right to Roam' as dubbed by walkers, came into effect in 2005 after a long campaign to allow greater public access to areas of countryside in England and Wales deemed to

---

❏ THE COUNTRYSIDE CODE

The Countryside Code, originally described in the 1950s as the Country Code, was revised and relaunched in 2004, in part because of the changes brought about by the CRoW Act (see below); it was updated again in 2012 and also in 2014. The Code seems like common sense but sadly some people still appear to have no understanding of how to treat the countryside they walk in. An adapted version of the 2014 Code, launched under the logo 'Respect. Protect. Enjoy.', is given below:

Respect other people

● **Consider the local community and other people enjoying the outdoors** Be sensitive to the needs and wishes of those who live and work there. If, for example, farm animals are being moved or gathered keep out of the way and follow the farmer's directions. Being courteous and friendly to those you meet will ensure a healthy future for all based on partnership and co-operation.

● **Leave gates and property as you find them and follow paths unless wider access is available** A farmer normally closes gates to keep farm animals in, but may sometimes leave them open so the animals can reach food and water. Leave gates as you find them or follow instructions on signs. When in a group, make sure the last person knows how to leave the gates. Follow paths unless wider access is available, such as on open country or registered common land (known as 'open access land'). Leave machinery and farm animals alone – if you think an animal is in distress try to alert the farmer instead. Use gates, stiles or gaps in field boundaries if you can – climbing over walls, hedges and fences can damage them and increase the risk of farm animals escaping. Also be careful not to disturb ruins and historic sites.

Protect the natural environment

● **Leave no trace of your visit and take your litter home** Take special care not to damage, destroy or remove features such as rocks, plants and trees. Take your litter with you (see p51); litter and leftover food doesn't just spoil the beauty of the countryside, it can be dangerous to wildlife and farm animals.

  Fires can be as devastating to wildlife and habitats as they are to people and property – so be careful with naked flames and cigarettes at any time of the year.

● **Keep dogs under effective control** This means that you should keep your dog on a lead or keep it in sight at all times, be aware of what it's doing and be confident it will return to you promptly on command.

  Across farmland dogs should always be kept on a short lead. During lambing time they should not be taken with you at all. Always clean up after your dog and get rid of the mess responsibly – 'bag it and bin it'. (See also p28 and pp170-1).

Enjoy the outdoors

● **Plan ahead and be prepared** You're responsible for your own safety: be prepared for natural hazards, changes in weather and other events. Wild animals, farm animals and horses can behave unpredictably if you get too close, especially if they're with their young – so give them plenty of space. See also p52.

● **Follow advice and local signs** In some areas there may be temporary diversions in place. Take notice of these and other local trail advice.

be uncultivated open country; this essentially means moorland, heathland, downland and upland areas. Some land is covered by restrictions (ie high-impact activities such as driving a vehicle, cycling, horse-riding are not permitted) and some land is excluded (such as gardens, parks and cultivated land). Full details are given on ⌨ www.naturalengland.org.uk.

With more freedom in the countryside comes a need for more responsibility from the walker. Remember that wild open country is still the workplace of farmers and home to all sorts of wildlife. Have respect for both and avoid disturbing domestic and wild animals.

Outdoor safety

AVOIDANCE OF HAZARDS

With good planning and preparation most hazards can be avoided. This information is just as important for those out on a day walk as for those walking the entire Dales Way.

Always make sure you have suitable **clothing** (see p37) to keep warm and dry, whatever the conditions, and a change of inner clothes. Carrying plenty of food and water on those stages where eateries and shops are scarce is vital too. The **emergency signal** is six blasts on the whistle, or six flashes with a torch, best done when you think someone might see or hear them.

Safety on the Dales Way
It may be one of the shortest and easiest of the long-distance paths in Great Britain, but that doesn't mean that it's a completely 'safe path' – for no path can ever be said to be entirely danger-free. The most dangerous section is the stage between Buckden and Dentdale, where the elevation, comparative lack of signage and the sometimes inclement weather all combine to imperil walkers.

Minimising the risks on the Dales Way
All rescue teams should be treated as very much the last resort and it's vital you take every precaution to ensure your own safety:

● Avoid walking on your own if possible.
● Make sure that somebody knows your plans for every day that you're on the trail. This could be a friend or relative whom you have promised to call every night, or the place you plan to stay in at the end of each day's walk. That way, if you fail to turn up or call that evening, they can raise the alarm.
● If the weather closes in suddenly and mist descends while you're on the trail, particularly on the moors or fells, and you become uncertain of the correct trail, do not be tempted to continue. Just wait where you are and you'll find that mist often clears, at least for long enough to allow you to get your bearings. If you're still uncertain, and the weather does not look like improving, return the way you came to the nearest point of civilisation.

● Fill up with water at every opportunity and carry some high-energy snacks.
● Always carry a torch, compass, map, whistle, mobile phone and wet-weather gear with you.
● Wear sturdy boots or shoes, not trainers.
● Be extra vigilant if walking with children.

WEATHER FORECASTS

It's only sensible to try to find out what the weather is going to be like before you set off for the day, especially if heading between Buckden and Dentdale where chances to call for help are limited. Many hostels and tourist information centres will have pinned up somewhere a summary of the weather forecast.

The **Mountain Weather Information Service** (🖳 www.mwis.org.uk) gives detailed online forecasts for the upland regions of Britain including the Lake District and Yorkshire Dales. Online weather forecasts are also available at 🖳 www.bbc.co.uk/weather or 🖳 www.metoffice.gov.uk/public/weather/forecast.

Pay close attention to the forecast and consider altering your plans accordingly. That said, even if a fine sunny day is forecast, always assume the worst and pack some wet-weather gear.

BLISTERS

It's essential to try out new boots before embarking on your long trek. Make sure they're comfortable and once on the move try to avoid getting them wet on the inside and remove small stones or twigs that get in the boot. Air and massage your feet at lunchtime, keep them clean, and change your socks regularly. As soon as you start to feel any hot spots developing, stop and apply a few strips of low-friction zinc oxide tape. Leave it on until the foot is pain free or the tape

---

❑ Dealing with an accident/emergency

If you find yourself in an emergency situation anywhere on the fells, the procedure should be the same: dial ☎ 999, ask for the police and ask them to connect you with Mountain Rescue. For most of the Dales Way, it will be the Upper Wharfedale Fell Rescue Association (UWFRA, 🖳 www.uwfra.org.uk) who will come to your aid. They cover a wide area of the Dales including Nidderdale, Littondale and Mid-Airedale, as well as Wharfedale itself. Based in Grassington, in 2015 they were called out 55 times for a variety of incidents including fell walkers with broken ankles and potholers who had become lost underground.

All the people who work for UWFRA, which operates 24 hours a day, 365 days a year, are volunteers and the association itself is a charitable body relying entirely on donations for their survival.

● Use basic first aid to treat the injury to the best of your ability.
● Work out exactly where you are. If possible leave someone with the casualty while others go to get help. If there are only two people, you have a dilemma. If you decide to get help leave all spare clothing and food with the casualty.
● In an emergency dial ☎ 999 (or the EU standard number ☎ 112). Don't assume your mobile won't work up on the fells.

starts to come off. As you're walking continuously the chances are it won't get better, but it won't get worse so quickly. If you know you have problems apply the tape pre-emptively.

If you've left it too late and a blister has developed you should apply a plaster such as Compeed (or the slightly cheaper clone now made by Boots). Many walkers have Compeed to thank for enabling them to complete their walk; they can last for up to two days even when wet and work with a combination of good adhesive, a gel pad and a slippery outer surface. Popping a blister reduces the pressure but can lead to infection. If the skin is broken keep the area clean with antiseptic and cover with a non-adhesive dressing material held in place with tape. Blister-avoiding strategies include rubbing the prone area with Vaseline or wearing a thin and a thick sock as well as adjusting the tension of your laces. All are ways of reducing rubbing and foot movement against the inside of your boot.

HYPOTHERMIA, HYPERTHERMIA & SUNBURN

Also known as exposure, **hypothermia** occurs when the body can't generate enough heat to maintain its normal temperature, usually as a result of being wet, cold, unprotected from the wind, tired and hungry. It's usually more of a problem in upland areas such as in the Lakes and on the fells.

Hypothermia is easily avoided by wearing suitable clothing, carrying and consuming enough food and drink, being aware of the weather conditions and checking the morale of your companions. Early signs to watch for are feeling cold and tired with involuntary shivering. Find some shelter as soon as possible and warm the victim with a hot drink and some chocolate or other high-energy food. If possible give them another warm layer of clothing and allow them to rest until feeling better. If allowed to worsen, erratic behaviour, slurring of speech and poor co-ordination will become apparent and the victim can very soon progress into unconsciousness, followed by coma and death. Quickly get the victim out of wind and rain, improvising a shelter if necessary.

Rapid restoration of bodily warmth is essential and best achieved by bare-skin contact: someone should get into the same sleeping bag as the patient, both having stripped to the bare essentials, placing any spare clothing under or over them to build up heat. Send or call urgently for help.

Not an ailment that you would normally associate with the north of England, **hyperthermia** (heat exhaustion and heatstroke) is a serious problem nonetheless. Symptoms of **heat exhaustion** include thirst, fatigue, giddiness, a rapid pulse, raised body temperature, low urine output and, if not treated, delirium and finally a coma. The best cure is to drink plenty of water. **Heatstroke** is another matter altogether, and even more serious. A high body temperature and an absence of sweating are early indications, followed by symptoms similar to hypothermia (see above) such as a lack of co-ordination, convulsions and coma. Death will follow if treatment is not given instantly. Sponge the victim down, wrap them in wet towels, fan them, and get help immediately.

Sunburn can happen, even in northern England and even on overcast days. The only surefire way to avoid it is to stay wrapped up or smother yourself in sunscreen (with a minimum factor of 15) and apply it regularly throughout the day. Don't forget your lips, nose and the back of your neck.

COLLAPSE OF MORALE

This is not something that can be quickly treated with medication, but is probably the biggest cause of abandoned attempts on the Dales Way. Weather and injury which add up to exhaustion might be presumed to be the most common culprit, but as I know plenty manage the walk in monsoonal conditions and hobble into Bowness-on-Windermere with a great experience behind them. Others though, can suddenly think: 'What's the point, I'm not enjoying this'.

What it all boils down to is this: knowing your limitations and addressing your motivation; matching expectations with your companions; avoiding putting yourself under stress and being flexible rather than insisting on hammering out every last mile without repetition, hesitation or deviation. You can add having good equipment to that list too.

Map key

ⓘ	Tourist Information	□	Building
📖	Library/bookstore	●	Other
@	Internet	CP	Car park
🎩	Museum/gallery	🚌	Bus station/stop
✝	Church/cathedral	▬🚌▬	Rail line & station
☏	Telephone	▨	Park
☑	Public toilet	📱082	GPS waypoint
♠	Where to stay (G) = groups only		
○	Where to eat and drink		
Λ	Campsite		
⊠	Post Office		
£	Bank/ATM		

⁄⁄	Dales Way	⁄⥿	Gate	🪨	Stone Wall
⁄	Other path	⥿	Stile	~ ~ ~	Water
⁄⁄⁄	4 x 4 track	⤚	Kissing gate	🌳	Trees/woodland
⁄⁄	Tarmac road		River and bridge	⊓ᴛᴛ	Bench, table
⁄	Steps		Hedge	⌐	Signpost
🏷	Slope/ Steep slope	⁄	Fence	**21**	Map continuation

THE ENVIRONMENT & NATURE

Conserving the Dales Way

That the Dales Way is such a beautiful walk is not entirely down to luck. Over the past 50 years, while the predations of the modern world continue to gobble up significant swathes of this sceptered isle, various enlightened agencies and organisations have been established to ensure parts of this country, at least, remain as green and pleasant as William Blake promised.

GOVERNMENT AGENCIES AND SCHEMES

Natural England

The main government body charged with preserving the beauty, diversity, flora and fauna of this country is Natural England. It is this body that decides if a location is worthy of protection and what that level of protection should be. For example, it is Natural England who decides whether a long-distance path is worthy of being afforded the status of National Trail (and thus presumably is the body that, surprisingly, considers that the Dales Way *isn't* worthy of National Trail status!). It is also the agency that determines whether an area is worth being considered a National Park, an Area of Outstanding Natural Beauty, a National Nature Reserve, or a Site of Special Scientific Interest.

Which is all well and good – but what exactly do these designations mean? Well, the highest level of landscape protection is the designation of land as a **national park** which recognises the national importance of an area in terms of landscape, biodiversity and as a recreational resource. At the time of writing there were ten national parks in England. Two of these are visited by the Dales Way, the Yorkshire Dales and Lake District national parks. Indeed, most miles of the Dales Way are spent within these two national parks. This designation does not signify national ownership and these are not uninhabited wildernesses, making conservation a knife-edged balance between protecting the environment and the rights and livelihoods of those living in the parks.

The second level of protection is **area of outstanding natural beauty** (AONB). The only AONB visited by the Dales Way is Nidderdale AONB, which you enter – briefly – at the very start of the walk between Ilkley and Bolton Abbey. The primary objective for an

THE ENVIRONMENT & NATURE

AONB is conservation of the natural beauty of a landscape. As there is no statutory administrative framework for their management, this is the responsibility of the local authority within whose boundaries they fall.

National nature reserves (NNRs) are places where the priority is protection of the wildlife habitats and geological formations. There are currently 224 in England (including Ingleborough, one of the Yorkshire Dale National Park's so-called 'Three Peaks') and they are either owned or managed by Natural England or by approved organisations such as wildlife trusts.

Local nature reserves (LNRs) are places with wildlife or geological features that are of special interest to local inhabitants; there are nine in Cumbria and 17 in North Yorkshire, though none is on the trail.

Sites of Special Scientific Interest (SSSIs) range in size from little pockets protecting wild flower meadows, nesting sites or special geological features, to vast swathes of upland, moorland and wetland. SSSIs, of which there are currently over 4000 in England, covering about 8% of the country, are a particularly important designation as they have some legal standing. Owners and occupiers of SSSI land must give written notice before initiating any operations likely to damage the site and cannot proceed without consent from Natural England. Many SSSIs are also either a NNR or a LNR.

The region in which you'll be walking is littered with SSSIs though it seems the Dales Way takes a perverse delight in avoiding them wherever possible. That said, several are visited on the way: Strid Wood on the first stage north of Bolton Abbey (renowned for its oaks); Bastow Wood, north of Grassington (which overlies an old Celtic field system); River Wharfe, and the adjacent Upper Wharfedale, both north of Kettlewell; Yockenthwaite Meadows, west of Hubberholme; Deepdale Meadows, Langstrothdale; and Oughtershaw and Beckermonds, both west of Deepdale Bridge; Upper Dentdale Cave

---

❏ **Statutory bodies**
● **Department for Environment, Food and Rural Affairs** (🖥 www.gov.uk/defra) Government ministry responsible for sustainable development in the countryside.
● **Natural England** (🖥 www.naturalengland.org.uk) See p59.
● **Historic England** (🖥 historicengland.org.uk) Created in April 2015 as a result of dividing the work done by English Heritage (see p62). Historic England is the government department responsible for looking after and promoting England's historic environment and is in charge of the listing system, giving grants and dealing with planning matters.
● **Forestry Commission** (🖥 www.forestry.gov.uk) Government department for establishing and managing forests for a variety of uses.
● **National Association of Areas of Outstanding Natural Beauty** (🖥 www.landscapesforlife.org.uk); for further information on the North Pennines AONB visit 🖥 www.northpennines.org.uk.
● **Lake District National Park Authority** (🖥 www.lakedistrict.gov.uk); **Yorkshire Dales National Park Authority** (🖥 www.yorkshiredales.org.uk). The government authorities charged with managing the respective areas. They might be worth contacting to find out the latest developments to the path.

❏ **Conservation areas**

While the schemes mentioned in this section have all been introduced to preserve the natural glories of the UK, there is also a Conservation Areas programme (💻 historic england.org.uk). This scheme was actually introduced way back in 1967 to protect the 'man-made' features of the country. Defined as 'an area of special architectural interest, the character or appearance of which it is desirable to preserve or enhance', there are some 8000 Conservation Areas in England covering everything from registered parks and gardens to scheduled monuments, old wreck sites and listed buildings. There are a total of 37 conservation areas in the Dales National Park, and the Dales Way is unusual in that it passes through 11 of them: Bolton Abbey, Appletreewick, Burnsall, Hebden, Grassington, Kettlewell, Starbotton, Buckden, Hubberholme, Dent and Sedbergh. The Settle-Carlisle Railway is also protected under the scheme.

As you pass through these areas you'll struggle to see any significant sign that they are part of any conservation programme, though it's undeniable that they are very pretty. But in these conservation areas the locals are required to seek permission if they want to fell, or even prune, a tree; permission may also be required to modify the exterior appearance of a building, eg by fixing a satellite dish or changing the windows. In spite of these limitations on what a property owner can do, surveys suggest that residents actually enjoy living within a conservation area, and property prices, which are usually higher than similar properties outside these areas, are further evidence of this.

System; River Kent and its tributaries (a good spot for crayfish, apparently); and High Lickbarrow Mires and Pasture, just before Bowness.

Finally, there's the **Special Area of Conservation** (SAC), an international designation which came into being as a result of the 1992 Earth Summit in Rio de Janeiro, Brazil. This European-wide network of sites is designed to promote the conservation of habitats, wild animals and plants, both on land and at sea. Every land SAC is also an SSSI.

CAMPAIGNING AND CONSERVATION ORGANISATIONS

Voluntary organisations started the conservation movement in the mid 19th century and are still at the forefront of developments. Independent of government but reliant on public support, they can concentrate their resources either on acquiring land which can then be managed purely for conservation purposes, or on influencing political decision-makers by lobbying and campaigning.

Managers and owners of land include well-known bodies such as the following organisations. The **Royal Society for the Protection of Birds** (RSPB; 💻 www.rspb.org.uk) has over 150 nature reserves and more than a million members. The **National Trust** (NT; 💻 www.nationaltrust.org.uk), a charity with over three million members, aims to protect, through ownership, threatened coastline, countryside, historic houses, castles and gardens, and archaeological remains for everyone to enjoy. On the Dales Way, the NT's only property is quite an important one: the Upper Wharfe valley, which you'll march through for much of the second and third stages.

Often seeming to overlap the work of the National Trust, **English Heritage** (🖥 www.english-heritage.org.uk) actually looks after, champions and advises the government on historic buildings and places, whereas the National Trust focuses more on country houses. However, in April 2015 English Heritage was divided into a new charitable trust that retains the name English Heritage and a non-departmental public body, Historic England (see box p60).

Campaign to Protect Rural England (CPRE; 🖥 www.cpre.org.uk) exists to promote the beauty and diversity of rural England by encouraging the sustainable use of land and other natural resources in both town and country. Their valuable work is supplemented by the **Woodland Trust** (🖥 www.woodland trust.org.uk), which restores woodland throughout Britain for its 'amenity, wildlife and landscape value'.

As for the fauna, the umbrella organisation for the 47 wildlife trusts in the UK is **The Wildlife Trusts** (🖥 www.wildlifetrusts.org). Two relevant to the Dales Way are **Yorkshire Wildlife Trust** (🖥 www.ywt.org.uk) and **Cumbria Wildlife Trust** (🖥 www.cumbriawildlifetrust.org.uk).

Flora and fauna

From woodland and grassland to heathland, bog and beach, the variety of habitats one encounters on the Dales Way is surpassed only by the number of species of flower, tree and animal that each supports.

The following is not in any way a comprehensive guide; if it were, this book would be so big you would not have room for anything else in your rucksack. Instead, it's merely a brief guide to the more commonly seen flora and fauna of the trail, together with some of the rarer and more spectacular species.

TREES

There's some terrific woodland in Wharfedale. The most memorable that's actually along the path is, of course, Strid Wood, a large area of acidic oak woodland. Elsewhere, the limestone woodlands of Wharfedale, which are characterised by trees such as ash (*Fraxinus excelsior*), downy birch, hazel, hawthorn (*Crataegus monogyna*) and rowan (*Sorbus aucuparia*), several of which have been planted at Little Town (see p135), tend to dominate.

The tree most associated with the River Wharfe is the **willow** (*Salix*) and a number of varieties survive along the banks of the Wharfe including the **weeping willow** (*Salix sepulcralis*), **white willow** (*Salix alba*), which can be easily identified by its long and narrow leaves which taper to curled tips and are hairy underneath, and the **crack willow** (*Salix fragilis*), with its bright green leaves.

PLANTS AND FLOWERS

The river is imperative to the life of the local flora and many plants and wild-flowers abound along the banks and in the meadows which often line the Wharfe.

By the river

Perhaps the two most striking plant species that you'll come across time and again on your riparian ramble are both non-native. The giant-leaved **gunnera** (*Gunnera manicata*) thrives by rivers and in marshy places where they grow in large colonies, often to the exclusion of other plants. And then there's the incredibly prolific pink-flowered **himalayan balsam** (*Impatiens glandulifera*), which is actually a member of the busy lizzy family. You may not be particularly enamoured with the way this tall, aggressive foreign invader has monopolised many a prime riverside site at the expense of the less rapacious native wildflowers but you do have to admit it puts on a lovely display.

Even in the relatively few places where balsam hasn't managed to gain a foothold, the riverbanks are still a riot of colour, provided by, amongst others, the **yellow iris** (*Iris pseudacorus*), the pink flowers of the flowering **rush** (*Butomus*), the lilac of **water violet** (*Hottonia palustris*) and an abundance of white-flowered **water crowfoot** (*Ranunculus aquatilis*). You should also see the reddish stem and fluffy pink flowers of **hemp-agrimony** (*Eupatorium cannabinum*), while below them reside the dark green kidney-shaped leaves of **marsh marigold** (*Caltha palustris*), the blue petals of water **forget-me-nots** (*Myosotis scorpioides*) and the floating oval leaves of yellow water-lilies (*Nymphaea lutea*) – a good sign of nutrient-rich water.

Meadows, woodland and moorland

Perhaps the most famous – and one of the rarest – flowers of the Dales – indeed, it's almost become its emblem – is the **bird's-eye primrose** (*Primula farinosa*). Flourishing in June in soggy grassland, this beautiful flower, taller (at 3-20cm in height) than the more common, yellow, ground-hugging primroses, with pinky-lilac petals surrounding a yellow 'eye' – hence the name – is native to the north of England, with its biggest population in the Dales. Occasionally they can still be seen in Wharfedale though they no longer flourish where the ground has been drained or fertiliser has been used.

The **common rock-rose** (*Helianthemum nummularium*) is an evergreen trailing plant with bright yellow flowers which the Northern Brown Argus butterfly finds irresistible.

Synonymous with spring and the start of the walking season are **bluebells** (*Hyacinthoides non-scripta*), the bluish-purple bell-shaped flowers of which adorn the woodland and hedgerows. Appearing at a similar time of year are **cowslips** (*Primula veris*), **cuckooflower** (*Cardamine pratensis*), aka Lady's Smock, and meadow **buttercups** (*Ranunculuc acris*). The latter can grow up to one metre in height.

By June the pinkish-lilac petals of the **common valerian** (*Valeriana officinalis*) should be on display in the meadows, as should yellow-centred white petaled **oxeye daisies** (*Leucanthemum vulgare*), the purple florets of **common** (*Centaurea nigra*) and **greater knapweed** (*Centaurea scabiosa*), **bird's foot trefoil** (*Lotus corniculatus*), the tall and fragrant **meadowsweet** (*Filipendula ulmaria*), the golden-yellow **lady's bedstraw** (*Galium verum*), and the highly poisonous bright yellow flowers of the invasive **common ragwort** (*Senecio jacobaea*), which, sensibly avoided by grazing animals, thrives, particularly in pastures.

Britain's rarest native orchid, the **lady's slipper orchid** (*Cypripedium Calceolus*), which was thought extinct until a single plant was discovered in 1930 growing in Yorkshire, has now found a home at the Kilnsey Park Estate, below the path near Conistone (see p106). There is rumoured to be one still growing in the wild; but should you by some miracle stumble upon it, note that it is illegal to even touch this plant, while trying to dig it up and steal it could leave you facing a six-month jail sentence!

Perhaps the most spectacular display by any flower, however, is one that you will usually see from a distance. In August the **heather** (*Calluna vulgaris*) comes into bloom, leaving the top of the fells ablaze with colour. It's a wonderful sight.

INSECTS

Of course, whilst you walk, head deep in England's history or dizzy from another spell of meandering, there is another world in existence all about you: that of the insect.

Whizzing past your ears on the riverbank you will experience **dragonfly** (*Anisoptera*) and the smaller **damselfly** (*Zygoptera*), amongst them the brilliant-green **banded demoiselle** (*Calopteryx splendens*), and the rare and relatively slow flying **club-tailed dragonfly** (*Gomphus vulgatissimus*). Also airborne are the splendidly named **marmalade hoverfly** (*Episyrphus balteatus*), the amber-winged **brown hawker** (*Aeshna grandis*), **mayfly** (*Ephemeroptera*), and the obligatory bees and wasps.

Meanwhile, on the ground you may come across one of the 70 species of **longhorn beetle** (*Cerambycidae*) native to Britain, the yellow and black **Cinnabar caterpillar** (*Tyria jacobaeae*) and **yellow meadow ants** (*Lasius flavus*). The singing of grasshoppers and crickets is ubiquitous in summer; those you'll possibly see springing about in the grass include meadow grasshoppers (*Chorthippus parallelus*), **field grasshoppers** (*Chorthippus brunneus*) and **Roesel's Bush crickets** (*Metrioptera roeseli*).

Butterflies

The meadows and waterside pathways of the Dales Way are rich in many species, even though, for many of the UK's native species, the Yorkshire Dales is pretty much at the northernmost extremity of their distribution.

The only rarity of the UK's 54 or so native species that has found a home in Wharfedale is the Northern Brown Argus (*Aricia artaxerxes*) which can be seen mainly in June and particularly in Grassington and Upper Wharfedale where its food-plant, the rockrose, grows.

Foxglove
Digitalis purpurea

Rosebay Willowherb
Epilobium angustifolium

Himalayan Balsam
Impatiens glandulifera

Common Vetch
Vicia sativa

Harebell
Campanula rotundifolia

Red Campion
Silene dioica

Lousewort
Pedicularis sylvatica

Meadow Cranesbill
Geranium pratense

Common Dog Violet
Viola riviniana

Wood Sorrel
Oxalis acetosella

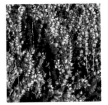

Heather (Ling)
Calluna vulgaris

Bell Heather
Erica cinerea

Common Ragwort
Senecio jacobaea

Hemp-nettle
Galeopsis speciosa

Cowslip
Primula veris

Gorse
Ulex europaeus

Meadow Buttercup
Ranunculis acris

Marsh Marigold (Kingcup)
Caltha palustris

Bird's-foot trefoil
Lotus corniculatus

Water Avens
Geum rivale

Tormentil
Potentilla erecta

Primrose
Primula vulgaris

Yellow Rattle
Rhinanthus minor

Honeysuckle
Lonicera periclymemum

Common Knapweed
Centaurea nigra

Yarrow
Achillea millefolium

Hogweed
Heracleum sphondylium

Rowan (tree)
Sorbus aucuparia

Dog Rose
Rosa canina

Forget-me-not
Myosotis arvensis

Ramsons (Wild Garlic)
Allium ursinum

Bluebell
Hyacinthoides non-scripta

Ox-eye Daisy
Leucanthemum vulgare

Colour photos (following pages)

● **C4 Top**: Burnsall (see p95) – a treat for tired legs and empty stomachs. **Bottom**: Beautiful Sedbergh (see p140), lying snugly in the valley beneath Winder Fell.

● **C5**: The lethal Strid (see p90) – narrow enough to tempt the foolhardy to attempt to leap across; though slip and you'll be dragged under the water by the deadly currents. Better to stick to the riverbank and admire from a safe(-ish!) distance.

● **C6-7** There are numerous photogenic 19th century viaducts (see pp125-4) and old stone bridges on this walk. **Top**: The best view of Lowgill Viaduct is probably this one, from the fields above Half Island House. **Bottom**: The golden arches of the bridge over the River Wharfe at Burnsall, on a sunny summer evening.

That said, many of the species in the Dales are thriving and some previously unseen species are moving into the Dales, such as the speckled wood and ringlet (*Aphantopus hyperantus*), which have become abundant as the climate warms. Walking in September, the most common species I saw were the **small tortoiseshell** (*Aglais urticae*), **large** and **small white** (aka **cabbage white**; *Pieris brassicae/Pieris rapae*) and the **red admiral** (*Vanessa atalanta*); though, particularly with this last one, which is famous for being one of the last butterflies to be seen before winter sets in, the fact I saw more of these species than others has more to do with the time of year I was walking than the relative populations of each species in the Dales. Arrive in early spring, for example, and the species you're most likely to see is the aptly named **orange tip** (*Anthocharis cardamines*).

Other common species include the **small copper** (*Lycaena phlaeas*), **comma** (*Polygonia c-album* – look for the obvious white comma shape on the underwing), gorgeous **peacock** (*Aglais io*) and the plain but plentiful **meadow brown** (*Maniola jurtina*). Most of these I saw while walking by the Wharfe but it's worth noting that I also saw several tortoiseshells near the watershed and the highest point of the trail!

MAMMALS

For much of its length the Dales Way is a riverside walk, whether accompanied by the Wharfe, the Dee, the Lune or one of their minor tributaries. So in addition to the usual wildlife you'll see on most long-distance paths – the rabbits, foxes, badgers, deers and hares – you'll also find some more unusual creatures.

Most prized amongst trekkers would be a sighting of the rarely glimpsed and charismatic **otter** (*Lutra lutra*). This sleek and graceful beast is actually enjoying something of a renaissance thanks to concerted conservation efforts and, though more common in the south-west, otters are still present in the north of England. In addition to being mesmerising to watch, they are also a good indicator of a healthy unpolluted environment. Don't come to the north expecting otter sightings every day though – indeed, if you see one at all you should consider yourself *extremely* fortunate, for they remain rare and very elusive. There are said to be some by Birks Bridge near Sedbergh but they've also been seen as far downstream as Addingham.

❏ **Lambing**
Lambing takes place from mid-March to mid-May when dogs should not be taken along the path. Even a dog secured on a lead can disturb a pregnant ewe.
If you see a lamb or ewe that appears to be in distress contact the nearest farmer. Also, be aware of cows with calves.

(Opposite) Top and bottom: Much of this walk is through or near farming communities and you'll attract friendly interest from most of the locals, which include Highland cattle and Dalesbred sheep. Keep your dog on a lead near livestock. **Middle left**: Small Tortoiseshell butterfly (*Aglais urticae*) on a thistle. **Middle right**: Red Admiral butterfly (*Vanessa atalanta*) on Hemp Agrimony (*Eupatorium cannabinum*). (Photo © Jane Thomas).

THE ENVIRONMENT & NATURE

Even rarer than the otter, the **water vole** (*Arvicola amphibius*) is England's fastest disappearing mammal thanks in large part to the predations of the introduced American mink, small enough to squeeze through the entrance of the water vole's burrow. A concerted conservation campaign is underway to improve the vole's chances of survival but they remain rare and unless you're very lucky you'll have to content yourself with views of their burrows on the riverbank. Away from the river but just as rare, the Yorkshire Dales provide one of the last wild sanctuaries for the **red squirrel** (*Sciurus vulgaris*), particularly around Patterdale and Haweswater. While elsewhere in the country these small, tufty-eared natives have been usurped by their larger cousins from North America, the **grey squirrel** (*Sciurus carolinensis*), in the Dales the red squirrel maintains a precarious foothold. Your best bet for seeing one is to visit Kilnsey Trout Farm, near Conistone, over a mile off the path, where a protected population thrives.

One creature that you will see everywhere along the walk is the **rabbit** (*Oryctolagus cuniculus*). Timid by nature, most of the time you'll have to make do with nothing more than a brief and distant glimpse of their white tails as they stampede for the nearest warren at the first sound of your footfall. Because they are so numerous, however, the laws of probability dictate that you will at some stage get close enough to observe them without being spotted; trying to take a decent photo of one of them, however, is a different matter.

If you're lucky you may also come across **hares**, often mistaken for rabbits but much larger, more elongated and with longer back legs and ears.

Rabbits used to form one of the main elements in the diet of the **fox** (*Vulpes vulpes*), one of the more adaptable of Britain's native species. Famous as the scourge of chicken coops, their reputation as indiscriminate killers is actually unjustified: though they will if left undisturbed kill all the chickens in a coop in what appears to be a mindless and frenzied attack, foxes will actually eat all their victims, carrying off and storing the carcasses in underground burrows for them and their families to eat at a later date. These days, however, you are far more likely to see foxes in towns, where they survive mostly on the scraps and leftovers of the human population, rather than in the country. While generally considered nocturnal, it's not unusual to encounter a fox during the day too, often lounging in the sun near its den.

One creature that is strictly nocturnal, however, is the **bat**, of which there are 17 species in Britain, all protected by law. Your best chance of spotting one is just after dusk while there's still enough light in the sky to make out their flitting forms as they fly along hedgerows, over rivers and streams and around street lamps in their quest for moths and insects. The most common species in Britain is the pipistrelle (*Pipistrellus pipistrellus*).

The **badger** (*Meles meles*) is relatively common throughout the British Isles, these nocturnal mammals with their distinctive black-and-white-striped muzzles are sociable animals that live in large underground burrows called setts, appearing after sunset to root for worms and slugs. In addition to the above, keep a look out for other fairly common but little-seen species such as the carnivorous **stoat** (*Mustela erminea*), its smaller cousin the **weasel** (*Mustela nivalis*), the **hedgehog** (*Erinaceus europaeus*) – these days, alas, most commonly seen as roadkill – and a number of species of **voles**, **mice** and **shrews**.

Some trekkers are lucky enough to encounter deer. Mostly this will be the **roe deer** (*Capreolus capreolus*), a small native species that likes to inhabit woodland, though some can also be seen grazing in fields. Britain's largest native land mammal, the **red deer** (*Cervus elaphus*), is rarely seen on the walk though it does exist in small pockets around the Lakes. As with most creatures, your best chance of seeing one is very early in the morning or late in the evening.

BIRDS

One of the most exciting sights on the Dales Way is watching a **kingfisher** (*Alcedo atthis*) flit across the water. Usually all you'll get is a brief glimpse of its dazzling iridescent blue and gold plumage as it crosses the Wharfe from one perch to another, but occasionally, particularly, I've found, in the evenings, one can take a seat on the riverbank and watch as it hunts for fish, plunging under the water to emerge a fraction of a second later with a beak full of fish. The **dipper** (*Cinclus cinclus*) is the kingfisher's rotund, monochromatic cousin, often swooping above the water in a similar fashion though without some of the agility and with none of the colour of the king.

Another bird you'll see on the Wharfe is the **heron** (*Ardea Cinerea*), an elegant, angular, grey bird with a sinewy neck. Often spied standing motionless in the river's shallows, though sometimes, particularly near the source of the Wharfe by Beckermonds, you'll find them surveying the land from the top of one of the old stone barns, like a feathered weather vane. If you don't believe that birds are descended from dinosaurs, watch as a heron takes flight and opens up its mighty wings; this always put me in mind of those artists' drawings of a pterodactyl on the wing. It's a magnificent sight.

Other water birds that occasionally pop up on the trail to say hello are the **goosander** (*Mergus merganser*) which, with their tufted crest and slightly wild, staring eyes, always look slightly unhinged to me.

More familiar waterfowl that you'll probably encounter along the way include the **swan**, usually the mute version (*Cygnus olor*) – orange beak, prominent black nob on the forehead – though occasionally the odd **whooper swan** (*Cygnus cygnus*) may land (long, wedge-shaped yellow beak, occasionally brown-stained neck); it has perhaps separated from the main flock that usually winters around the Ouse Washes further east. The only bird that can rival swans for pure whiteness is the **snow goose** (*Anser caerulescens*), a pair of which were hanging around downstream of the Crook of Lune Bridge when I was researching this guide. Ducks include the ubiquitous **mallard** (*Anas platyrhynchos*), **teal** (*Anas crecca*) and its close relative the **garganey** (*Anas querquedula*). Not strictly a water bird, though one you'll see frequently on the water's edge, is the elegant **wagtail**, both pied (*Motacilla alba yarrellii*) and grey (*Motacilla cinerea*), the latter's rather dull moniker failing to do justice to a beautiful, 'exotic' bird with a lovely yellow chest and a long, almost bird-of-Paradise tail. If you see a bird perched on a rock in the river or on the river's rocky shore with its tail twitching up and down you can be pretty sure it's a wagtail.

THE ENVIRONMENT & NATURE

Birds of prey near the path include the commonly seen **kestrel** (*Falco tinnunculus*) and **buzzard** (*Buteo buteo*), as well as the much less-spotted, nocturnal **barn owl** (*Tyto alba*), **tawny** (*Strix aluco*) and little **owls** (*Athene noctua*).

One of the most common birds seen on the path, particularly in the latter half of the walk, is the **pheasant** (*Phasianus colchicus*). Ubiquitous on the moors, the male is distinctive thanks to his beautiful long, barred tail feathers, brown body and glossy green-black head with red at the side, while the female is a dull brown. Another way to distinguish them is by the distinctive strangulated hacking sound they make. Rather stupid, ungainly birds, they nevertheless have the capacity to scare the life out of walkers by flying up noisily from the long grass as you approach, their wings slapping together loudly as they fly off. Another reasonably common sight on the fells of Yorkshire is the **lapwing** (*Vanellus vanellus*), also known as the peewit. Black and white with iridescent green upper parts and approximately the size of a pigeon or tern, the lapwing's most distinctive characteristic is the male's tumbling, diving, swooping flight pattern when disturbed, believed to be either a display to attract a female or an attempt to distract predators from its nest, which is built on the ground.

Less common but still seen by most walkers is the **curlew** (*Numenius arquata*), another bird that, like the lapwing, is associated with coastal and open fields, moors and bogs. With feathers uniformly streaked grey and brown, the easiest way to identify this bird is by its thin elongated, downward curling beak. Both the lapwing and the curlew are actually wading birds that nest on the moors in the spring, but which winter by the coast.

LAPWING/PEEWIT
L: 320MM/12.5"

Other birds that make their nest on open moorland and in fields include the **redshank** (*Tringa totanus*), **golden plover** (*Pluvialis apricaria*), **snipe** (*Gallinago gallinago*), **dunlin** (*Calidris alpina*) and **ring ouzel** (*Turdus torquatus*).

In the deciduous woodland areas on the trail, look out for **treecreepers** (*Certhia familiaris*), **tits** (family *Paridae*), including blue, coal, long-tailed and great), **nuthatches** (*Sitta europaea*), **pied flycatchers** (*Ficedula hypoleuca*) and **redstarts** (*Phoenicurus phoenicurus*), while in the conifers watch out for **crossbills** (*Loxia curvirostra*) and **siskins** (*Carduelis spinus*).

CURLEW
L: 600MM/24"

THE LINK ROUTES 4

From Harrogate, Bradford or Leeds

The Dales Way runs for approximately 81 miles (130km) from Ilkley, just outside the southern border of the Yorkshire Dales National Park, to Bowness, just inside the eastern boundary of the Lake District National Park. Walk between those two points on the designated path and nobody can argue that you haven't completed the entire trail – and with a clear conscience you can purchase your 'I've done the Dales Way' certificate and, if you're feeling so inclined, can even wear a T-shirt emblazoned with a similar sentiment.

However, the Dales Way has also sprouted three 'link' routes, that is to say three paths that run between the start of the Dales Way and the three main towns and cities nearest to it (other than Ilkley), namely Harrogate, Bradford and Leeds.

I have always been a bit suspicious of 'link routes' on national trails; having used several, I fail to really see the point of them. You don't ask a marathon runner to run an extra couple of miles before they even get to the starting line so why ask someone on a long-distance path to cover even more mileage before hitting the trail proper? And that's my main problem with these link routes: they add nothing extra (other than mileage) to the 'proper' path and, scenery-wise, they bear little in common with the dramatic scenery of the trail itself. On these link routes you often feel like you're reading the prologue of one book, before putting that tome down and reading a completely separate novel. Furthermore, with Ilkley well supplied with pretty much every facility a trekker could want, and with a perfectly adequate train and bus service running between there and the three towns listed above, it's not as if these feeder routes provide the only link between the trail and 'civilisation'.

Anyway, it matters not, of course, whether I like feeder routes or not; they are part of the Dales Way furniture and, as such, it's my duty to write about them. And besides, according to the main founder of the Dales Way, Colin Speakman, they have existed for almost as long as the Way itself. In truth these three paths are not without their charms. So, having just spent the last three paragraphs telling you in a fairly forthright fashion why I'm not a fan of a feeder route, in the interest of balance I'd better now tell you what advantages these routes may bestow on those who do attempt them.

(continued on p72)

Link routes to the start of the Dales Way at Ilkley

NOTE: ONLY MAIN ROADS SHOWN

HARROGATE

Royal Pump Room Museum

Swinsty Reservoir

Otley

Burley in Wharfedale

Middleton

ILKLEY

Dales Way

0 1 2 3km
0 1 2 miles

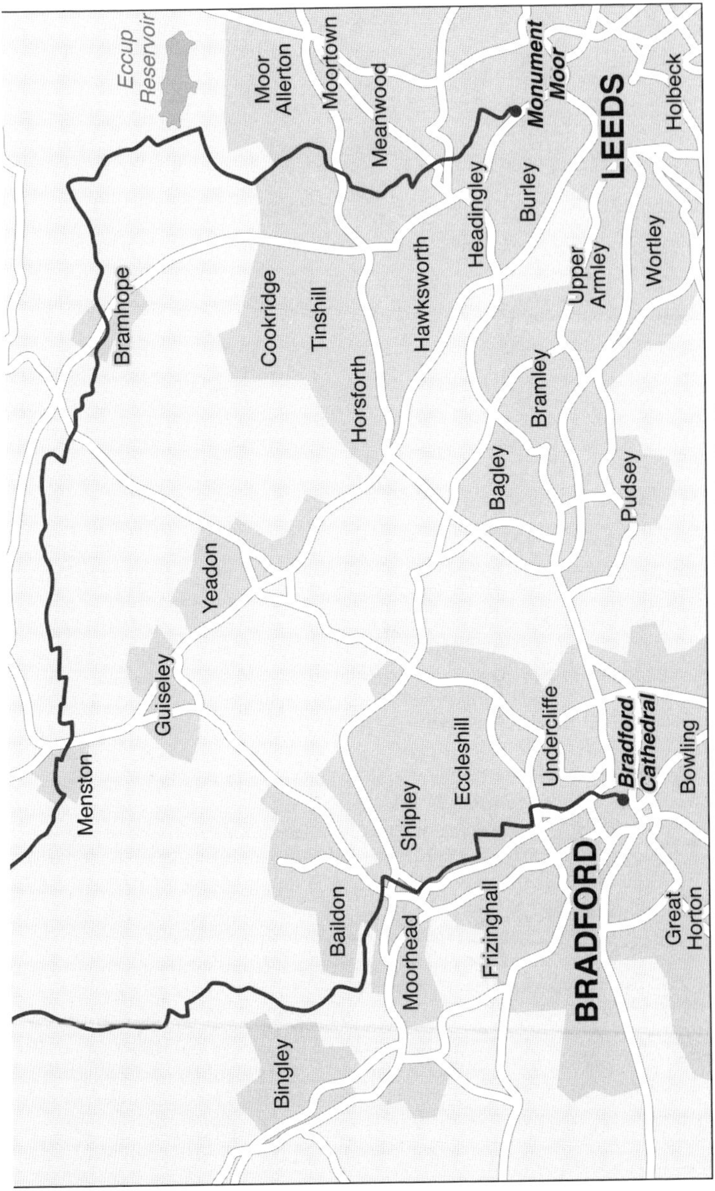
Eccup Reservoir
Moor Allerton
Moortown
Meanwood
Monument Moor
LEEDS
Holbeck
Headingley
Burley
Hawksworth
Upper Armley
Wortley
Bramhope
Cookridge
Tinshill
Horsforth
Bramley
Bagley
Pudsey
Yeadon
Guiseley
Menston
Undercliffe
Bradford Cathedral
Bowling
Eccleshill
Shipley
BRADFORD
Baildon
Frizinghall
Moorhead
Great Horton
Bingley

(continued from p69) For one thing, they will push you nearer to the magic 100-mile mark for the entire walk once you've completed the actual Dales Way – and in the case of the Leeds link, 21 miles (34km) long, over it.

You do also get to see three of the more interesting cities and towns in England: bustling, lively Leeds; cosmopolitan (and surprisingly charming) Bradford; and the tourist magnet of Harrogate, a proud Victorian spa town and, according to more than one poll, the 'happiest place to live in the UK' for the past couple of years! If the 21-mile Leeds link is biting off more than you can chew, the link from nearby Bradford is much shorter: 12½ miles (20km). My favourite, however, is the Harrogate Link at 16½ miles (26.5km). In my opinion it is the one trail which really stands out as a lovely walk in its own right, taking you as it does from the heart of Harrogate across the Nidderdale AONB – a region that seems so very much part of the Yorkshire Dales National Park, and in terms of beauty stands comparison with any valley within the park, yet for some reason lies outside the park's borders. It is this route I describe in greater detail first in the section below, with the other two routes in much less detail afterwards. If you wish to undertake any of these link routes I strongly urge you to get a copy of the relevant OS maps as indicated in the descriptions below.

HARROGATE LINK [see map pp70-1]

For a thorough description of this **16½-mile (26.5km) link route**, including some excellent detailed 'Wainwright-style' hand-drawn maps, visit the **Harrogate Ramblers** website (🖳 www.harrogateramblers.org.uk). Note that this is actually the second link route from Harrogate, the first having been all but abandoned now due to rights of way issues – so if you're using old maps do check that it is the new route you're following. The relevant OS map you'll require for this route is Explorer No 297 (Lower Wharfedale) which covers the entire path.

This new link route begins at the northern end of the town's **Valley Gardens**, across from the famous Pump Rooms, from where you should make your way towards the floral 'roundabout' at the heart of the park, just past the café. From there, you enter into the woods (with Jesus looking on), following the waymarked trail across the road and on to Crag Lane, with the car park for the Royal Horticultural's **Harlow Carr Gardens** on your right. The trail, too, leads right along the road for 100m then left to the Harrogate Arms, now closed. Here the tarmac comes to an end but you should continue into the woods with the fence of Harlow Carr Gardens on your left. It feels as if you are almost looping back on yourself but eventually the trail emerges at Pot Bank Cottage.

Go past the houses rather than taking the detour on your left and you'll soon emerge onto the road with a gate on your right leading steeply down to the bridge over Oak Beck. Cross over the bridge and hurry up the hill avoiding (hopefully!) the fast-moving traffic until you reach the sanctuary of Pot Bridge Farm, at the brow of the hill on your left. Follow this track through the farm to the small plot of trees after scruffy Oatlands Farm; an arrow daubed onto the side of an old water tank points the way. A series of fields follows, passing farmsteads including Central House Farm and, at the end of this stretch, Long Liberty

Farm. The first of the great reservoirs on this trail, **Beaver Dyke Reservoir**, and its adjoining neighbour John O'Gaunt's Reservoir, lie close by, reached by turning left on hitting the farm's access road, then right off it past the cow barns and through the gate. This latter reservoir is named after nearby **John of Gaunt's Castle**, a ruin of an old hunting lodge which is visible across the water from the trail (a couple of benches have been conveniently placed to encourage you to stop and savour the views).

At the end of the reservoir you hit a grassy lane, where you should turn left then right (don't drop down to the reservoir itself), to continue onto the old track known as Bank Slack. You are now entering Nidderdale AONB and should continue your south-westerly bearing across occasionally boggy fields to Brame Lane and *The Sun Inn* (💻 www.thesun-inn.com; food served Mon-Fri noon-2.30pm, Wed-Fri 6-8pm, Sat noon-8pm, Sun noon-5pm).

Cross the road to take the track down through fields and forest to **Swinsty Reservoir**. Follow the water's eastern edge, crossing over the dam to the reservoir's western side. The next bit can be slightly tricky to follow: a path at the dam's western end takes you up the bank and right, into the woods. A few hundred metres in take a left (waymarked) and then a couple of hundred metres later turn left again (unmarked) on the main path heading up the hill to the edge of the wood and a gate with a blue 'Yorkshire Water' sign. You'll know you're on the right track if, having gone through the gate, you cross a bridleway to a second gate, then follow a path that leads eventually, after several fields, to lovely **Timble**. Over a mile of road walking follows now, but the roads are quiet; heading over the crossroads onto a road that's forbidden to vehicles, you find yourself – eventually – entering the forest at **Great Timble**.

Keep straight on, ignoring paths that shoot out on both sides, until you finally emerge from the forest and via two gates onto Denton Moor. The obvious path here takes you along Lippersley Ridge to the first stone boundary marker, with a 'D' carved into its southern side. Continuing further along the path you come to a round cairn cum open shelter, which marks the high point of the walk. Retracing your steps for just a couple of metres, a small path leads you past several numbered stone shooting butts. The path seems to be taking you towards a stone lodge but before you reach it a vague path heads off west. Follow this and keep on looking west and in time you should spy **March Ghyll Reservoir**. At a path junction take the left-hand trail that aims right towards the reservoir, the path descending to a gate in a wall and a couple of sheep fields. Descending off the moor to **Hollingley Farm**, keeping the wall to your left all the way, turn right at the farmyard to pretty Fairy Dell, continuing onwards and upwards to East Moor Farm and further on to West Moor Farm.

At neighbouring **Hill Top Farm** they have a cottage industry baking chocolate brownies (☎ 07810 201 386, 💻 www.lovebrownies.co.uk); there's also a little café where they sell their wares. From here you should follow the road that heads south through Middleton and down to Curly Lane. At the lowest point of the lane, just before it starts to rise again, there's a footpath leading you past a swimming pool and on to the river; a right turn takes you to the main, metal bridge leading into Ilkley (see p77).

BRADFORD LINK   [see map pp70-1]

The **12½-mile (20km)** Bradford Link route is uneven, with patches of pure beauty interspersed with the occasional, less-impressive stretches where business parks and busy roads dominate. Bradford Council produce an excellent guide to the trail with four clear maps and four pages of detailed instructions; visit 🖥 www.bradford.gov.uk for details. For further back-up, OS map Nos 288 and 297 cover the entire trail (as well as the first few miles of the Dales Way).

The walk starts at the ornate metal gates of **Bradford Cathedral** and ends, beautifully, with a crossing of Ilkley Moor, passing stone circles and ancient milestones along the way, before you drop down into the town centre to arrive at the railway station. The first part of the path between Bradford and Shipley is largely urban in nature, though even here there are some charming spots including the Boars Well Urban Wildlife Reserve and some great views of the old mill buildings, which provided Bradford with so much of its wealth and status during its 19th-century heyday. (In fact, the original Bradford Link started at Shipley and was only extended to Bradford's city centre fairly recently.)

At **Shipley**, where refreshments are available, you join a canal towpath west for over a mile before heading north at Hirst Lock to reach Bingley Moor and the stone circle known as the **Twelve Apostles**. **Ilkley Moor** follows in short order, and soon the town itself is reached.

LEEDS LINK   [see map pp70-1]

Though it's my least favourite link, this is also the official link path according to the Dales Way Association. At **21 miles (33.8km)** it's also the longest and many people may want to divide the hike, booking two nights in Leeds and taking advantage of the excellent public transport links to convey them back to the city after a day on the trail. The suburb of Bramhope is approximately halfway along the trail and well connected by bus to both Leeds and Ilkley; the **X84 bus** (see box pp48-9) travels between Leeds and Skipton via Bramhope and Ilkley.

One of my problems with the route is the amount of time you spend walking out of Leeds itself. Indeed, it's only when you reach the reservoir at **Eccup** – around 6½ miles (10.5km) from the start of the walk at the **stone statue of Henry Marsden** – that you feel as if you've entered the countryside (though to be fair, the trail does its best to stick to the greener parts of the city as it makes its way northwards, including lovely **Adel Woods**).

Highlights of this link include the red kites that fly above Eccup, and the gorgeous **Chevin Forest Park**, about five miles further north, with its excellent birdlife and timid roe deer. Towards the end of the trail you finally get to fill your lungs with pure, unpolluted countryside air as you enjoy the wide-open expanse of the **Burley** and **Ilkley Moors**, culminating in a visit to the famous **Cow and Calf Rocks** on the edge of Ilkley town.

OS map Nos 288, 289 and 297 will be required to cover the whole trail.

Using this guide

The route guide has been divided into stages but these should not be taken as rigid daily stages since people walk at different speeds and have different interests. The route summaries below describe the trail between significant places and are written as if walking the path from south to north, from Ilkley to Bowness.

To enable you to plan your own itinerary, practical information is presented clearly on each of the trail maps. This includes walking times in each direction, places to stay and eat, as well as shops where you can buy supplies. Further service details are given in the text; note that the hours stated for pubs relate, for the most part, to when food is served; most venues serve drinks outside these hours. For **trail profiles** of the various stages see the **colour overview maps** at the end of the book.

For an overview of this information see the suggested itineraries (p31) and the town and village facilities table (p32).

TRAIL MAPS   [see map key p58]

Scale and walking times
The trail maps are to a scale of 1:20,000 (1cm = 200m; $3^1/8$ inches = one mile). Each full-size map covers about two miles but that's a very rough estimate owing to the variety of terrain.

Walking times are given along the side of each map; the arrow shows the direction to which the time refers. Black triangles indicate the points between which the times have been taken. These times are merely a tool to help you plan and are not there to judge your walking ability. After a couple of days you'll know how fast you walk compared with the time bars and can plan your days more accurately as a result. **See note on walking times in the box below**.

❏ **Important note – walking times**
Unless otherwise specified, all times in this book refer only to the time spent walking. You will need to add 20-30% to allow for rests, photography, checking the map, drinking water etc. When planning the day's hike count on 5-7 hours' actual walking.

Up or down?

The trail is shown as a dashed line. An arrow across the trail indicates the gradient; two arrows show that it's steep. Note that the arrow points towards the higher part of the trail. If, for example, you are walking from A (at 80m) to B (at 200m) and the trail between the two is short and steep it would be shown thus: A— — — >> — — – B. Reversed arrow heads indicate a downward gradient. Note that the *arrow points uphill*, the opposite of what OS maps use on steep roads.

GPS waypoints

The numbered GPS waypoints refer to the list on p169.

Other features

Features are marked on the map when they are pertinent to navigation. To avoid clutter, not all features have been marked each time they occur.

ACCOMMODATION

Accommodation marked on the map is either on or within easy reach of the path. Many B&B proprietors based a mile or two off the trail will offer to collect walkers from the nearest point on the trail and take them back the next morning.

Details of each place are given in the accompanying text. The number of **rooms** of each type is given at the beginning of each entry, ie: **S** = single, **T** = twin room, **D** = double room, **Tr** = triple room and **Qd** = quad. Note that many of the triple/quad rooms have a double bed and either one/two single beds, or bunk beds, thus in a group of three or four, two people would have to share the double bed but it also means the room can be used as a double or twin.

Rates quoted for B&B-style accommodation are **per person (pp)** based on two people sharing a room for a one-night stay; rates are usually discounted for longer stays. Where a single room **(sgl)** is available the rate for that is quoted if different from the rate per person. The rate for single occupancy **(sgl occ)** of a double/twin may be higher, and the per person rate for three/four sharing a triple/quad may be lower. At some places the only option is a **room rate**; this will be the same whether one or two people (or more if permissible) use the room. See p30 for more information on rates.

Your room will either have **en suite** (bath or shower) facilities, or a **private** or **shared** bathroom, or shower room, just outside the bedroom.

The text also indicates whether the premises have: **wi-fi** (WI-FI); if a **bath** (⚭) is available either as part of en suite facilities, or in a separate bathroom – for those who prefer a relaxed soak at the end of the day; if a **packed lunch** (Ⓛ) can be prepared, subject to prior arrangement; and if **dogs** (🐾 – see also pp170-1) are welcome, again subject to prior arrangement, either in at least one room (many places have only one room suitable for dogs), or at campsites. The policy on charging for dogs varies; some charge an extra £5-20 – a fee that usually covers their entire stay whether it's for just one night or much longer, while others may require a refundable deposit against any potential damage or mess.

The route guide

ILKLEY [see map p79]

The starting point for the 'official' Dales Way is Ilkley (⌨ ilkley.org), an attractive place of wide streets and handsome architecture. Best known as a Victorian spa town, Ilkley actually boasts some ancient origins. The Mesolithic carvings in the hills around the town are testimony to that, including some 250 'cup and ring' marks and a curved swastika carved on the rocky outcrops above the town which are estimated to be at least 11,000 years old. The Romans moved in during the 1st century AD and built a fort (believed by some to be called Olicana), near to the modern town centre; a person from Ilkley is still called an Olicanian. And there are three crosses in All Saints' Church at the northern end of the main boulevard, Brook St, that date back to the 7th-century Saxons. The town had to wait until the 19th century, however, to enjoy its heyday when the springs at Wheatley, a mile to the east, were developed by the Victorians into the huge Ben Rhydding Hydropathic Establishment; this has now been demolished, though Wheatley is now called Ben Rhydding in its honour. But where once folk used to flock to Ilkley to take the waters, now they arrive to drink the beer, with both the Ilkley and Wharfedale breweries located in town. See p14 for details of Ilkley's festivals.

Ilkley is a friendly place and, facilities-wise, there's pretty much everything a trekker could want, including some fine places to eat and stay. But with Ilkley Moor to the south and the Wharfe snaking away to the north, it's a rare trekker who doesn't want to pull on their boots, strap themselves into their backpack – and get on the trail as soon as they can.

Services

There's a **tourist information centre** (☎ 01943 602319, ⌨ www.visitilkley.com;

Mon-Sat 9.30am-4.30pm), at the top of the town opposite the railway station, while within the station itself is the **post office** (Mon-Fri 9am-5.30pm, Sat 9am-12.30pm) and a **supermarket**, M&S Simply Food (Mon-Fri 8am-8pm, Sat 8am-7pm, Sun 11am-5pm). A little further east on Station Rd is a large Tesco (Mon-Sat 6am-midnight, Sun 10am-4pm), and on the main drag, Brook St, there's a Co-op (daily 6am-11pm). This same road also hosts a branch of the **chemist's**, Boots (Mon-Sat 8.30am-5.30pm, Sun 11am-4pm), the **boot repairers** Timpson (Mon-Sat 9am-5.30pm), and an **outdoor/trekking shop**, Mountain Warehouse (Mon-Sat 9am-5.30pm, Sun 10.30am-4.30pm), for those who've forgotten their boots altogether. On Leeds Rd there's a second outdoor outlet, Backcountry (Mon-Sat 9.30am-5.30pm).

Transport

[For details see pp43-50] Ilkley is a stop on Northern Rail's **train** service (from Preston) which calls at Oxenholme Lake District, which is on the West Coast Line.

Ilkley bus station, on Station Rd, is a stop on several **bus** services. The X52 operates here from Harrogate; the X84 Leeds to Skipton service (journey time over an hour from Leeds to Ilkley) calls here as does the 762 (Keighley to Addingham) and the 962 from Otley. Services with stops on/near the Dales Way include Nos 74/74S to Grassington, with the Sunday/Bank Holiday 874 service continuing onto Buckden; other Sunday services include the 873 (Skipton to Ilkley), the 875 (Wakefield to Buckden via Ilkley) and the 884 (Skipton to Addingham).

Where to stay

Ilkley rather lets itself down on the accommodation front, with no campsites, bunk barns or hostels within its borders and a dearth of B&Bs in the town centre too. If you're having trouble, don't forget Addingham, just a few miles along the trail and with a couple of good options.

About 5-10 minutes east of the tourist information centre and at No 1 on the street of the same name is *Tivoli Place* (☎ 01943 600328, 🖳 www.tivoliplace.co.uk; 2D/1T all en suite, 1Tr private bathroom; ✆; WI-FI). It's a pleasant place, a Victorian terrace surrounded by high hedges and with every room equipped with TV and DVD player. Rates are £32.50pp (sgl occ £45, £85 for three adults sharing).

Across town, 19th-century *Dales View Cottage* (Map 1, p83; ☎ 07768 764719, 🖳 www.dales view-ilkley.co.uk; 1D or T en suite/1D with private bathroom; ✆; WI-FI), at 142 Skipton Rd, which is on the A65 and is about 10 minutes west of the town centre but less than five to both the start of the trail and one of the best places to eat in town, Ilkley Moor Vaults (see Where to eat). Both the rooms are at the rear of the property and both overlook the start of the trail; there is also a guest lounge. Rates are £35pp rising to £37.50pp on Fri & Sat (sgl occ £45).

The most appropriate – and central – place to stay is *The Dalesway* (☎ 01943 605438, 🖳 www.thedaleswayhotel.co.uk; 1T/7D or T/1Tr, all en suite; ✆; 🐾; WI-FI), on New Brook St, a slightly scruffy hotel on the outside though the rooms, all of which are named after places on the trail, are fine. Rates are £35-60pp (sgl occ rates on request; three sharing room rate plus £10), with midweek rates lower than the weekend tariff. Breakfast costs £11.95.

Up the hill due south of the railway station, the Georgian *Rombalds Hotel* (☎ 01943 603201, 🖳 www.rombalds.co.uk; 2S/12D/1T, all en suite; 🐾; £10; WI-FI) is part of the Best Western chain though under various guises it's been welcoming guests since 1835. Rates vary throughout the year but expect to pay from £54pp (sgl from £77.50, sgl occ from £87.50). Note that the single rooms are on the 3rd floor and the hotel does not have a lift.

Finally, just 200 yards from the start of the trail and overlooking the Wharfe, *The*

Riverside Hotel (☎ 01943 607338, 🖳 www.ilkley-riversidehotel.com; 1S/7D/3T/1Qd, all en suite; 🐾 £10; Ⓛ; WI-FI) is a lovely spot. The hotel has been run by the same family for the past 44 years and is reasonable value (B&B £42.50-47.50pp, sgl £55, from £145 for the quad). A little busy in the daytimes, particularly at weekends when the sun is shining and the world and his wife seem to want to hang out by the riverbank here.

Where to eat and drink
There are several choices for those who want to head off on the trail early in the morning, and are looking for something to nibble on before they go, including branches of those ubiquitous cafés, **Costa** (Mon-Fri 7am-6.30pm, Sat 7.30am-6.30pm, Sun 8.30am-5.30pm) and **Caffe Nero** (Mon-Sat 7am-6.30pm, Sun 8.30am-6pm), with the latter allowing dogs inside.

If you want to avoid the high-street chains, **La Stazione** (Mon-Fri 6am-5pm, Sat 7.30am-5pm, Sun 9am-5pm) also boasts a very early opening time. **Loafer Bakery** (Mon-Sat 7.30am-3.30pm) charges just £4 for their large takeaway breakfast in a box, which includes toast, bacon, egg, sausage, black pudding, mushrooms, tomatoes and beans. Nearby on Brook St there's also a branch of **Greggs** (Mon-Sat 8am-5pm, Sun 10am-4pm).

For lunch, I liked **Café J** (🖳 www.cafejilkley.co.uk; Mon-Fri 10am-3pm, Sat 10am-4pm) hunkered down in a cellar on The Grove, a cosy place with a lovely burner nestling beneath an old stone mantlepiece. Dog friendly and with WI-FI, the menu is of the standard sarnis-and-jacket-spuds variety but it often has a great specials board that elevates the food above the mundane.

There are also several great speciality choices on Church St. **Veggie** (🖳 www.the veggiecafe.co.uk; Tue-Fri 11am-4pm, Sat 9.30am-4pm) employs lovely smiling staff who exude the joy of vegetarianism. Their veggie mezze (£7.50) is a great way to sample the range of fare on offer, their marinated portobello mushroom burger is delicious (£7.25) – or you can stick to the regular

River Wharfe

To Harrogate

1
To Riverside Hotel &
start of the Dales Way

Middleton Ave

0   50   100m

Castle Rd

★ trailblazer

Castle Rd

Wharf View Rd

New Brook St

Weston Rd

Leeds Rd A65

Castle Hill

Bridge Lane

Castle Rd

**Flying
Duck**

Moody Cow ○

Moo-oooo ○

Lishman's ●

Veggie ○

The Dalesway

● **Backcountry**

**Toast
House** ○

Church St A65

To Dales View Cottage
& Ilkley Moor Vaults

○ **Box Tree**

Caffe Nico ○

Nile Rd

Victory Rd

Timpson ●

Boots ●

Cunliffe Rd

West St

Brook St

● **Barça**

Trafalgar Rd

**Ilkley
Sandwich
Company** ○

Co-op ●

**Bistro
Saigon** ○

Costa ○

Railway Rd

Greggs ○

**M&S
Simply
Food** ●

**Railway
station**

Café J ○

Caffe Nero ○

**Pizza
Express** ○

**Bus
stops**

The Grove B6382

Mountain ●
Warehouse

✉

**Post
Office &
La Stazione**

Station Rd B6382

To Tivoli
Place

Back Parish Ghyll Rd

Riddings Rd

**Loafer
Bakery** ○

ⓘ

**Tourist
information**

Wells Walk

Wells Promenade

Wells Rd

Whitton Croft Rd

Chantry Dr

Ilkley

To Rombalds Best
Western Hotel,
Bradford & Leeds

Chantry Dr

sandwiches (£5.50) and paninis (£6.25). Just up the street, **Toast House** (Tue-Fri 9am-4.30pm, Sat 9am-5pm) is an unusual place, where two slices of toast with various toppings are £2.60, a toast-based lunch is £4.95 (eg beetroot & mint dip with feta on two slices of sourdough toast), or there is, unexpectedly, a range of porridges available too (£3-4.50).

Across the way, **Moo-oooo** (🖳 www .moo-oooo.co.uk; Tue-Sat 11am-5pm, Sun noon-4pm) serves coffee, shakes and ice-cream; it's mainly a kid's place but no less tasty for that. On the same side, **Lishman's** (☎ 01943 609436; Mon-Fri 8am-5.30pm, Sat 8am-4.30pm) is a first-class butchers (they even offer butchery courses) which also does a nice byline in hot pork rolls with apple sauce (and even crackling if requested) for less than £3. Finally, for takeaway sandwiches the **Ilkley Sandwich Company** (Mon-Fri 9am-4pm, Sat to 5pm) offers over 50 fillings (sandwiches from £2.50) as well as jacket spuds (£3-5), toasties (£3.20-3.70) and salad boxes (£3-3.90) to take away.

Back on Brook St, **Caffe Nico** (Mon-Sat 8.30am-5.30pm) is a good option if you're looking for coffee but don't want to patronise the chains. Despite the name it actually offers fairly standard English café fare (full English breakfasts, for example, £6.10) but occasionally with an Italian twist (the sandwiches are on ciabatta and they do a delicious special mozza melt (mozzarella, chopped tomato, oregano, spicy sausage & rocket with olive oil melted on an open ciabatta) for £6.30, or half for £3.60.

In the evenings, the place that got the most recommendations was **Ilkley Moor Vaults** (☎ 01943 607012, 🖳 www.ilkley moorvaults.co.uk; Tue-Sat noon-2.30pm & 5.30-9pm, Sun noon-6pm), known locally as 'The Taps'; it lies above the start of the trail on Stockeld Rd. The menu is, perhaps surprisingly, largely made up of standard pub grub but the food itself is anything but, with most of the ingredients locally sourced and the dishes served absolutely scrumptious. The specials board changes regularly but allows the chef to show off his creative side; if it's available don't miss the Yorkshire burger, with Yorkshire blue cheese, black pudding, bacon & spicy chips (£13.45). Great atmosphere, great food, great drinks selection ... overall, it's just great.

Back near the town centre, **Moody Cow Steakhouse, Bar & Grill** (Tue-Thur noon-2.30pm & 5.30-9.30pm, Fri & Sat to 10pm, Sun noon-8pm) is good for a slap-up meal, with a 5oz steak and half a rack of ribs for £17.95. A few yards to the south, **The Dalesway Hotel** (Mon-Fri noon-2.30pm & 6-9pm, Sat & Sun noon-4pm & 6-9pm) does the usual pub favourites as well as their own take on a local delicacy, basically a meal of roast beef, roast potatoes, veg and onion gravy, all served in a giant Yorkshire pudding, for £7.95. Beer fans should head to the **Flying Duck** (🖳 www.wharfedalebrew ery.com; Sun-Thur noon-11pm, Fri & Sat noon-midnight), home to Wharfedale Brewery (see box p23).

For those who want something other than British food there are several choices: **Barca** (☎ 01943 604408) is on the 1st floor of a building on Brook St, a Mediterranean restaurant with mains in the evening from £7 (for a basic Arrabiata pasta dish) to £19.95 for the rib-eye, and with sharing platters for £24.95-29.95. At 11 Station Plaza is a branch of **Pizza Express** (☎ daily 11.30am-11pm), while one block north on Railway Rd is **Bistro Saigon** (🖳 www .bistrosaigon.co.uk; Tue-Sat 11.30am-2pm, Sun noon-2.30pm, Tue-Thur 6.30pm to late, Fri & Sat from 6pm, Sun 6-8.30pm) with Vietnamese mains running from £10.75 for lemongrass chicken to £15 for Vietnamese yellow duck curry.

Finally, the place with the best reputation for fine dining in Ilkley is the Michelin-starred, flower-fronted **Box Tree** (☎ 01943 608484, 🖳 www.theboxtree .co.uk), where celebrated chef and stock-cube ambassador Marco Pierre White trained. The pricing is fairly simple, with four courses for £65, and the food is, of course, terrific. The menu regularly changes though – when I called in, wild-caught seabass, San Marzano tomatoes, aubergine purée and a caper beurre noisette was seen swimming across its pages. It's lovely but, really, shouldn't you be saving this sort of treat for the end of your walk?

STAGE 1: ILKLEY TO BURNSALL [MAPS 1-7]

Traditionally, the destination for walkers at the end of their first day on the Dales Way is Grassington, and with its superior choice of B&Bs, eateries and other facilities, it does at first sight seem a sensible choice. But there is no getting away from the fact that walking over 16 miles on the first day is, as sports commentators are wont to say, 'a big ask'. Furthermore, by attempting to hike all that way in one day you're leaving yourself little time to savour the sights and settlements – Addingham Church and its ancient stone cross, magnificent Bolton Abbey, the pubs at Appletreewick and pretty Burnsall – that you'll encounter along on the way.

So for this reason, I'm going to break with tradition and recommend that you actually reduce your ambitions on this first stage. If you're camping, this means stopping at Appletreewick, which at 12 miles (19.6km) from the trail's start is a sensible distance for the first day (and you get the chance to enjoy the best pub of the whole trail, the characterful Craven Arms, too). While those relying on B&Bs and pubs for their accommodation can choose to end their first day either in Appletreewick, or a mile further on in Burnsall (**13¼ miles/21.5km; 5hrs 40 mins**), another lovely spot and one with everything a walker would want. In both cases, Grassington, around 3½ miles (5.7km) further on from Burnsall, can then be treated as an early lunch stop the next day.

As for the highlights on this first stage, well the magic really starts once you cross the boundary into the Yorkshire Dales National Park and are confronted by the fabulously photogenic Bolton Abbey, an enigmatic ruin set against a backdrop of mighty mature woodland. Thereafter the Way takes you on a stroll through **Strid Woods**, the longest unbroken stretch of woodland on the entire trail (and boy, is it lovely!) before embarking on an unchallenging amble along the banks of the Wharfe, past aqueduct, angler, wildflowers and white waters, to **Appletreewick**, whose main pub, the Craven Arms, is just a few minutes from the trail. **Burnsall**, with a wider choice of B&B-style accommodation, is a mere mile of pleasingly unproblematic promenading further along the trail.

The route

The first half of this initial stage can best be summed up as 'pleasant'. Not 'jaw-dropping' or 'spellbinding' – I'll save those adjectives for later in the walk, when the sights and scenery truly justify them. Instead, this initial section is an attractive but unremarkable hike, necessary to convey you from the hubbub of Ilkley to the delights of the Dales.

The trail is not without interest – and this begins right at the start with the lovely 17th-century humpbacked **Old Bridge** at Ilkley. A hostage to both kismet and climate, its exterior ravaged by time, it nevertheless stands stoically and silently, bent but unbowed. Which is, coincidentally, how you'll be loc'' once the Dales Way has finished with you.

The start of your odyssey begins at the bridge's southern end, and initially feels more like a Sunday afternoon stroll than a long-distance trail, the path dodging a course between back garden and riverbank, through sheep fields and wild meadows alive with birdsong and butterflies as it follows, more or less, the line of the Wharfe to Addingham's venerable church.

ADDINGHAM   [Map 2, p84]

The chances are you'll see little of Addingham (🖥 addingham.info) save its churchyard, through which the Dales Way passes, and a couple of outlying streets. In one sense this is a bit of a shame, for the village itself is said to have more listed buildings than any in the Dales, even though it actually lies outside the boundary of the national park.

On the other hand, the centre of Addingham, Main St, is a 5- to 10-minute walk from the path and, given that you've not long left Ilkley, you probably won't want or need to visit Addingham proper. If you do wish to, on joining North St (after the church), cross the road and walk down Church St until you hit Main St, where you should turn right to reach the centre. Here you'll find several of these venerable listed buildings, the majority of which date back to the 18th and 19th centuries when Addingham was a mill town. Many of the listed buildings are the former residences either of the mill owners or the simple terraced cottages of those who worked for them.

Also on Main St is a Co-op **supermarket** (daily 7am-10pm) and two pubs that offer accommodation. With a devastating fire having swept through the popular Fleece Inn, that pub's operations have moved, hopefully temporarily, to its sister establishment about 700m down the road, *The Craven Heifer* (☎ 01943 830106, 🖥 www.thecravenheifer.com; 7D, all en suite; 🍴; WI-FI; rates £37.50-75pp, sgl occ £60-135; breakfast is £9.95) with gorgeous rooms and a fantastic – if expensive – menu (food served Mon-Sat noon-2pm & 6-9pm, Sun noon-7pm, and afternoon tea Mon-Sat 2-5pm), for example cumin-rubbed monkfish, curried mussels, ratte potatoes, pink grapefruit and a mini onion bhaji (£17). The second option is *The Crown Inn* (☎ 01943 830278, 🖥 www.thecrowninnaddingham .co.uk; 2T or D, both en suite; 🐾 £5; 🍴; WI-FI) a 17th-century 'pie and mash' coaching inn with B&B from £40pp (sgl occ £60) and a very cheap menu (food served daily noon-9pm; mains all £7.95).

The Nos 74/74S and 874 **bus** services call in along Main St (outside the fire-damaged Fleece Inn). Other services stopping in Addingham are the X84, 762, 873 and 884 (the latter two are Sun/bank holiday services only).

But as pleasant as Addingham undoubtedly is, most walkers content themselves with just a quick peek inside **St Peter's Church** (🖥 www.stpeters addingham.org.uk) before heading out. Parts of the current church date back to the 15th century, though Christians have been worshipping on this site for well over a thousand years, as the discovery in 1947 of an ancient stone cross and several Anglo-Saxon burial sites goes some way to proving. The cross is usually on display on the left-hand side of the church, although it sometimes gets removed when the church is being redecorated.

After Addingham, the path hugs the river more closely, bisecting caravan park and cow field, diverting only to cross the busy B6160 to **Farfield Friends' Meeting House**. The building is undecorated and tranquil, its simplicity masking its importance historically for the Quaker movement (see box p86).

(continued on p86)

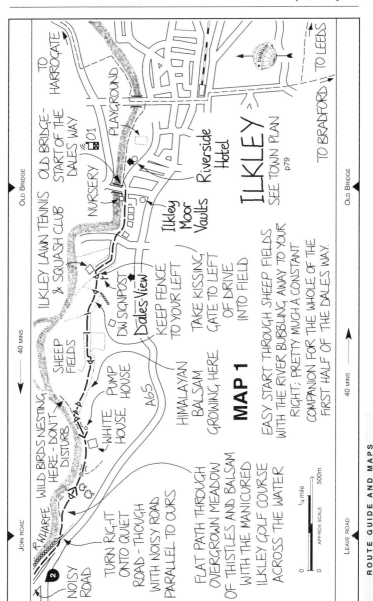

OLD BRIDGE

TO HARROGATE

OLD BRIDGE – START OF THE DALES WAY

PLAYGROUND

NURSERY

ILKLEY LAWN TENNIS & SQUASH CLUB

← 40 MINS →

Riverside Hotel

ILKLEY
SEE TOWN PLAN
p79

Ilkley Moor Vaults

KEEP FENCE TO YOUR LEFT

TAKE KISSING GATE TO LEFT OF DRIVE INTO FIELD

DW SIGNPOST
Dales-View

SHEEP FIELDS

HIMALAYAN BALSAM GROWING HERE

PUMP HOUSE

A65

WHITE HOUSE

MAP 1

EASY START THROUGH SHEEP FIELDS WITH THE RIVER BUBBLING AWAY TO YOUR RIGHT; PRETTY MUCH A CONSTANT COMPANION FOR THE WHOLE OF THE DALES WAY.

40 MINS

TO BRADFORD

TO LEEDS

OLD BRIDGE

R.WHARFE

WILD BIRDS NESTING HERE – DON'T DISTURB

JOIN ROAD

← 40 MINS →

NOISY ROAD

TURN RIGHT ONTO QUIET ROAD – THOUGH WITH NOISY ROAD PARALLEL TO OURS

FLAT PATH THROUGH OVERGROWN MEADOW OF THISTLES AND BALSAM WITH THE MANICURED ILKLEY GOLF COURSE ACROSS THE WATER

LEAVE ROAD

¼ mile
500m
APPROX SCALE
0

ROUTE GUIDE AND MAPS

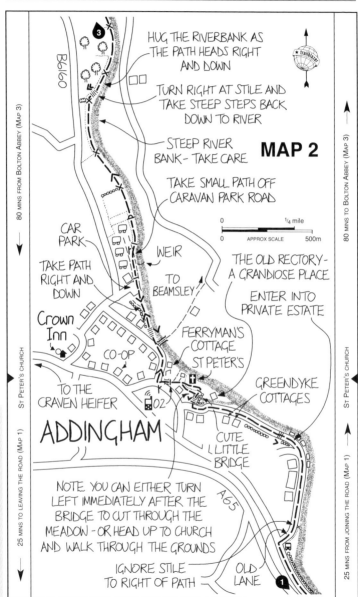

HUG THE RIVERBANK AS THE PATH HEADS RIGHT AND DOWN

TURN RIGHT AT STILE AND TAKE STEEP STEPS BACK DOWN TO RIVER

STEEP RIVER BANK - TAKE CARE

MAP 2

TAKE SMALL PATH OFF CARAVAN PARK ROAD

B6160

CAR PARK

TAKE PATH RIGHT AND DOWN

WEIR

TO BEAMSLEY

Crown Inn

CO-OP

TO THE CRAVEN HEIFER

ADDINGHAM

THE OLD RECTORY - A GRANDIOSE PLACE

ENTER INTO PRIVATE ESTATE

FERRYMAN'S COTTAGE

ST PETER'S

GREENDYKE COTTAGES

CUTE LITTLE BRIDGE

O2

NOTE YOU CAN EITHER TURN LEFT IMMEDIATELY AFTER THE BRIDGE TO CUT THROUGH THE MEADOW - OR HEAD UP TO CHURCH AND WALK THROUGH THE GROUNDS

IGNORE STILE TO RIGHT OF PATH

OLD LANE

A65

0   ¼ mile
0   500m
APPROX SCALE

80 MINS FROM BOLTON ABBEY (MAP 3)

ST PETER'S CHURCH

25 MINS TO LEAVING THE ROAD (MAP 1)

80 MINS TO BOLTON ABBEY (MAP 3)

ST PETER'S CHURCH

25 MINS FROM JOINING THE ROAD (MAP 1)

ROUTE GUIDE AND MAPS

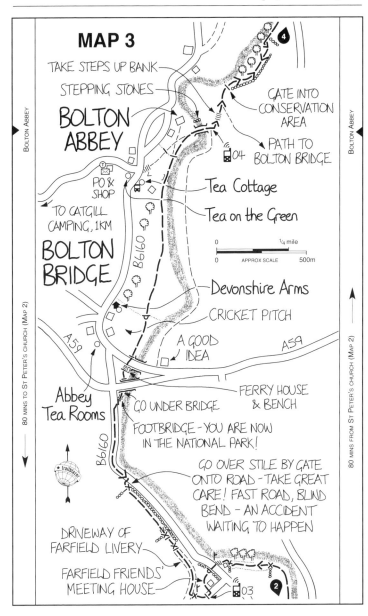

MAP 3

BOLTON ABBEY

TAKE STEPS UP BANK

STEPPING STONES

BOLTON ABBEY

GATE INTO CONSERVATION AREA

PATH TO BOLTON BRIDGE

04

PO & SHOP

Tea Cottage

Tea on the Green

TO CATGILL CAMPING, 1KM

BOLTON BRIDGE

B6160

0		¼ mile
0	APPROX SCALE	500m

Devonshire Arms

CRICKET PITCH

A GOOD IDEA

A59

A59

FERRY HOUSE & BENCH

Abbey Tea Rooms

GO UNDER BRIDGE

FOOTBRIDGE - YOU ARE NOW IN THE NATIONAL PARK!

GO OVER STILE BY GATE ONTO ROAD - TAKE GREAT CARE! FAST ROAD, BLIND BEND - AN ACCIDENT WAITING TO HAPPEN

B6160

★ trailblazer

DRIVEWAY OF FARFIELD LIVERY

FARFIELD FRIENDS' MEETING HOUSE

03

2

BOLTON ABBEY

80 MINS TO ST PETER'S CHURCH (MAP 2)

80 MINS FROM ST PETER'S CHURCH (MAP 2)

ROUTE GUIDE AND MAPS

(continued from p82) The Meeting House provides as good a place as any to make peace with your God before you tackle the most dangerous stretch of walking on the whole trail, as you join the pavement-less B6160 on a blind downslope in the road.

If you need a stiff drink to settle the nerves, after walking under the A59 turn left on the road and call in at the super-smart 17th-century ***Devonshire Arms Hotel & Spa*** (☎ 01756 710441, 🖥 www.thedevonshirearms.co.uk; 40D

❏ The Quakers and the Farfield Friends' Meeting House

The Religious Society of Friends started life back in the middle of the 17th century when a young man, George Fox, from Leicestershire, became dissatisfied with the established Church of England and its teachings. In particular, George believed that the ordained clergy of the Church were unnecessary, even an obstruction, hindering the relationship between a believer and his God and that one could communicate with Him without their intervention. An egalitarian group, Quakers believe that there is something of God in everybody and thus one needed neither clergy nor their rites and rituals in order to pray and speak with their Lord. Even the church buildings themselves were deemed by Fox to be unnecessary, for one could just as easily pray in a field or orchard as in a chapel or church.

Unfortunately, for the first few decades his followers faced wholesale persecution; the English Civil War (1642-51) was still fresh in many people's minds and any dissent or deviation from the orthodox was viewed as unsettling and potentially dangerous. Indeed, George himself was brought before the magistrates in 1650 on charges of religious blasphemy. It was during this trial that the judge, on being told by Fox to 'tremble at the word of the Lord', dubbed him and his religious group 'Quakers' – a nickname that stuck and was eventually adopted by the Society itself.

The Toleration Act of 1689 gave the Friends a little more religious freedom – as long as they pledged allegiance to the king – and it was in this year that the **Farfield Friends' Meeting House** was built, the land having been given to the society by the tenants of Farfield Hall, the Myers family, who were followers. As is typical of the movement, the building lacks any sort of ornamentation – in stark contrast to the ruins of Bolton Priory nearby. Attend a Friends' meeting today (note it's not called a 'service') and you'll find no priests, no singing nor set prayers; just a group of like-minded individuals sitting in a circle in noiseless contemplation, the silence broken only when one of the members feels compelled to speak.

The seats you see around the walls at Farfield today are the original 17th-century benches, though the ones in the centre are from a meeting house in Skipton and date back *only* to 1761. The elaborate tombs outside are something of an anomaly for such a humble, unostentatious sect and house the members of the Myers family – the benefactors who gave the land to the Friends. The hall is today in the care of the Historic Chapels Trust, who replaced the roof in 1998, though the meeting hall has not actually been used regularly by the Quakers for over 150 years.

Incidentally, later on in the walk, just after Sedbergh, you will pass **Brigflatts**, which perhaps holds an even more prominent position in the history of the Quaker movement. For it was here in 1652 that Fox repaired to after he had had his 'great vision' atop Pendle Hill – which Quakers often count as the beginning of their story. Subsequently a meeting house was built here in 1675 (the second oldest in the UK after one in Hertford, built – but older even than the one at Farfield), a simple whitewashed affair that you can visit to this day.

or T en suite; ☞; WI-FI; 🐾 £10). Rates for B&B midweek are around £87.50pp, single occ £157; add dinner in their fine-dining Burlington restaurant to the B&B and the total is nearer £152.50pp (£245 single occ), while in the cheaper brasserie it's £120pp (£210 single occ). Or, for more flaccid thirst quenchers, the *Abbey Tea Rooms* (☎ 01756 710797; daily 10am-4pm) is just across the road. Alternatively and more convenient, turn right and head over the bridge to *A Good Idea* (Fri 10am-5pm, Sat 10am-5.30pm, Sun 10.30am-5pm) which sells the odd cold drink and sausage roll.

That said, in terms of choice and setting, better off waiting until you get to the lovely tearooms at Bolton Abbey, beckoning you ahead....

BOLTON ABBEY   [Map 3, p85]

It's hard not to love Bolton Abbey (🖥 boltonabbey.com) and the neighbouring hamlet that shares its name. This is one of those rare places where the modern world has to make concessions for the ancient one, rather than the other way round. If you don't believe me, take the Sunday bus (see p88) that runs through the village and watch as the driver is forced to stop, remove the wing mirror so that the bus can squeeze through an ancient stone arch, then re-attach it once through.

Considering there can't be more than half a dozen buildings in Bolton Abbey village, there are more services here than there is any right to expect. There's a **post office**

for a start (Mon 9am-12.30pm, Tue-Sat 10am-12.30pm), which is part of the **shop** (Mon 9am-5.30pm, Tue-Sun 10am-5.30pm) next to the car park. The shop has a **call box** outside – useful, given the weak signal experienced by most mobile users here.

There's no accommodation in the centre of the village but there is a **campsite**, *Catgill* (☎ 01756 710247, 🖥 www.catgill campsite.co.uk; 🐾), about 700m from the post office along the pavement-less but quiet road. It's a decent place with nice people running it; expect to pay £8pp midweek or £10pp weekends, there is a handy onsite shop for basic provisions.

❏ The Priory of Bolton Abbey

Bolton Abbey is, despite the name, technically actually a priory rather than an abbey. Originally founded in 1154 by the Augustinian order, it has suffered down the centuries from raids by the Scots and, most devastatingly, from the Dissolution of the Monasteries in 1540, which left most of the eastern end of the structure in ruins. The western half of the site, however, has served as the parish church since around 1170 and survived the Dissolution's devastation. Much of the intact church you see today is Gothic in style but with Victorian embellishments, including the stained-glass windows by celebrated artist August Pugin.

It's hard not to look upon the ruins of Bolton Abbey today and not be inspired, and down the years the priory has been the subject of several paintings by JMW Turner and a long narrative poem by William Wordsworth, *The White Doe of Rylstone*, which starts with the deer entering the churchyard to lie down on a particular grave.

The dukes of Devonshire have owned the estate since the 18th century. The current owner is the septuagenarian Peregrine Andrew Morny Cavendish, the 12th Duke of Devonshire and the son of Dowager Duchess 'Debo', the youngest of the famous/notorious Mitford sisters who enjoyed a certain level of fame as the public face of the Duke's main family seat, Chatsworth, about which she wrote and in whose restoration she played a key role.

ROUTE GUIDE AND MAPS

[**Bolton Abbey**, cont'd] In their determination that no artery should go unclogged, this cholesterol-laden village also boasts not one but two wonderful **tearooms**. *Tea on the Green* (☎ 01756 711 834; daily 10am-4.30pm, winter 10am-3.30pm) operates a 'field to fork' philosophy, meaning that they serve local produce wherever possible including Kilburn reared beef and Escrick ham in their sandwiches (all £4.75) – as well as serving toasted teacakes with lashings of butter (£2.20). Note that dogs are not allowed inside but dog treats and a bowl of water are thoughtfully provided by the front door for all passers-by. Opposite, *Tea Cottage* (☎ 01756 710495; daily 10am-4pm; WI-FI) is an even more traditional tearoom, the inside very quaint and olde-worlde (again no dogs allowed). But it's the outside space I love, including a covered area with blankets and again, dog treats and a bowl of water provided free of charge. What's more, it's only from outside that you can truly appreciate the cottage's magnificent setting as you overlook the abbey grounds while munching on a scone with jam and clotted cream (£2.75), or fruitcake with Wensleydale cheese (£2.85). The nearest defibrillator, by the way, is at the New Inn in Appletreewick.

The 74/74S **bus** services call here between Ilkley and Grassington, with the Sunday 874 service continuing onto Buckden. The 873 runs between Ilkley and Skipton (Sun/bank hols only). Bolton Abbey is also a stop on some No 75 services. For further details see pp47-50.

So far, so-so. But Bolton Abbey is more than just a lovely place to get indigestion. As you've already discovered it also confirms that you are now very much in the national park (and have been since you crossed the small footbridge prior to passing under the A59). And isn't it strange how, almost as soon as you enter the park, the scenery becomes that much prettier, the grass that little bit more lush, the trees mightier and, overall, the landscape that much more attractive. It's as if someone flicked the pretty switch.

So when you finally manage to extricate yourself from your chair at one of Bolton Abbey's tearooms and waddle back down to the path, you're in for a treat! Taking the lovely footbridge at the eastern end of the ruins (or, for adrenaline junkies in search of a cheap hit, the stepping stones that lie parallel to it), there now follow two stretches of divine wood walking, first on one side of the Wharfe and then an even more gorgeous stretch on the other, western side. Between the two is the *Cavendish Pavilion* or, as Dales Way veterans call it, the 'Cav Pav' (☎ 01756 710245; daily 10am-5pm, to 4pm in winter), a sunny-looking place with loads of outdoor seating. Too big, perhaps, to be completely charming, there are nevertheless several things here that you may find useful, including a **gift shop-cum-tourist office** (open same times as the café), some **public toilets** and a **phone**. It's also been at least 30 minutes since you left the tearooms at Bolton Abbey; ample time, methinks, to develop an appetite for the pizzas, cakes and sandwiches that they serve here.

The stretch of woodland walking after the pavilion takes you through **Strid Wood**, named after the small but deadly section of violent rapids that lie at their centre. Before you even get there, however, you'll come to **Flying Shavings**, where the owner, universally known as 'The Bodger', runs wood-turning courses using local materials. If nothing else, you have to admire the location of his office!

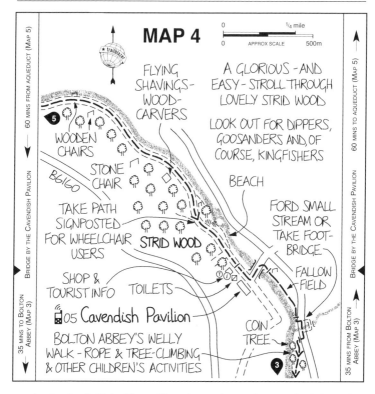

As for the Strid itself, you'll read enough warnings on the information boards dotted about the place but just to reiterate: no matter how narrow The Strid looks, don't even think of jumping across it. The ground can be slippery, the consequences of any mistake are often fatal – and if you've been indulging at the Bolton Abbey's tearooms, you're probably not as mobile as you were at the start of the walk.

A little further along from the Strid itself and a couple of hundred metres off the path, on the B6160, lies the **Strid Wood Tearooms** (☎ 01756 711745; daily 9.30am-4.30pm; 🐾; WI-FI), a cheerful place catering more to the passing motorist than the walker, though it has a decent menu, with their Cornish pasties (£3.90) particularly recommended. It has a big outside toilet block, too, though note that camping is not allowed anywhere near here – even though many a walker would consider it an ideal spot. For those who've had enough, the same **bus** services (74/74S Mon, Wed, Fri & Sat, 873 & 874 Sun/bank hols only; see pp47-50) that serve Bolton Abbey also call in at the Tearooms, 5-6 minutes earlier or later depending, of course, on which way they're heading.

❏ The Strid

Given the deadly reputation of this small, 20m-long section of rapids in the heart of the forest that took its name, and the legends that have grown up around it, your first impression maybe that it all looks a little, well, tame. Indeed, you may well be thinking that, with one decent-sized stride, you'll be safely on the other side. But I strongly advise you don't test this hypothesis.

For the fact of the matter is that for all the noise and fury of the foaming surface, the real danger lies under the rocks. Undertows drag you into underwater caverns from where the force of the water ensures there's no escape. It's an unpleasant way to go.

The roll call of those who have perished at the Strid is lengthy, though the most famous remains The Boy of Egremond (sometimes spelt Egremont), the son of Alizia de Romille, the lady of Skipton Castle in the 12th century. The tragedy is recounted in a 19th-century poem by Samuel Rogers, which was illustrated by JMW Turner.

In tartan clad and forest-green,
With hound in leash and hawk in hood,
The Boy of Egremond was seen.
Blithe was his song, a song of yore
But where the rock is rent in two,
And the river rushes through,
His voice was heard no more!
'Twas but a step! the gulf he passed;

But that step – it was his last!
As through the mist he winged his way,
(A cloud that hovers night and day,)
The hound hung back, and back he drew
The Master and his merlin too.
That narrow place of noise and strife
Received their little all of Life!

In her grief, Lady Alizia is said to have given the Augustinians at nearby Embsay some land near the Strid on which to build Bolton Abbey (though as the Boy of Egremond was a signatory to this transfer, this version of events seems unlikely). It is said, however, that shortly before the Strid claims its next victim the ghostly apparition of a white horse is seen nearby.

More delights await as you finally leave the wood behind for good, for in a matter of metres you're confronted by the 19th-century crenellated **Barden Aqueduct**. I hope that you see this for the first time as I did, on a gorgeously sunny day with the kingfishers dazzling and the river lazily drifting by, blissfully unaware of the chaos that awaits it just a little way downstream at the Strid. Surprisingly, the aqueduct is actually still in use, carrying the waters from Nidderdale, 15-20 miles away, towards Leeds. You'll see no sign of this, however, for the pipework is buried between the path that you take to cross it and the tops of the arches underneath.

Once across the Wharfe the water runs down inside the bridge abutment at the far (north-eastern) end, and continues its subterranean way towards the feeder reservoirs for Bradford and Leeds. Don't forget to look up too, to appreciate the lovely vista as the river ahead sweeps right towards Barden Bridge, with the ruin of Barden Tower overseeing everything.

BARDEN BRIDGE   [Map 5]

The main thing of interest to the Dales Way walker here is the **ice-cream van** that's often parked here during the summer. If you were to cross the bridge – which was largely rebuilt in 1659 to replace a much earlier crossing – and head up the hill (take the

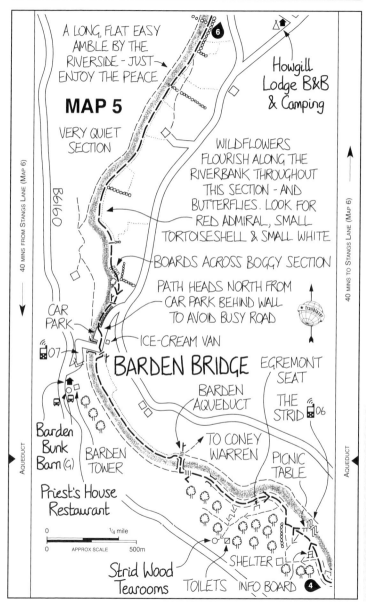

A LONG, FLAT EASY AMBLE BY THE RIVERSIDE - JUST ENJOY THE PEACE

MAP 5

VERY QUIET SECTION

Howgill Lodge B&B & Camping

WILDFLOWERS FLOURISH ALONG THE RIVERBANK THROUGHOUT THIS SECTION - AND BUTTERFLIES. LOOK FOR RED ADMIRAL, SMALL TORTOISESHELL & SMALL WHITE

BOARDS ACROSS BOGGY SECTION

PATH HEADS NORTH FROM CAR PARK BEHIND WALL TO AVOID BUSY ROAD

trailblazer

B6160

40 MINS FROM STANGS LANE (MAP 6)

40 MINS TO STANGS LANE (MAP 6)

CAR PARK

07

ICE-CREAM VAN

BARDEN BRIDGE

EGREMONT SEAT

BARDEN AQUEDUCT

THE STRID 06

Barden Bunk Barn (G)

BARDEN TOWER

TO CONEY WARREN

PICNIC TABLE

Priest's House Restaurant

AQUEDUCT

AQUEDUCT

0   1/4 mile

0   500m
APPROX SCALE

Strid Wood Tearooms

SHELTER

TOILETS   INFO BOARD

4

ROUTE GUIDE AND MAPS

stile on the left about halfway up to avoid the road), you come to **Barden Tower**, once a 15th-century hunting lodge (the name 'Barden' is said to be a corruption of the Anglo-Saxon for 'Valley of the Wild Boar') which was later turned into a lavish private residence by the 10th Lord Clifford, (1454–1523) who preferred it to his family seat at Skipton Castle. The main building is now a ruin and off-limits but the grounds play host to the 24-bed *Barden Bunk Barn* (☎ 01756 720616, 🖳 www.bardenbunk barn.co.uk) which, unfortunately, is only for **groups** of eight or more (£395 per night, £845 for the two-night minimum at weekends).

There's also a posh restaurant, *The Priest's House* (☎ 01756 720616, 🖳 www .thepriestshouse.co.uk). Decorated with pikes and halberds which, it is believed, saw battle against the Scots in the 16th century, the restaurant is open for Sunday lunch and occasional lunch and evenings, though it's mainly booked for functions by those seeking a little medieval atmosphere for their celebrations. Booking is essential.

The 74/74S **bus** services stop outside the restaurant (see pp47-50).

The stretch from Barden Bridge to Burnsall and beyond can accurately be described as classic Dales Way terrain. This is walking at its most serene and care-free, the ground flat and easy, the scenery absorbing, and with little to disturb the tranquillity. Your soundtrack on this stretch will be that of birdsong, and of the river bubbling lazily on your left; while keeping you company are the riverbank wildflowers that nod gently on the breeze and the butterflies – the small tortoiseshell, large and small whites, and maybe even the odd peacock and red admiral – that flit between them. (I am assuming, of course, that the weather will be good when you take this path – otherwise, the reality that greets you may be less serene than the picture painted here.)

It's all very straightforward and, in the right climate, idyllic. If you're enjoying it as much as I did you may want to stop, and luckily there are two options about a mile from Barden Bridge on **Stangs Lane**. The first is a simple **mobile home** (Map 6; ☎ 01756-720294; sleeps 5) just before you hit the road, in which a handwritten sign is displayed in the window offering it for £120 for the weekend (£315 for a week) – though they may, if bookings allow, offer it for less time. As you reach the road you'll also notice a footpath that takes you up to *Howgill Lodge* (see Map 6; ☎ 01756 720655, 🖳 www.howgill-lodge.co.uk; 3D/1Tr, all en suite; 🛏; WI-FI), which offers B&B in a 17th-century converted barn. Rates are from £41pp (single occ £82), two-night minimum booking at weekends. Note that they don't do evening meals and it's just over a mile to Appletreewick. They also offer **camping** (late Mar to late Oct) from £7 per night for hikers; dogs are allowed on the site for free if kept under close control.

Back on the path, and after passing some rapids that interject a brief note of sound and fury on an otherwise peaceful stretch, it's not long before the trail delivers you to the tiny but lovely village of Appletreewick.

APPLETREEWICK   [Map 6]

Little more than a one-street village, Appletreewick – often shortened to Ap'wick by the locals – boasts a fair history for a place of less than 250 souls. The most celebrated son is Sir William Craven, whose meteoric career saw him Sheriff and Lord Mayor of London at the beginning of the 17th century, and whose life is believed

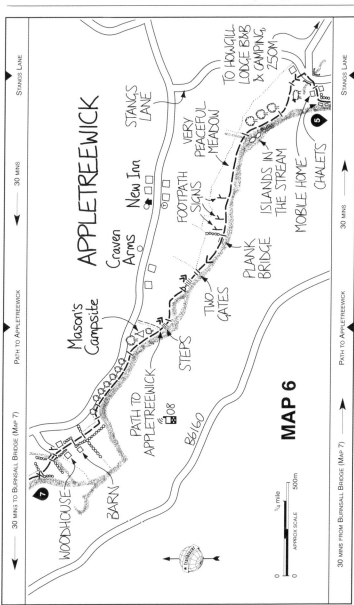

APPLETREEWICK

STANGS LANE

30 MINS

PATH TO APPLETREEWICK

30 MINS TO BURNSALL BRIDGE (MAP 7)

New Inn

STANGS LANE

Craven Arms

TO HOWGILL LODGE B&B & CAMPING, 250m

VERY PEACEFUL MEADOW

FOOTPATH SIGNS

ISLANDS IN THE STREAM

MOBILE HOME CHALETS

PLANK BRIDGE

TWO GATES

STEPS

Mason's Campsite

PATH TO APPLETREEWICK

B6160

WOODHOUSE

BARN

5

7

MAP 6

PATH TO APPLETREEWICK

STANGS LANE

30 MINS

30 MINS FROM BURNSALL BRIDGE (MAP 7)

¼ mile

APPROX SCALE

500m

0

0

by some to have been the basis for the Dick Whittington legend. On his return from London, Sir William spent some of his fabulous wealth enriching the area (in 2000 *The Sunday Times* named him as one of the 100 richest people who have lived in England since 1066, with a personal fortune in today's terms of around £6.3 billion). It was he who was responsible for building Burnsall Bridge and the nearby school too, and he also repaired St Wilfrid's Church in Burnsall. More recently, in fact in 2009, Appletreewick was awarded the title of 'Britain's Friendliest Town to Drive Through', a result based upon UK-wide data collected on road-rage incidents, driver communication, average speeds and so on.

Today, the village plays host to two pubs, a **phone box** (outside The New Inn), one very good campsite and .... not much else, though the 75 **bus** service calls here (see pp47-50).

The **campsite** is *Mason's* (☎ 01756 720275; ☐ www.masonscampsite.co.uk; ⏛ £1), a very popular place, unsurprisingly so given its location (by the river, near a great pub and abutting the Dales Way) as well as the quality of the facilities on site (the showers are particularly lovely). They have also adopted the concept of glamping in a big way, with yurts (sleeping two people) and a safari tent (sleeping up to six people) available for rent (£75-169 depending on the time of year). For walkers arriving on foot, the price is a more digestible £8pp.

As for the **pubs**, at the eastern end of town is *The New Inn* (☎ 01756 720252, ☐ www.the-new-inn-appletreewick.com; 1T/5D or T, en suite; ⏛; WI-FI), a friendly-

enough place where rates are £42.50pp (sgl occ £55) including breakfast. The **food** (daily from noon to around 8pm) is fine, with some interesting platters for sharing (fish platter £12.95, Tex-Mex platter £13.95), but what really marks this place out is its fine collection of world beers, including some from the Goose Eye Brewery in nearby Keighley.

However, as good as the grub is here, it suffers by comparison to the 16th-century *Craven Arms* (☎ 01756 720270, ☐ www .craven-cruckbarn.co.uk; food daily noon-9pm, Sun to 8.30pm), back down the hill. Indeed, this is pretty much the most fascinating pub on the trail, built with stone-flagged floors and real oak beams and equipped with a large open fire and pleasant beer garden – and all of it still lit by gaslight. Always the centre of the village, until 1926 the Court Leet was still held here to deal with local minor crimes, the wrongdoers being punished in the stocks that still stand to the left of the building. There is no accommodation at the pub but what they do offer – fine food and good beer – are areas in which they truly excel. The menu alone is enough to get the tastebuds tingling; try the whole roast grouse with onion purée, roast artichokes, fondant potato, wild mushroom and whisky cream (£19.95), for example. Suffice to say it's the first time in adulthood that I've literally licked a plate clean. If I have a criticism, it's that it gets so busy you need to get here early to secure a table. That, and the fact that the dishes tend to be tasty rather than hearty; though, to be fair, the puddings are of the same quality as the mains that preceded them and can top up any holes left unfilled by the main course.

The river meanders a lot in this section, drifting here and there as if reluctant to head downstream, like a schoolchild on his way to an exam for which he hasn't revised. Soon, however, you leave the river for a brief stroll through farm and fields on the way to lovely Burnsall.

BURNSALL   [Map 7]

Though bisected by the B6160, the main road that runs along the length of the Wharfe from Addingham to Buckden and beyond, Burnsall is one of the most exquisite villages

on the Dales Way. It can be quite beautiful at times, particularly in the late evening when the bridge glows a pale honey hue in the evening light, or during the day when

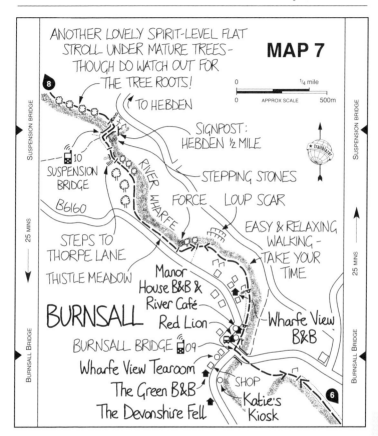

ANOTHER LOVELY SPIRIT-LEVEL FLAT STROLL UNDER MATURE TREES - THOUGH DO WATCH OUT FOR THE TREE ROOTS!

MAP 7

0 ___ ¼ mile
0 ___ APPROX SCALE ___ 500m

8

TO HEBDEN

SIGNPOST: HEBDEN ½ MILE

SUSPENSION BRIDGE

SUSPENSION BRIDGE

10 SUSPENSION BRIDGE

B6160

RIVER WHARFE

STEPPING STONES

FORCE   LOUP SCAR

EASY & RELAXING WALKING - TAKE YOUR TIME

25 MINS

STEPS TO THORPE LANE

THISTLE MEADOW

Manor House B&B & River Café

BURNSALL   Red Lion

BURNSALL BRIDGE 09

Wharfe View Tearoom

The Green B&B

The Devonshire Fell

Wharfe View B&B

SHOP

Katie's Kiosk

6

25 MINS

BURNSALL BRIDGE

SUSPENSION BRIDGE

kids splash about in the water while on the nearby green the parents gently sizzle and get sozzled under the scorching sun.

Surprisingly for such a small place, Burnsall has most things a trekker could want, including a decent pub, a tearoom, a fast food kiosk, a couple of friendly B&Bs, a smart hotel, a pizzeria and a **small shop** (Mon, Tue, Thur-Sat 8am-4pm, Sun 10am-2pm), of limited stock but with a good range of pork pies for around £1.30 each. The 74/74S and 874 **bus** services call here en route between Ilkley and Grassington; the Sunday 874 service continues to Buckden via Kettlewell. For details pp47-50.

For accommodation, there are four options. *The Green* (☎ 01756 720163; www.burnsallaccommodation.co.uk; 2D en suite; ✙; WI-FI; Ⓛ) is right in the heart of the action, just down from the tearoom and next door to the village shop; they charge £37.50pp (sgl occ £40). About 100m past the primary school, *Wharfe View Farm House* (☎ 01756 720643, 🖳 www.burnsall .net; 1T en suite, 1T/1Tr share facilities; 🐾 prebook £5; WI-FI; Ⓛ); from £35pp, from £40 sgl occ, more at weekends) has amiable hosts and large rooms. They also have a holiday cottage (1T/1D; ✙; no 🐾) that they offer as B&B when free.

Dominating the centre of the village, *The Red Lion* (☎ 01756 720204, 🖥 www .redlion.co.uk; 1S/13D or T, en suite; 🐾; 🐕 £20; WI-FI in the public areas; Ⓛ) was originally a ferryman's inn built in the 16th century (ie before the bridge was built) and remains the focus of village life today. Some of the rooms are a little small but the rates are fair (with B&B at £76-81pp, single £70, sgl occ is £10 less).

The owners also run the Victorian *Manor House* (8D/3D or T, all en suite; 🐾; WI-FI in public area; B&B £37.50-51pp, sgl occ rates on request), just over 100m away, with most of the rooms boasting river and village views. In addition they also have **four cottages** (2D or T) in the village and the three-bedroomed *Old Police House* (1S/1D/1T), both of which they are willing to let for one night's B&B (£60-85pp) if vacant.

Finally, on the outskirts of town is the Edwardian *Devonshire Fell Hotel* (☎ 01756 718111, 🖥 www.devonshirefell.co .uk; 14D/2T/1Tr, all en suite; 🐾; WI-FI; 🐕) Another place named in honour of the local aristocrats, the hotel's bold décor is said to have been chosen by the Duchess of Devonshire herself. Rates vary greatly according to demand and season but start at around £44.50pp (from £76 for sgl occ) for B&B, check online for special offers.

For **food**, *Katie's Kiosk* (☎ 07793 408910; Mon-Fri 9am-5 or 6pm, Sat 10am-4 or 6pm, Sun 9am-5 or 6pm) is a simple snack shack in a car park selling mugs of tea for 50p and Yorkshire Dales ice-cream for a pound. The sarnis are only £2.20-3.90, with a bacon, sausage and egg butty only £3.60. For something slightly more formal, *Wharfe View Tearooms* (☎ 01756 720237; Sat-Wed 9.30am-5.30pm) does a good Yorkshire cheese on toast for £5.50 and a homemade steak and potato pie for £6.50. Note that they accept only cash here.

The Red Lion has two menus, one for the bar (Mon-Fri noon-2.30pm & 6-9.30pm, Sat noon-9.30pm, Sun noon-9pm), where their beef & venison casserole with port, apricots and mashed potatoes is delicious (£15.50); and one for their restaurant (noon-2pm & 7-9.30pm, Sun to 9pm), with all the bar menu dishes plus more imaginative options including pan-fried pigeon breast with black pudding, broad beans, watercress, hazelnuts and cauliflower puree (£16.50) and corn-fed guinea fowl supreme, artichoke & truffle ravioli, serrano ham and wild garlic hollandaise (£16.10). The riverside seating out back by the path is lovely on a warm summer's evening. They also offer pizzas at their *River Café* (see Where to stay; Fri, Sat & Sun 5-9pm), to eat in at the Manor House or take away.

STAGE 2: BURNSALL TO BUCKDEN VIA GRASSINGTON
MAPS 7-13

Up to now the Dales Way has stuck with limpet-like tenacity to the valley floor, hugging the riverbank closely and avoiding, where possible, any hint of a slope or gradient. On this **14¾-mile (23.4km; 5hrs 55 mins)*** section, however, the path shows what treats await those who head for the heights. True, the first part of this stage, to Grassington, couldn't have been flatter if God had used a spirit level. The last stretch from Kettlewell to Buckden covers familiar riparian terrain, too – and both of these stretches are lovely in their own way. But it's the middle section, from Grassington to Kettlewell, that will stick in your mind the longest. Free of the valley walls that have been hemming you in and the vast shadows they cast, you are now able to savour Yorkshire's very own Big Sky Country. It's bracing, there's little shelter, and it can be quite windswept and lonely; but there's no denying its beauty, the isolation is glorious – and the views down the valley frequently verge on the breathtaking.

*(You need to add another 200m to take you from the trail to Buckden itself)

Logistically, there are plenty of options for this stage. The 874 bus service (Sun/bank hols only; see pp47-50) bumbles along between Burnsall and Buckden, and there are several places to stop and eat on the way – or indeed, stop altogether for the day if the whim takes you, with Grassington and Kettlewell both directly en route and Hebden and Starbotton both just off it.

The route

What a lovely – and gentle – way to start a stage. Heading round the back of the Red Lion on a path so flat that it's even accessible for wheelchairs, the trail continues its love affair with the Wharfe for this first stretch to Grassington, passing **Loup Scar**, a limestone escarpment and the final resting place of poor Dr Petty, the victim of homicidal Tom Lee (see box p100). This stretch of the river up to the bridge is popular with anglers, canoeists, kingfishers and those who just want to spend a sunny summer afternoon splashing around. It's a very pretty stretch, with the springy old suspension bridge at Hebden (which is not the same as Hebden Bridge, a town about 40 miles to the south) and its accompanying stepping stones a particular highlight.

HEBDEN   [Map 8, p98]

Where the path turns left (west) after the bridge, those in need of sustenance can continue straight on to Hebden and *The Old School Tea Room* (☎ 01756 753778; daily 10am-5pm) where if the weather's right you can sit in their lovely garden and watch their pygmy goats play. I think it's pretty much the most charming tearoom on the trail, the only drawback being that it's the best part of 1½ miles (2.4km) from the trail.

Nearby, for accommodation, *Court Croft* (☎ 01756 753406, 🖥 www.bedand breakfasthebden.co.uk; 3T, 2 en suite; ✒; wi-fi; 🐾; Ⓛ) sits next to the church on Church Lane and is good value at £30pp (£35 sgl occ).

North Barn (☎ 01756 752816, 🖥 www.northbarnhebden.com; 2D, en suite or private facilities; ✒; wi-fi; Ⓛ) lies a little further north on Brayshaw Lane at the end of a farm track. Rates are £40pp for one night (£50 sgl occ), with evening meals

£15.95 if booked in advance (bring your own wine). Still further north, just off the B6265, *Orchard House* (☎ 01756 752597, 🖥 www.orchardhousehebden.co.uk; 1D with private bathroom/1D or T en suite; ✒; wi-fi) is at the far (northern) end of the village and charges from £37.50pp, single occupancy £50. Nearby, at the far northern end of Hebden – though simultaneously its spiritual centre – *Clarendon Hotel* (☎ 01756 752446, 🖥 www.clarendonhebden .co.uk; 4D/1T en suite; 🐾; wi-fi; rates £30-40pp, £40-50pp at weekends; £60 for single occupancy) is the place to go in the evenings for **food** (Mon-Sat noon-2.30pm & 6-9pm, Sun noon-7pm); mains start from £9.95 for sausages and mash, or gammon, egg and chips.

The Nos 75 (Mon/Wed/Fri only), 802 (Sat only) and 812 (Sunday/bank hols only) **bus** services call here; see pp47-50 for details.

Back at the bridge, on the northern side of the Wharfe the path becomes slightly quieter but no less level as you amble beneath a row of mighty chestnut trees. A further set of stepping stones to the left of the path, before you reach the fish farm, leads to **Linton**'s **St Michael and All Angels Church**, Norman in origin though much restored over the centuries. Back on the trail and sticking to the path through open, saturated sheep fields, eventually you turn right up a dreamy little country lane lined by two impressive stone walls.   *(cont'd on p101)*

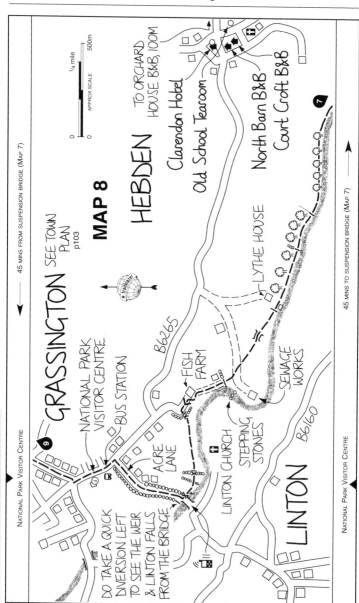

NATIONAL PARK VISITOR CENTRE

45 MINS FROM SUSPENSION BRIDGE (MAP 7)

GRASSINGTON

SEE TOWN
PLAN
p103

MAP 8

NATIONAL PARK
VISITOR CENTRE

BUS STATION

ACRE
LANE

B6265

FISH
FARM

HEBDEN

TO ORCHARD
HOUSE B&B, 100M

Clarendon Hotel
Old School Tearoom

North Barn B&B
Court Croft B&B

LYTHE HOUSE

SEWAGE
WORKS

¼ mile

APPROX SCALE   500m

0

7

DO TAKE A QUICK
DIVERSION LEFT
TO SEE THE WEIR
& LINTON FALLS
FROM THE BRIDGE

LINTON CHURCH

STEPPING
STONES

LINTON

B6160

NATIONAL PARK VISITOR CENTRE

45 MINS TO SUSPENSION BRIDGE (MAP 7)

9

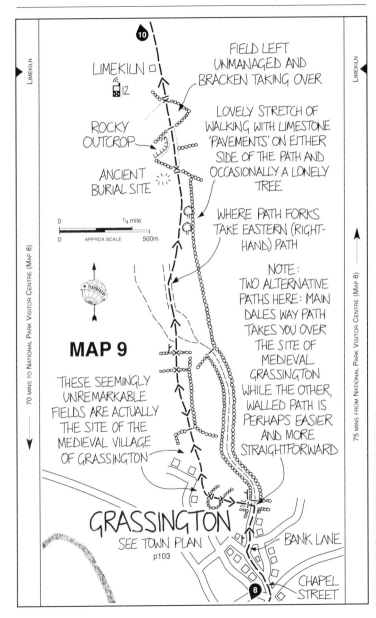

❑ The tale of Tom Lee

The year was 1779 and the main protagonist of the story is a hot-headed young man in his late 20s. On the face of it life was pretty sweet for young Tom Lee. Married, with a good business as a blacksmith in the centre of pretty Grassington, there would have been many at that time who looked upon his life with more than a degree of envy. They would also probably have resented the fact that such blessings had fallen to one who so little deserved it, for Tom Lee had a reputation as an intimidating bully, with a legendary temper that could be as hot as the metal that he worked with all day.

Things started to go very wrong for Tommy when he tried to hold up and rob the 'running postman', whose job it was to deliver the wages of the local lead miners to the counting house at Yarnbury, 1½ miles away. The attack, which occurred on Grassington's Moor Lane, failed largely because of the efforts of the postman himself who successfully fought back against his assailant, with Tom Lee receiving a bullet in the shoulder for his troubles.

Badly injured, Tommy sought the help of the local doctor, a cheerful middle-aged gentleman who went by the name of Dr Petty. Clearly a man of probity, Dr Petty adhered to the principle of patient/doctor confidentiality, and made no attempt to tell the authorities about Tom Lee's injuries – even though the attack on the running postman was by now common knowledge amongst the townsfolk – and such an attack was punishable by death.

Unfortunately for Dr Petty, this decision not to grass on the Grassington blacksmith was to have fatal consequences. For while the good doctor had saved the young man's life by treating his wounded shoulder, in return Tom Lee hatched a plot to kill Dr Petty, presumably because he couldn't live with the knowledge that all the doctor had to do was tell someone about his injuries and arrest – and execution – was sure to follow. Which was how it came to pass that, a few months later, the good doctor could be found lying wounded on the ground (near the path of the modern Dales Way; see p97), having been dragged from his horse by Tom who had been hiding behind a drystone wall. Under the light of the moon, he then set about beating the doctor to death, raining blow after sickening blow down upon his victim with a heavy cudgel, before dragging the limp body of Dr Petty into the undergrowth to cover his crime.

As the previous episode with the postman had already shown, however, Tom's wickedness was matched only by his incompetence. Returning to the scene of the crime with his young apprentice, Bowness, to bury the body, they quickly realised that the doctor was still – just – alive. This time Tommy made sure, killing the doctor 'again' before burying the body in a nearby peat bog. (Several weeks later Tommy moved the body for a second time, on this occasion with the help of his wife to the River Wharfe and Loup Scar, near Burnsall. Incidentally, the nearby lane is still called Skull Lane to this day.) Though the body was eventually discovered, and suspicion immediately fell upon Tom Lee, initially no charges were brought against him due to lack of evidence. Indeed, it was only three years later that his apprentice, Bowness, unable to live with the guilt any longer, went to the authorities to confess. Tom Lee was immediately arrested, tried, convicted and hanged, his body then suspended by chains in Grass Wood, near the scene of the murder.

Today, the life and crimes of Tom Lee are recounted in song, poem and play. You may, quite properly, think his rather unsavoury deeds unworthy of such celebration. But while nobody would describe the Dales Way as 'murderous', there is nevertheless a certain symmetry between the short, brutal life of Tom Lee, which was eventually ended by Bowness – and the short (and just occasionally brutal) Dales Way – which also, of course, ends by Bowness.

(continued from p97) The lane leads all the way to Grassington, the town that marks the border between Lower Wharfedale and Upper Wharfedale. Before you do so, however, turn left at the stile to admire the view of **the weir** from the bridge.

GRASSINGTON [see map p103]

You have to have a sneaking admiration for a place that decides not to cover up the fact that its most famous son is a murderer, (see box opposite), but opts instead to celebrate it openly and fervently. Visit the smart glass bus shelter, for example, by the National Park Centre and you'll find a poem recounting Mr Lee's deeds etched into the glass, while head to the town centre and you'll find his former home is even marked with a plaque. But this is Grassington, Wharfedale's largest town and a lovely looking place, with a great character and, refreshingly for a tourist hotspot, a wonderful sense of community too.

The town's somewhat sedate façade also hides a rather lengthy and lively history that stretches back at least 1500 years, for the Romans farmed these slopes for grain way back in the 4th and 5th centuries AD. Since medieval times, however, Grassington has gone downhill – quite literally, for the remains of the medieval town lie in fields above the modern Grassington, as you'll see when you continue the Dales Way on to Kettlewell (see p106). The current town prospered on the back of the lead-mining industry, which had been carried out in the local hills since the 15th century. As the mining industry thrived at the end of the 17th century so more people were attracted to the town and Grassington became a wild and rather lawless place during most of the 18th and early 19th centuries. No surprise, then, that the local police force is said to have been the first in the UK to have been armed! This was also the era of Tom Lee, his grisly acts adding even more notoriety to the town.

Eventually, as the mining industry died so the workforce drifted away, leaving only a few hardy souls and a couple of grand buildings behind, such as the Mechanics Institute at the top of town, donated in the 1870s by concerned benefactor, the Duke of Devonshire, after whom it is now named.

The town enjoyed a renaissance in the middle of the 20th century, thanks largely to the tourist industry; these days it's awash with Gore-Tex in the warmer months as trekkers come from all around to explore the surrounding hills. This summer influx helps to keep the town's economy thriving and ensures, too, that there are plenty of B&Bs, cafés and pubs to serve the weary walker.

You can find more about the history of the town and its local environment by visiting **Grassington Folk Museum** (Mar-Oct daily 2-4.30pm if volunteer staff available; free but donations welcome), on the main square (which is called, rather unimaginatively, The Square). Exhibits include some locally panned gold and a few mesolithic arrow points and scrapers.

Even though Grassington is not at the end of a stage in this book it's only a few easy miles from Burnsall and many will say that the extra effort is definitely worth it.

Services

The **National Park Visitor Centre** (late Mar to end Oct daily 10am-5pm; weekends only in winter 10am-4pm) sits on the Dales Way at the start of town, next to the main bus stop. Full of useful info, it's a great place to sort out the rest of your trip, find out about bus services and buy souvenirs. Lots and lots of souvenirs. By the way there is a fee of 20p to use the **toilets** next door – rather annoying if you've been saving yourself on the walk for this moment!

Another option for tourist information is **The Hub** (Grassington Hub & Community Library; 🖵 www.grassington .uk.com; Mon & Wed 10am-6pm, Tue, Thur & Fri to 5pm, Sat to 4pm).

Moving to the centre you'll find the **post office** (Mon-Fri 9am-5.30pm, Sat 9am-12.30pm) and general store (Mon-Fri 9am-5.30pm, Sat 9am-5pm, Sun 10am-4.30pm), while down the hill is a small Spar **supermarket** (daily 8am-9pm).

Reflecting the popularity of Grassington amongst walkers, there is not one but two **outdoor stores**: Mad About Mountains (Mon-Sat 9am-5.30pm), below the Spar; and, round the corner on Wood Lane, Mountaineer (Mon-Sat 9am-4.30pm, every other Sun 10am-4.30pm).

The only **cashpoint** is at Barclays Bank at the bottom of Main St.

There's plenty of accommodation but during the **Grassington Festival**, which traditionally takes place over the last two weeks of June, and the end-of-year **Dickens Festival**, rooms may be a little harder to come by.

Transport

[See public transport map & table pp47-50] Grassington is a stop on several **bus** routes but services are limited. The X43 from Manchester, 812 from Ripon, 874 from Ilkley and 875 from Leeds/Wakefield (all Sun/bank hols only); the 800 to Hawes via Kettlewell & Buckden (Tue & Sat only); the 801 (Tue only) from Bradford; the 802 (Sat only) from Wakefield and Leeds.

The various forms of the 72 service (72/72A/72B/72R) provide a more regular service here from Skipton/Buckden. The 74/74S and 75 also connect Grassington with places along the trail.

Where to stay

There are **no campsites** in Grassington (the nearest one, **Bell Bank**, is over two miles away across the river in Threshfield; ☎ 01756 752321; £5pp, simple facilities, nice people) and **no hostels** either. What's more, the local **Grassington Bunk Barn** (☎ 01756 753882, 🖥 www.grassingtonbunk barn.co.uk; sleeps 34 in four bedrooms; £340 per night, rising to £980 at weekends; WI-FI; 🐾), about 800m above the town on Moor Lane (opposite the junction with Edge Lane), mostly accepts **group bookings**; individuals may stay during the week for £25 per night if bookings allow.

As such, a **B&B** is pretty much your only option in Grassington. Thankfully there are plenty here; the only problem is finding them. Apart from the half-dozen or so upmarket options on or just off Main St,

there are several 'minor' B&Bs that don't advertise, don't have a sign outside – and yet provide good-value accommodation for walkers in a decent, central location. I've written about the ones I could find but I'm sure there are others. Unfortunately, locating them could be tricky as even the tourist office has no information on them. Ask the other B&Bs and pubs if they know of any – it'll be your best bet.

Among these 'anonymous' B&Bs are: friendly **Banks Farm** (☎ 0776 6257555, 🖥 www.banksfarmgrassington.co.uk; 1D en suite; 🐾 £5; WI-FI; ⓛ); rates £45pp, sgl occ £55), which is pretty much the last house on Chapel St before Bank Lane, right on the Dales Way; pleasant **Croft House** (☎ 01756 751759, 🖥 www.crofthousegrassington .co.uk; 1D en suite, 1D private bathroom; 🐾; WI-FI; rates £37.50pp, £40pp at weekends and bank hols, single occ rate on request) on the cul-de-sac, Chapel Croft; **Town Head** (☎ 01756 752811; 3D en suite; 🐾; B&B rates are £35pp, sgl occ £45), opposite the top of Main St just along from the town hall; and **Craven Cottage** (☎ 01756 752205, 🖥 www.grassington.uk .com/craven-cottage; 2D en suite; 🐾; WI-FI; B&B £35pp, sgl occ £40) centrally placed at the top of Main St.

Virtually opposite this last B&B is **Rokeby Guest House** (☎ 01756 753839, 🖥 www.rokebybandb.co.uk; 2D en suite; 🐾; WI-FI; ⓛ), a pretty former farmhouse off the north end of Main St on Garrs End Lane; sitting in their front garden with a cup of tea watching the bustle of the main drag is a very pleasant way to spend a lazy hour or two. Rates are from £57.50pp for B&B (served in front of a lovely inglenook fire-place), with single occupancy £75 rising to £115 at weekends.

Moving down the hill, on the same side of Main St (though tucked away down its own private cul-de-sac below Dales Books/Mephisto) is the 17th-century, Grade II listed **Ashfield House** (☎ 01756 752584, 🖥 www.ashfieldhouse.co.uk; 4D/ 4D or T; most en suite; 🐾; WI-FI; ⓛ), a supremely smart place that was once just a row of humble lead-miners' cottages. Rates are generally £55-62.50pp (sgl occ rates on

To Croft House, 175m
& Banks Farm, 250m **9**

Moor La

To
Grassington
Bunk Barn (G),
850m

Town Hall

Gars End La

**Rokeby ♠
Guest
House**

**♠ Town
Head**

**Craven
Cottage**

Moody Sty La

High La

0   25   50m

**Springfield ○
Tearoom**

Gars La

Water St

**Tom Lee's ●
House**

★ trailblazer

**Corner
House
Café**

**Dales
Book Centre**

**Foresters
Arms**

Mephisto ♠

Main St

**Retreat
Café &
Tearoom**

○ ○ **TA's Fish & Chips**

**Ashfield
House**

**♠ Black Horse
Hotel**

The Devonshire ○

**Rozi's
Tandoori**

Gars La

**ⓘ▣ The Hub (Grassington
Hub & Community Library)**

**Walkers ○
Bakery**

**Grassington
fi Folk Museum**

The
Square

ⓣ Public phone

Post Office ✉

**♠ Grassington
House
& No 5 Restaurant**

**♠ Grassington
Lodge**

Wood La

○
**Cobblestones
Café**

Spar ●

Mountaineer ●

**Mad About ●
Mountains**

○ **CoffeeEco**

ⓔ Barclays (ATM)

Station Rd   B6265

B6265

**To Bell Bank
Campsite,
1½ miles**

Toilets ▣

ⓘ
**National Park
Visitor Centre**

Haden Rd

Bus station 🚍

Grassington

8

Acre La

request), but rise to £105pp (based on two sharing) for the garden suite for B&B. Note that there is a minimum two-night stay policy at weekends.

Ashfield House's position as the smartest address in Grassington has two real challengers. Firstly, no review of the town's accommodation can ever be complete without *Grassington House* (☎ 01756 752406, 🖳 www.grassingtonhousehotel.co .uk) 8D/1D or T en suite; ➤; WI-FI; ⓛ); after all, it was their decision way back in the late 19th century to change their home from a private residence to a boarding house which kicked off the tourist industry in Grassington. The place itself is very salubrious and comfy – as you'd expect from a hotel that's had over a hundred years to get it right. The rooms are all individually furnished and the rates are similarly varied, with B&B ranging from £60 to £120pp (sgl occ is £105 for B&B, £147.50 for dinner, B&B). Not to be confused with the above, *Grassington Lodge* (☎ 01756 752518, 🖳 www.grassingtonlodge.co.uk; 7D/5D or T, en suite; ➤; WI-FI) is an endearingly eccentric place opposite the police station at 8 Wood Lane; look out for the ibis sculpture in the front garden. There's no disputing the quality of the accommodation or the warmth of the welcome, however. Rates for B&B are 47.50-75pp at weekends, cheaper midweek but only by £5 or so. There is no discount on the room price for single occupancy during peak periods.

Finally, in addition to the B&Bs there are the **pubs**. *The Devonshire* (☎ 01756 752525, 🖳 www.thedevonshiregrassington .co.uk; 4D or T/4Qd, all en suite; ➤; wi-fi; ➤; ⓛ; B&B £50-60pp, three/four sharing room rate plus £20pp, sgl occ rates on request) is large and centrally located and has reopened after major refurbishment following a change of ownership. On Main St the noisy *Foresters Arms* (☎ 01756 752349, 🖳 www.forestersarmsgrassington .co.uk; 3D/1T/1D or T/2Tr; all en suite; ➤; ➤; WI-FI; ⓛ) currently gets the lion's share of guests. This 18th-century former coaching inn is a down-to-earth place and remains the most popular place to eat at night (see opposite) so there's not far to

crawl back to bed afterwards. B&B costs from £40pp (sgl occ from £45). However, now under new ownership, *Black Horse Hotel* (☎ 01756 752770, 🖳 www.black horsehotelgrassington.co.uk; 3T/6D/2Tr/ 1Qd/1x6-bed bunk room; all en suite; ➤; ➤; WI-FI) is starting to provide a decent alternative, with B&B from a reasonable £45pp (£60 sgl occ) and with some tempting special offers on their website too. There is a minimum 2-night stay here at weekends.

Where to eat and drink

While Grassington can't quite feed you round the clock, it certainly does its best. Those in need of an early morning fix of caffeine and cholesterol should find that *Walkers Bakery* (Mon, Wed-Sat 8am-4pm, Tue 8am-2pm) is often open much earlier than advertised and seems happy to serve you. There's no seating inside but for those wanting to set off on the trail early, their roll with egg and bacon (£2.60) is a great value way to start the day.

If caffeine is your drug of choice, you certainly won't be suffering withdrawal symptoms in Grassington. My favourite place is the *Retreat Café & Tearoom* (☎ 01756 751887, 🖳 www.theretreatcafe.co .uk; Thur-Tue 10am-4pm), which is currently the most popular place with locals too; indeed, come here some mornings when the local wives gather to gossip and it's like sitting in the middle of an Alan Bennett play. The café allows dogs, doesn't have wifi, but does have great coffee and a sizeable menu of vegetarian options with sandwiches from £3.60 and main meals such as vegetarian chilli from £6.80. Stiff competition on the coffee front is provided both further up Main St at *Springfield Tearoom* (☎ 01756 753208), housed in a former chemist's shop, where the regular menu is dominated to some extent by sandwiches though this is supplemented by an excellent specials board offering more substantial meals such as lasagne and chicken curry (both £9.95); and down the hill at the southern end of The Square at *CoffeEco* (☎ 01756 751835, 🖳 www.grassingtoncoffee .com; daily 9am-5pm) where both dogs and boots are welcome, the coffee carries the

Fairtrade mark and the food is locally sourced where possible. Just up the hill a few paces and also on The Square, **Cobblestones Café** (☎ 01756 752303; Fri-Wed 9.30am-5pm) is also dog friendly, though only outside at the rear of the building. A good choice for those seeking something more substantial than sandwiches, their mains (traditional English dishes) are all around the £7.25-7.75 mark. Continuing up the hill there's also the family-run, dog-friendly, wifi-connected **Corner House Café** (☎ 01756 752414; Wed-Sun 10am-4pm) with sandwiches about £5.50, though their delicious steak sandwich is £9.

In the evenings, you're pretty much confined to a takeaway, a pub or fine-dining. For takeaway there's **Rozi's Tandoori** (☎ 01756 753342, 🖳 www.rozis.co.uk; daily 5-11.30pm) or **TA's Fish and Chips** (☎ 01756 752436; Wed, Fri & Sat 11.45-1.15pm, Tue & Wed 4.45-6.30pm, Thur-Sat 4.45-7pm).

For pubs, **Foresters Arms** (see Where to stay; food served Mon-Sat noon-2.30pm, Mon-Thur 6-8.30pm, Fri & Sat to 9.30pm,

Sun noon-8.30pm) is very popular with walkers and locals alike, which is always a good sign. Their reputation for serving huge portions of grub is justifiable, with mains starting at £8.95 for bangers and mash, rising to £15.95 for the slow-roasted shoulder of lamb. There's also the **Black Horse Hotel** (see Where to stay; daily noon-2.30pm & 6-8.30pm, Fri & Sat to 9pm) again offering traditional English fare but with a simpler pricing system, with one course £12, two courses £15.

The Devonshire (see Where to stay; food served Mon-Sat noon-9pm, Sun noon-8pm) serves standard pub food and mains cost from £9.95,

Finally, Grassington House plays host to the town's very own fine-dining option, called **No 5 Restaurant** (see Where to stay Grassington House; Mon-Fri noon-2.30pm & 6-9.30pm, Sat noon-4pm & 6-9.30pm, Sun noon-4pm & 6-8.30pm) with mains £13.95 rising to £25.50 for the 28-day-aged Pateley Bridge 6oz beef fillet with tomatoes, mushrooms and chips.

It's after Grassington that things – literally – begin to look up. You can tell from the fact that you leave Grassington from the top end of the village that the riparian walking you've been used to thus far on the trail is, for the moment at least, suspended. Yet in spite of the bleak, lonely nature of this section, curiously the area is rich in archaeological treasures with plenty of tell-tale signs that man once lived and worked here – and died up here too.

The evidence that man once lived up here can be found in the **medieval village of Grassington**, which you come upon almost as soon as you leave the modern-day version. To the layman there's little remarkable about these first few fields that you cross, save that they seem a bit more lumpy than usual. But when seen from the air a clear series of enclosures and building platforms can be discerned, etched into the pasture. The area has yet to be fully surveyed, but a small dig in the 1960s uncovered a *midden* (an old dump for kitchen waste) containing pottery from the 14th century as well as a few rectangular buildings built in a row, one with a paved floor.

A little way along is proof that man died and was buried up here too. A turf-covered **burial cairn**, situated to the left of the path before the kiln, dates back to the early Bronze Age, around 4000 years ago. Excavated in 1892 by the local vicar, the cairn consisted of a central chamber that contained the bones of at least five individuals, as well as several flint arrowheads and an early Bronze Age beaker.

As for the evidence that man worked here too, well about half a mile further on the path passes a **lime kiln** on the left, dating back to about the mid 19th century. These kilns were used to super-heat limestone, producing quicklime which was then spread on the fields to improve the fertility of the soil by controlling the acidity. The limestone could also be used for mortar in buildings.

These days, of course, where man has finally moved out, the cows have moved in, and it is their disconcerting, unblinking gaze that will follow your progress now as you cross field after field, finally ending up overlooking a tall communications mast – proof that modern man hasn't abandoned these uplands altogether. Don't make the mistake, as so many do on this stage, of heading down the slope here on Scot Gate Lane, a path that leads to Conistone and Kilnsey but which will entail either a long schlep back up the slope to rejoin the path or a section of roadside trudging up the valley to the next destination, Kettlewell. Unless, of course, you specifically want to…

CONISTONE & KILNSEY [Map 10]

Two small settlements sit snugly in the valley, hidden from the trail a steep mile away.
Conistone (🖳 www.kilnseyandconis tone.co.uk) lies on the eastern side of the Wharfe and is, unfortunately, perhaps best known for the Mossdale Caverns tragedy, where six cavers were drowned in 1967 in what remains the most deadly speleological incident in the UK. A plaque marks the entrance to the caverns, which have been closed to cavers since the tragedy.

There's little for the trekker in the village – though it's pretty enough – but across the water in **Kilnsey** is *Kilnsey Park Estate*, just off the B6160, with its own café (Mon-Fri 10am-2pm, Sat & Sun to 4pm). The estate actually dates back to the 1100s,

when it was farmed by the monks from nearby Fountains Abbey, though these days it's better known for its trout farm and its meadows, in which grow the UK's rarest orchid, the lady's slipper orchid (see p64). To the north lies the 17th-century coaching inn *The Tennants Arms Hotel* (☎ 01756 753946, 🖳 www.thetennantsarms.co.uk; 8D/2T/1Qd, all en suite; ✆; WI-FI; 🐾) with smart rooms from £50 to £75pp (sgl occ £60-80) including breakfast. They also do **food** (Mon-Fri noon-2.30pm & 6-9pm, Sat & Sun noon-9pm) including their popular Friday steak night (£35 for two including a bottle of wine).

The Nos 800 & 875 **bus** services stop in Kilnsey; see pp47-50 for details.

For those who don't want to drop all that way to Conistone, keep instead to the high ground and the trail and you will eventually find yourself, after a period of valley-top tramping, descending via wood and field to the outskirts of Kettlewell. Within sight of the village, however, a rather nasty surprise awaits, with a lengthy series of stiles, gates, gaps and ladders across a series of narrow fields standing between you and Kettlewell. It's like an agrarian version of the Olympic 110m hurdles, except there's only sheep as spectators and there are no medals for those who complete the course…just the chance of a well-earned cup of tea.

KETTLEWELL [see map p109]

The charm of Kettlewell is an abiding charm, and to those of us whose life is spent amid the hurley-burley of city life, the village seems the peculiar abode of peace and quiet beauty; its limestone terraces, with

their fringes of hazel and rowan coppices give to the district a characteristic beauty. But the special glory of Kettlewell is not that of colour, but of line. Situated at the junction of the main valley of the Wharfe

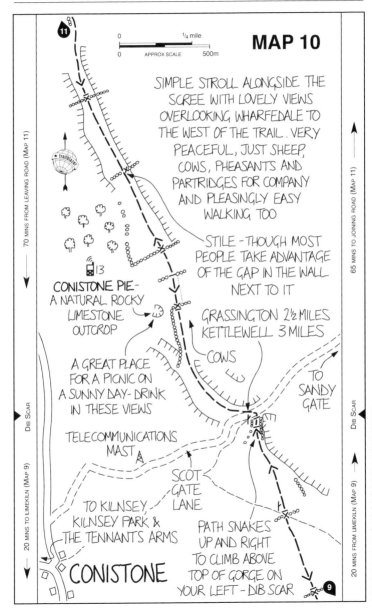

MAP 10

SIMPLE STROLL ALONGSIDE THE SCREE WITH LOVELY VIEWS OVERLOOKING WHARFEDALE TO THE WEST OF THE TRAIL. VERY PEACEFUL, JUST SHEEP, COWS, PHEASANTS AND PARTRIDGES FOR COMPANY AND PLEASINGLY EASY WALKING TOO

STILE - THOUGH MOST PEOPLE TAKE ADVANTAGE OF THE GAP IN THE WALL NEXT TO IT

GRASSINGTON 2½ MILES
KETTLEWELL 3 MILES

COWS

CONISTONE PIE -
A NATURAL ROCKY
LIMESTONE
OUTCROP

A GREAT PLACE FOR A PICNIC ON A SUNNY DAY - DRINK IN THESE VIEWS

TELECOMMUNICATIONS MAST

SCOT GATE LANE

TO KILNSEY,
KILNSEY PARK &
THE TENNANTS ARMS

CONISTONE

PATH SNAKES UP AND RIGHT TO CLIMB ABOVE TOP OF GORGE ON YOUR LEFT - DIB SCAR

TO SANDY GATE

13

trailblazer

70 MINS FROM LEAVING ROAD (MAP 11)

20 MINS TO LIMEKILN (MAP 9)

DIB SCAR

65 MINS TO JOINING ROAD (MAP 11)

DIB SCAR

20 MINS FROM LIMEKILN (MAP 9)

11

9

ROUTE GUIDE AND MAPS

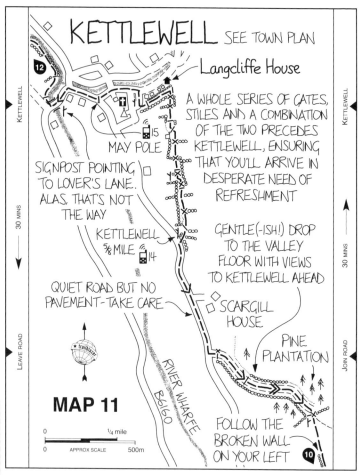

KETTLEWELL SEE TOWN PLAN

Langcliffe House

KETTLEWELL

KETTLEWELL

A WHOLE SERIES OF GATES, STILES AND A COMBINATION OF THE TWO PRECEDES KETTLEWELL, ENSURING THAT YOU'LL ARRIVE IN DESPERATE NEED OF REFRESHMENT

15 MAY POLE

SIGNPOST POINTING TO LOVER'S LANE. ALAS, THAT'S NOT THE WAY

KETTLEWELL 5/8 MILE 14

GENTLE(-ISH!) DROP TO THE VALLEY FLOOR WITH VIEWS TO KETTLEWELL AHEAD

30 MINS

30 MINS

QUIET ROAD BUT NO PAVEMENT-TAKE CARE

SCARGILL HOUSE

PINE PLANTATION

★ trailblazer

LEAVE ROAD

JOIN ROAD

MAP 11

RIVER WHARFE B6160

0   1/4 mile
0   APPROX SCALE   500m

FOLLOW THE BROKEN WALL ON YOUR LEFT

10

valley, which descends from the Coverhead Pass, Kettlewell is the converging point of many contour lines, and to the eye which delights in the flow and ripple of sky line there is a beauty in Kettlewell which is all its own. **Frederic William Moorman** (1872-1918), Professor of English Language and Literature at Leeds University. Moorman, incidentally, died in a tragic drowning accident and was succeeded in the post by one JRR Tolkien.

Kettlewell (🖳 kettlewellvillage.co.uk) is where Wharfedale and Coverdale meet, a cosy little village where the houses are huddled cheek-by-jowl on the valley floor while the sheer slopes of the fells rise loftily above. The name is believed to derive from the Anglo-Saxon 'Cetel Wella', which means a bubbling spring or stream, and in 1997 workmen digging near the village uncovered the skeleton of a woman that dates back to this era, being about 1400

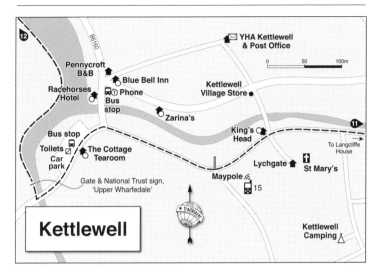

Kettlewell

years old. Like Grassington, however, Kettlewell only grew really prosperous with the establishment of the lead-mining industry that flourished in these parts back in the 17th and 18th centuries.

These days it's tourism that brings in the bucks, with walkers and cyclists in particular making up the majority of visitors. Most of them use the village as a base, of course, to explore the surrounding hills but if you've got a spare few minutes do visit the pretty local church, **St Mary's**, a 19th-century edifice built on the site of an original 12th-century Norman church.

Services

The **village store** (💻 www.kettlewellvil lagestore.co.uk; Mon-Thur 8am-5pm, Fri & Sat 8am-7pm, Sun 9.15am-5pm) is very much the heartbeat of Kettlewell. There is no tourist information in town but the people who run the store seem to be able to answer any questions you may have. In the absence of any ATM in the village the store's **cashback facility** is also rather vital. You can get up to £50 as long as you spend £5, which is not difficult given the variety of goods they have on sale. The pubs may also offer cashback, too, though check with them first. Sharing a building

with the YHA hostel, the village **post office** (Mon-Fri 10.30am-1pm) is on Westgate, just along from the store.

Transport

[See pp47-50] Kettlewell is a stop on the Nos 72A/72B **bus** routes and these provide the most frequent service. The 800 Grassington to Hawes (Tue & Sat only) service also stops here as do the 874 & 875 on Sunday/bank holidays.

Where to stay

There is a **campsite**, *Kettlewell Camping* (☎ 07930 379 079, 💻 www.kettlewellcam ping.co.uk; £7pp; 🐾), on the edge of the village and a short way off the trail. A convenient spot, then, and one with a smart and spotless toilet block where you can have a lovely hot shower, after which you can settle down for the night and sleep the sleep of the just... Until, that is, the church bells chime, and continue to chime, every 15 minutes throughout the night. Bring earplugs, or you'll be muttering some very sacrilegious thoughts the next day.

The village also plays host to one of the oldest **hostels** in the YHA network, having taken in guests for over 70 years. *Kettlewell YHA* (☎ 01756 760232, 💻 www

.yha.org.uk/hostel/kettlewell; 40 beds across 8 rooms of 2-6 beds each; WI-FI) also doubles as the local post office in town. As with most hostels, however, you may have to wait until 5pm when reception opens to check-in. Rates start at £22pp, with private rooms from £50. There's a self-catering kitchen and they offer evening meals, mains £8 – though I recommend you eat at one of the exceptional pubs in the village.

There is a choice of good **B&Bs** in Kettlewell. Friendly and helpful *Pennycroft* (☎ 01756 760845, 🖳 www .pennycroft.co.uk; 1D en suite/1D private bathroom; 🐾; WI-FI; Ⓛ); rates £32.50/40pp for smaller/bigger room, single occ £65) sits right next to the pubs and boasts of serving the 'best breakfast in the Dales'. *Lychgate* (☎ 01756 760355, 🖳 www.lych gate-bnb.co.uk; 1D en suite, 🐾, 1D/1T share shower facilities; 🐾; WI-FI; Ⓛ; rates £32.50-37.50pp, £55/65 sgl occ) is a new place in a lovely location next to the church gate. While up the road, *Langcliffe House* (☎ 01756 761180, 🖳 www.langcliffehouse .co.uk; 2D en suite; WI-FI; £45pp, sgl occ £70) overlooks all those stiles you've just struggled to negotiate. The year '1706' is carved into the stone above the door but as the owner will freely admit, the house's real construction date is nearer 1901 – though it's no less charming for that.

Both the village's tearooms and all the pubs offer accommodation. Of the tea-rooms, *Zarina's* (☎ 01756 761188, 🖳 www .zarinaskettlewell.co.uk; 1S/2D, en suite; WI-FI; B&B £39.50-44.50pp, sgl £45) is perhaps my favourite with three comfy rooms including one with a four-poster bed. The other, *The Cottage Tea Room* (☎ 01756 760405, 🖳 www.kettlewelltearooms .co.uk; 2D en suite; 🐾; 🐾; WI-FI) does offer a glass of sherry to greet new arrivals and while the rooms themselves are a little plain they are fine for a night or two. B&B rates are £32.50pp midweek or £35pp weekends (£65/70 sgl occ).

As for the pubs, *Racehorses Hotel* (☎ 01756 760233, 🖳 www.racehorseshotel.co .uk; 8D/9D or T en suite; 🐾; 🐾 £6; WI-FI; B&B rates £50pp, £62-5 sgl occ) dates back to the mid 1700s according to the date

above the large fireplace. It's a big place for such a small village with 17 rooms, though it's rather overshadowed at the moment by the older and more popular *Blue Bell Inn* (☎ 01756 760230, 🖳 www.bluebellkettle well.co.uk; 2T/4D/1D or T; all en suite; 🐾 £5; WI-FI; B&B from £42.50pp, sgl occ £65) where dogs are given just as warm a welcome as their owners. The third option, *The King's Head* (☎ 01756 761600, 🖳 www.thekingsheadkettlewell.co.uk; 5D/1T, en suite but one with private shower facilities), offers B&B for £35pp in the small double, £45pp otherwise (sgl occ £60-80). An attraction here is the good selection of DVDs which you can watch on the flat-screen TV in your room.

Where to eat and drink

You'd think that any village with 'kettle' in its title would have at least one place where you can get a decent cuppa, and in most people's opinion that place is *Zarina's* (see Where to stay; Fri-Wed 10am-5pm), which also serves some good hot food such as a bacon, sausage and egg butty for £5.95. The other tearoom in town, *The Cottage Tea Room* (see Where to stay; food daily 8.45am-sunset) stands opposite the car park on the way out of the village, a more traditional tearoom with decent teacakes.

For evenings, the place with the reputation for the finest food is *The King's Head* (see Where to stay; food served Mon-Thur noon-3pm & 5-9pm, Fri & Sat noon-3pm & 5-9.30pm, Sun noon-7pm). The fact they don't allow dogs didn't endear them to us but I can't reproach them for their cooking, which they describe as 'modern English' and includes such highlights as 'pork two ways' (slow-roast pork belly and pan-fried pork fillet with a bubble-and-squeak croquette, apple and chorizo and sherry sauce for £12.50). However, I preferred *The Blue Bell Inn* (see Where to stay; daily noon-9pm). I was already charmed by this place thanks to the little touches it employs – the miniature glasses by each of the beer pumps, for example, which allow you to 'try before you buy', and the welcome they give to people's dogs, which was possibly the warmest on the entire trail. And this was before they brought out their Famous Blue Bell Meat & Potato Pie (£14.65), which was enormous enough to take up most of the table and a couple of neighbouring postcodes as well. Thankfully, it was delicious too, which made the prospect of eating it all much less

daunting. Great stuff! The third option, *Racehorses Hotel* (see Where to stay: food served Mon-Fri noon-2pm, Sat & Sun to 3pm, daily 6-9pm), opposite, is not a bad choice either, with mains starting at £9.95 for the vegetarian curry, rising to £18.25 for the 10oz sirloin.

Leaving Kettlewell, note the garage on the right by the car park, which played a small but integral role in the 2003 film *Calendar Girls*. (In the movie, a calendar of topless 'glamour models' on the wall of the garage provides the inspiration for the WI ladies to get their kit off for charity.) Thereafter, things settle down into a pattern more familiar with Dales Way walkers as the trail once again adheres more or less to the river, passing through yet more arche-typal Dales fields and pasture meadows, each separated from its neighbour by an old drystone wall. After 2¼ miles (3.5km) a bridge conveys those seeking rest or refreshment across the water to teeny-tiny Starbotton.

STARBOTTON [Map 12, p112]

Those for whom the Dales Way is little more than a glorified pub crawl may wish to take the bridge across the Wharfe to the 70-house hamlet of Starbotton and the very decent, 400-year-old *Fox and Hounds* (☎ 01756 760269, ☐ www.foxandhounds-starbotton.co.uk; 3D/1T, en suite; ☛; WI-FI in the bar only; B&B rates are £40pp, £50 sgl occ). **Food** is served Tuesday to Sunday (noon-2pm & 6-8.30pm).

At the far (northern) end of the village, *Sweetbriar Cottage* (☎ 01756 761307, ☐ www.sweetbriarcottage.co.uk; 1F; ☛; ☚;

WI-FI; Ⓛ) is a converted 18th-century farm-house; the family room has a double bed and bunk beds, as well as its own private bathroom and lounge. B&B rates are £50/75/120 for single/double/family occu-pation. They also offer **camping** from £5pp per night (with shower on site); breakfast is available if requested in advance).

The 72A/72B **bus** services call here en route between Buckden, Kettlewell and Grassington (and on to Skipton); see pp47-50.

Back on the western side of the bridge, the call of Buckden continues to lure you onward, the path still flirting with the Wharfe. At one point you pass a copse of incongruous **redwoods**, the living remnants of a 19th-century estate, planted by local landowner Sir John Ramsden in 1850 – though now, like every-thing else round here, property of the National Trust. As trail and river diverge you'll notice the surrounding land becoming boggier (though thankfully not the path itself) and sedges and other moisture-loving plants dominate the fields, evidence of the fact you're now on a floodplain that is still occasionally inun-dated after heavy rain.

❏ **Important note – walking times**
All times in this book refer only to the time spent walking. You will need to add 20-30% to allow for rests, photography, checking the map, drinking water etc.

ROUTE GUIDE AND MAPS

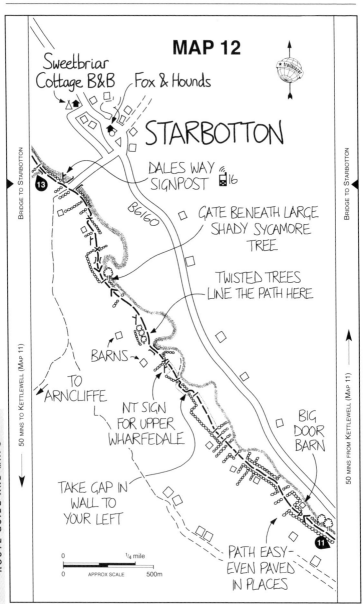

MAP 12

Sweetbriar Cottage B&B

Fox & Hounds

STARBOTTON

BRIDGE TO STARBOTTON

DALES WAY SIGNPOST 📶 16

B6160

GATE BENEATH LARGE SHADY SYCAMORE TREE

TWISTED TREES LINE THE PATH HERE

BARNS

TO ARNCLIFFE

NT SIGN FOR UPPER WHARFEDALE

BIG DOOR BARN

TAKE GAP IN WALL TO YOUR LEFT

50 MINS TO KETTLEWELL (MAP 11)

PATH EASY - EVEN PAVED IN PLACES

BRIDGE TO STARBOTTON

50 MINS FROM KETTLEWELL (MAP 11)

0   ¼ mile

0   APPROX SCALE   500m

ROUTE GUIDE AND MAPS

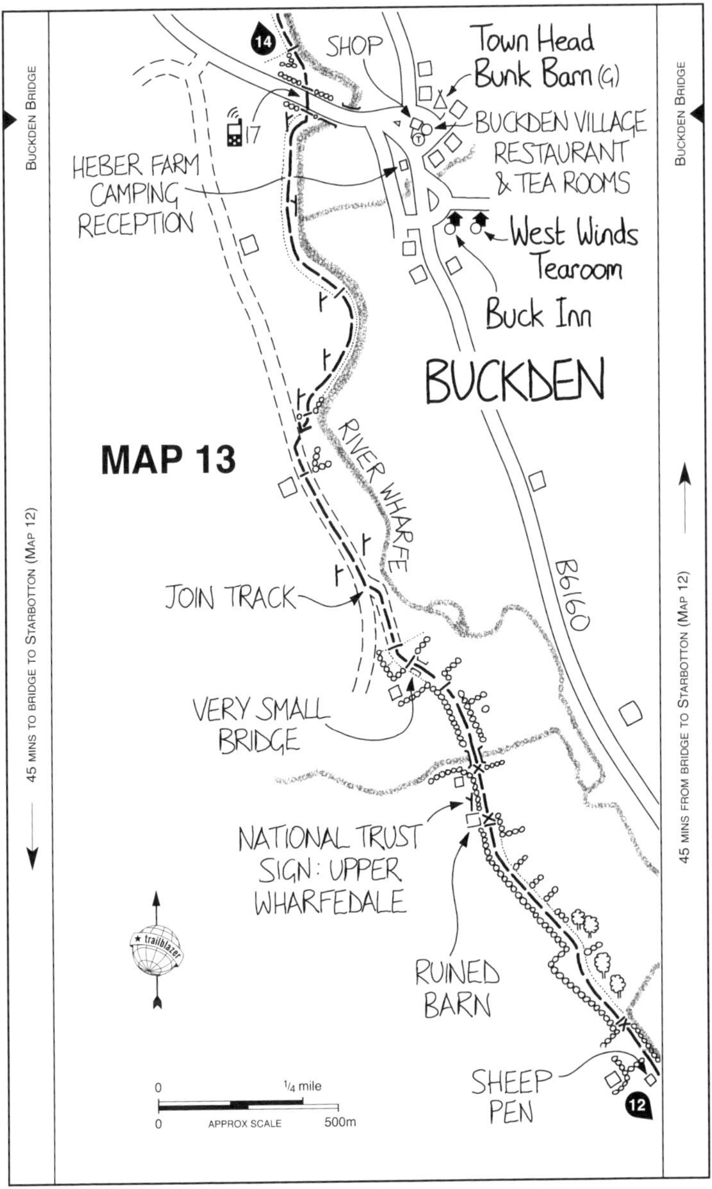

MAP 13

SHOP

Town Head
Bunk Barn (G)

BUCKDEN VILLAGE
RESTAURANT
& TEA ROOMS

HEBER FARM
CAMPING
RECEPTION

West Winds
Tearoom

Buck Inn

BUCKDEN

RIVER WHARFE

B6160

JOIN TRACK

VERY SMALL
BRIDGE

NATIONAL TRUST
SIGN: UPPER
WHARFEDALE

RUINED
BARN

SHEEP
PEN

trailblazer

0   ¼ mile
0   500m
APPROX SCALE

BUCKDEN BRIDGE

BUCKDEN BRIDGE

45 MINS TO BRIDGE TO STARBOTTON (MAP 12)

45 MINS FROM BRIDGE TO STARBOTTON (MAP 12)

ROUTE GUIDE AND MAPS

BUCKDEN [Map 13, p113]

The serene village of Buckden (🖳 www
.buckden.org) can feel like the final outpost
of civilisation: in all probability your
mobile phone signal will have abandoned
you back down the valley before
Kettlewell; the bus even stops following
your path here, chugging off to Hawes
instead. And after here there's just one
more pub, a church, and a few scattered
farmhouses providing lonely but lovely
accommodation before the inn at Cowgill is
reached in the neighbouring valley of
Dentdale, over 16 miles (25.7km) away.
What's more, the nearest shop from here
isn't until Dent, almost 22 miles (35.4km)
and one very long day's walk further along
the trail. So stock up in Buckden and plan
well, for there's little help along the way for
the next 20 miles and more. Worryingly,
even the future of the **village shop** (Thur-
Tue 8am-4pm, Wed 8-11am) is in danger,
with the owner having put it up for sale
(though he did reassure me that whoever
did buy it would be barmy to close it
down). Outside is a **phone box**, which
probably sees more action than most given
the lack of any mobile reception.

The 72A **bus** service calls here in
term-time only, but the 72B operates year-
round. The 800 (Tue & Sat only) also stops
here and on Sunday/bank holidays the 874
from Ilkley continues here. The 874 connects with the 857 (also Sun/bank hols)
between Hawes and Buckden. For details
see pp47-50.

See p14 for details of Buckden
Festival.

For **accommodation**, there's **camping**
at *Heber Farm* (☎ 01756 760304; 🐾 free)
where a pitch is £5. You should try to report
to reception at the farmhouse first, though
the site itself is above the car park. In the
same corner of the village is the National
Trust-owned *Town Head Bunk Barn* (☎

0344 335 1296; 13 beds, 4 bunk beds in 3
rooms plus one en suite single; 🐾; 🐾 up to
two OK) which has a fully equipped
kitchen that again, frustratingly, is for
groups only and costs £240 for a minimum
stay of two nights for the whole barn.

For **B&B**, there are two choices: the
tearoom, *West Winds* (☎ 01756 760883, 🖳
www.westwindsinyorkshire.co.uk; 2S/1D;
shared bathroom; 🐾; basins in rooms; WI-
FI; Ⓛ) offers complimentary tea and cake in
the tearoom (see below) for guests on arrival. Rates are a reasonable £30pp or £35 for
single occupancy of a double.

The alternative is to stay at the village
pub. *The Buck Inn* (☎ 01756 761401, 🖳
www.buckinnbuckden.co.uk; 8D or T/4Tr,
all en suite; 🐾; 🐾 £5; WI-FI; Ⓛ) is certainly the spiritual centre of the village and a
warm welcome is pretty much guaranteed.
Rates are £39.50-48.50pp (sgl occ from
£57, three sharing room rate plus £15pp).

The **food** at *The Buck Inn* has also
been recommended, for the quantity as
much as the quality (Mon-Thur noon-
8.30pm, Fri & Sat to 9pm, Sun to 8pm; note
bar snacks only Mon-Fri 2.30-6pm). *West
Winds Tearoom* (Easter-Oct Wed-Sun
12.30-5.30pm), behind the pub, is also a
decent place, renowned for its pies cooked
in its Aga (eg rabbit & juniper pie from
£7.60, cheese & cashew nut pie from
£6.80). The third alternative, *Buckden
Village Tearooms*, located directly behind
the shop (Thur-Tue 11am-4.30pm & 6-
8pm), serve their teapots with an extra pot
of water, a custom of which I heartily
approve. Dogs are welcome as long as others eating in the café aren't against the idea.
Note that they accept cash only. The menu is
fairly standard (cakes, sandwiches etc) with
a tuna and cheese toasted sandwich £3.95;
in the evenings things are more imaginative, with a plate of local trout topped with
dill butter and almonds costing £13.

STAGE 3: BUCKDEN TO COWGILL   MAPS 13-22

I don't know about you but I've just about had enough of Wharfedale. All those
effortlessly ravishing riparian landscapes start to make my eyes ache after a
while. And those lovely locals with their warm welcomes and lashings of home-
cooked food – well I was hoping to lose weight on this walk, not gain it. And

as for the delightful kingfishers with their acrobatics and their dazzling iridescent plumage – just show-offs, the lot of them!

So it's with a sigh of relief that you'll learn that today is the day that you
wave farewell to the Wharfe. Where you actually do so, however, is open to
debate. For one thing, soon after you leave Buckden, the valley you follow is
actually renamed **Langstrothdale**, even though the river you are following is
still the Wharfe. Then, at Beckermonds, 4 miles (6.3km) further on, the river is
joined by another tributary, **Green Field Beck**, and many people cite *this*
spot as the place where the River Wharfe actually begins. But that's not the end of
the matter: for though, officially, the waterway you follow upstream of
Beckermonds is called Oughtershaw Beck, others will maintain that it's still
called the Wharfe, and only at Nethergill (see p121) do Wharfe and Way finally separate for the last time, with the river bending north to its source at boggy
Fleet Moss.

Confused? Well, you're not alone. Suffice to say, whatever the correct version, your farewell to the Wharfe is a fairly protracted one. Nor is this the only
reason that this is such a red-letter day. For it is on this stage that you pass the
halfway point (occurring near Winshaw House on the regular route, or somewhere on the approach to Wold Fell from Newby Head Gate on the Alternative
(High Level) Route; see pp126-9 for details). The high point of the entire trail,
at 522m (or 574m on the Alternative Route), is also conquered. This is also
where the path turns from being one heading generally northwards, though with
a slightly westward drift, to being a more westerly path with a slightly northerly leaning. What's more, if you manage to reach Dentdale before the end of the
stage (which is one of the few valleys round here that's named after one of the
villages within it rather than the river that runs through it, which is called the
Dee; Wensleydale, incidentally, is another) then you're also in a new county,
Cumbria – even though you won't actually be leaving the Yorkshire Dales
National Park for a couple of days yet!

But such accomplishments are not gained easily and for many this **17-mile
(27.3km; 7hrs)** stage to the Sportsman's Inn at Cowgill – or it's **17¾ miles
(28.5km)** to Lea Yeat (remember to add on about 200m to get from Buckden to
the start of the trail too) – is the hardest walk of the entire Way. This is particularly true if the weather's against you, for there are lots of exposed stretches and
little shelter en route. Furthermore, with the nearest proper village not until
Dent, 22 miles away, and with some tricky walking in between, the average
Dales Way walker is usually compelled to find somewhere en route to bed down
for the night. For some, that could be one of several isolated farmhouses that
earn a little extra by offering B&B, or a place to camp. For others, there are a
couple of places away from the route that can put you up for the night. The
Station Inn (see p130) at Ribblehead, for example, near the mighty viaduct, is a
sensible choice, even though it's about 1½ miles (2.4km) from the path along a
busy-ish road, for it divides the walk into two manageable chunks: 12½ miles
(20km) from Buckden to Far Gearstones plus 1½ miles (2.4km) to Ribblehead
on the first day, then 1½ miles (2.4km) back to Far Gearstones and 10 miles

(16km) to Dent. Oh, and remember to add on the 200m between Buckden and the trail itself, and a similar distance between the trail and Dent too at the start/end of this stage.

But whatever your destination on this stage, an early start is recommended; in all probability you've got a lot of miles to cover and, if something does go wrong, it's good to have plenty of daylight to sort yourself out.

The route

The start of this stage is mundane enough (though to describe it as such probably says more about how you've been spoilt with the scenery and walking thus far and less about the quality of this stretch!) as you once again follow the river upstream. A significant moment occurs about 10 minutes from Buckden Bridge, however, as Cray Gill joins the Wharfe from the north – and the valley you follow is renamed **Langstrothdale** (though it is still the River Wharfe that will be accompanying you). Soon afterwards you join a road, Dubbs Lane, that leads all the way to Hubberholme.

HUBBERHOLME   [Map 14]

Though it may sound like someone breaking wind in the bath, the name Hubberholme is actually derived from the Norse for Hunberg's Homestead, which gives you an idea of the ancient origins of this village. It's a tiny place, little more than a pub, church and a couple of farmsteads squashed together by the river which is, for most of the day at least, by far the noisiest element.

Hubberholme's pub and church have an interesting relationship. Indeed, The George Inn started off life as the vicarage back in the 17th century, and the pub's tradition of having a lit candle on the bar dates back to a time when the vicar of the church would put a candle in his window to let his parishioners know that he was home. That candle later found secondary employment as the centrepiece of the **Hubberholme Parliament**.

Taking place on the first Monday of each year, the parliament is an auction where local farmers bid for the rights to 16 acres of pasture held by the church, with the proceeds traditionally going to the poor of the parish. The auction ends only when the candle finally burns itself out, with the vicar himself acting as auctioneer, overseeing the proceedings from the House of Lords (or the dining room as it's more commonly called), while the farmers

themselves stay in the House of Commons (ie the bar).

As for the **church** itself, it still revels in the endorsement it received from author JB Priestley, who described it as 'one of the smallest and most pleasant places in the world'. You can see why Priestley, who was born in nearby Bradford, was so captivated, for it remains the most characterful and absorbing church on the entire path. Do pay a visit (it's usually open), looking out in particular for the altar, rescued in 1862 from the pub where it was seeing service as the bar and returned to the church. The keen-eyed amongst you may also wish to seek out the mice carved into the pews by the famous Mouseman of Kilburn, the carpenter Robert Thompson. The mice are said to commemorate a time when the church was flooded after the Wharfe broke its banks and rodents got into the chapel. Priestley's ashes incidentally, were scattered in the churchyard after his death in 1984, and there's a memorial plaque dedicated to him in the church.

The pub also likes to claim that it was Priestley's favourite watering hole, and it wouldn't be a surprise if this, too, were true. *The George Inn* (☎ 01756 760223, 🖳 www.thegeorge-inn.co.uk; 1S/3D/2D or T/1Tr, en suite; 🛏; 🐾 £5; WI-FI; B&B rates £42.50pp, plus £5 for single-night stay over

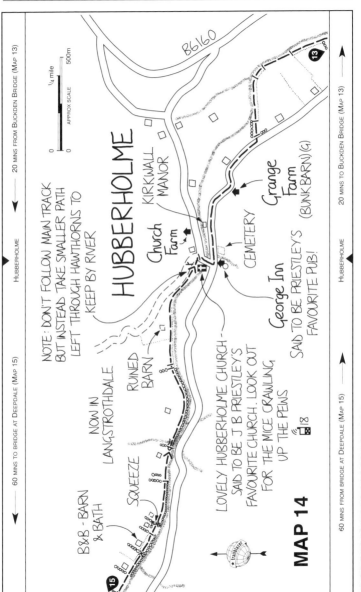

a weekend, single £65, single occ £70) is a throwback to a less cacophonous age, with a lovely lack of piped music and gaming machines inside. The **food's** good too (Wed-Mon; food noon-2.30pm & 6-8pm), fairly standard pub grub but with the odd stand-out dish such as vegetable and chestnut stew with sage crust and crispy kale served with garlic and smoked cheese ciabatta and mash or chips (£13.95).

Other accommodation includes the **groups-only bunk barn** at *Grange Farm*

(☎ 01756 760259; room for 18 people across four rooms; 🐾 one per weekend; WI-FI; rates from £480), just before the village, which is open weekends only; or for **B&B**, 16th-century *Church Farm* (☎ 01756 760240 or ☎ 07833 702055, 🖳 www .churchfarmhubberholme.co.uk; 1D or T en suite/1T with private bathroom; 🍴; WI-FI; £37pp, £60 sgl occ), a short distance down Stubbing Lane.

The trail continues on its riparian route with the Wharfe now to its left, taking you past ruined barns and ruminating sheep to **Yockenthwaite**, an isolated, chilly huddle of houses. Fans of British children's TV programmes in the 1990s may recognise the name as one of the main characters in *The Rottentrolls*, narrated by Martin Clunes. (Kettlewell, Little Strid and Penyghent are just some of the other characters in the show, and all of the names used are taken from place names from this corner of the Dales.)

Though there's no accommodation in Yockenthwaite itself, you can leave the path to cross the river here and make your way back down to *Low Raisgill B&B* (☎ 01756 760351, 🖳 www.lowraisgill.co.uk; 1S private facilities, 2D/1T all en suite; 🍴; WI-FI; Ⓛ; £42.50-47.50pp, sgl £50, sgl occ £65-75) now under new ownership and a lovely spot, with Aga-cooked breakfasts and a wood burner in the dining room; lifts are offered to and from the pub for evening meals.

Continuing on the trail from Yockenthwaite, a fine **lime kiln**, more complete even than the restored one you saw outside Grassington, lies directly on the path. Of even more interest, further along you come to a **stone circle**, two dozen or so stones placed in a slight oval by the path. The current consensus amongst academic circles is that rather than conforming to the official definition of a stone circle, this is actually a **ring cairn**, a construction most commonly seen in Wales and Cornwall but which can also be found in neighbouring Derbyshire to the south. (The distinction between stone circles and ring cairns is minor, though one difference is that the stones that form a ring cairn tend to be lower.) Whatever it's called, the actual purpose for the Bronze Age people who constructed it about 4000 years ago is still very much open to debate to this day.

Continuing on, weather permitting you'll love the next stretch of easy strolling, the open expanse of moor on either side and the far-reaching views providing a welcome contrast to the more enclosed scenery of much of what's gone before. The trail decides to cross back to the southern bank at **Deepdale**, though this is not to the detriment of the trail, which seems to grow lovelier with every step around here. Herons stand sentinel on the old stone barns, kings of all they survey, while the river, now a shallow shadow of its downstream self, bubbles merrily away on your right.

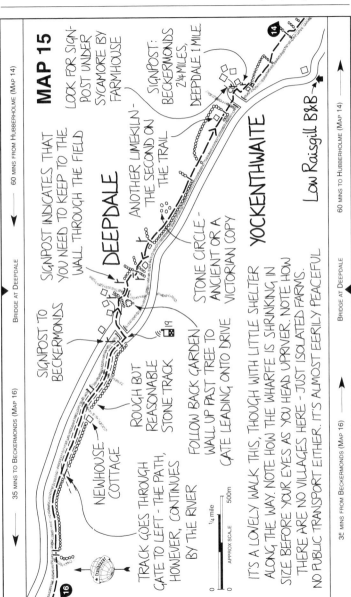

MAP 15

60 MINS FROM HUBBERHOLME (MAP 14)

LOOK FOR SIGN-POST UNDER SYCAMORE BY FARMHOUSE

SIGNPOST INDICATES THAT YOU NEED TO KEEP TO THE WALL THROUGH THE FIELD

SIGNPOST: BECKERMONDS 2¼ MILES, DEEPDALE 1 MILE

DEEPDALE

ANOTHER LIMEKILN - THE SECOND ON THE TRAIL

SIGNPOST TO BECKERMONDS

ROUGH BUT REASONABLE STONE TRACK

NEWHOUSE COTTAGE

FOLLOW BACK GARDEN WALL UP PAST TREE TO GATE LEADING ONTO DRIVE

STONE CIRCLE - ANCIENT OR A VICTORIAN COPY

YOCKENTHWAITE

Low Raisgill B&B

TRACK GOES THROUGH GATE TO LEFT - THE PATH, HOWEVER, CONTINUES BY THE RIVER

¼ mile

500m

APPROX SCALE

IT'S A LOVELY WALK THIS, THOUGH WITH LITTLE SHELTER ALONG THE WAY. NOTE HOW THE WHARFE IS SHRINKING IN SIZE BEFORE YOUR EYES AS YOU HEAD UPRIVER. NOTE HOW THERE ARE NO VILLAGES HERE - JUST ISOLATED FARMS. NO PUBLIC TRANSPORT EITHER. IT'S ALMOST EERILY PEACEFUL

35 MINS TO BECKERMONDS (MAP 16) — BRIDGE AT DEEPDALE — 60 MINS FROM HUBBERHOLME (MAP 14)

35 MINS FROM BECKERMONDS (MAP 16) — BRIDGE AT DEEPDALE

16

14

ROUTE GUIDE AND MAPS

At lovely **Beckermonds** the two sources of the Wharfe – Green Field Beck and Oughtershaw Beck – unite for the first time. It also may be possible to camp here at *East House Farm* (☎ 01756 760816; £6pp), but at the time of writing the property was on the market so may have been sold by the time you get here. So, walkers **must** call in advance, likewise if they want any meals: evening meal, breakfast or packed lunch – this is only sensible, as there's nowhere else to eat around here. Facilities here include a shower, toilet and an outside tap. Dogs are allowed on the site.

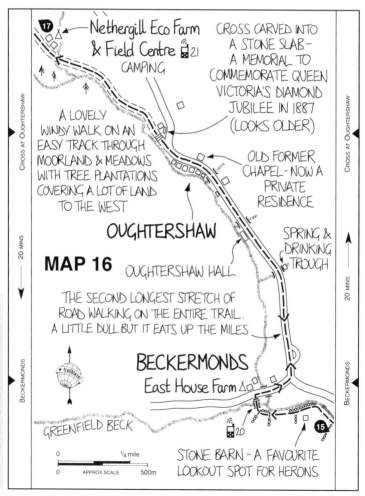

17 — Nethergill Eco Farm & Field Centre 📱21
CAMPING

CROSS CARVED INTO A STONE SLAB – A MEMORIAL TO COMMEMORATE QUEEN VICTORIA'S DIAMOND JUBILEE IN 1887 (LOOKS OLDER)

A LOVELY WINDY WALK ON AN EASY TRACK THROUGH MOORLAND & MEADOWS WITH TREE PLANTATIONS COVERING A LOT OF LAND TO THE WEST

OLD FORMER CHAPEL – NOW A PRIVATE RESIDENCE

OUGHTERSHAW

MAP 16   OUGHTERSHAW HALL

SPRING & DRINKING TROUGH

THE SECOND LONGEST STRETCH OF ROAD WALKING ON THE ENTIRE TRAIL. A LITTLE DULL BUT IT EATS UP THE MILES

★ trailblazer

BECKERMONDS
East House Farm

GREENFIELD BECK

📱20

15

STONE BARN – A FAVOURITE LOOKOUT SPOT FOR HERONS

0 — ¼ mile
0 — APPROX SCALE — 500m

CROSS AT OUGHTERSHAW
20 MINS
BECKERMONDS
CROSS AT OUGHTERSHAW
20 MINS
BECKERMONDS

Those not stopping for the night will need to steel themselves for one of the longest stretches of road walking on the trail, a schlep of over a mile – though thankfully you'll rarely encounter traffic on the way save for summer week-ends. The road takes you through the hamlet of **Oughtershaw**, at the end of which the path leaves the road, just by the old stone cross carved to celebrate Queen Victoria's Diamond Jubilee in 1887 (the spring you passed on the road before Oughtershaw commemorates the same event).

Things are starting to feel very remote now, the landscape opening up with every stride but revealing little for those seeking civilisation. There are, how-ever, two path-side options for those who've had enough for the day. First up is *Nethergill Eco Farm* (☎ 01756 761126, 🖳 www.nethergill.co.uk); ostensibly a field centre but also a working hill farm with sheep, rare-breed white shorthorn cattle, a working Dales pony, and chickens. You can **camp** here for £10 (which goes towards bird food), and though there's no shower there is a basin and toi-let and you can use the tea centre to make yourself a cup of tea or coffee and have a flapjack (please pay the honesty box). The tea centre is open for walkers passing through as well.

About a mile further along the track, *Swarthghyll Farm* is a lovely place to rest your corns (☎ 01756 760466, 🖳 www.swarthghyll-farm.co.uk; WI-FI; 🐾) They offer superior self-contained, **self-catering accommodation** in three flats surrounding a courtyard (1D/1T plus one Courtyard Flat with 1D/1T). Rates are £40pp in the double or twin flats, sgl occ £60 or it's £150 in the studio. Note that breakfast is not included. On the north side of the courtyard is a **bunkhouse** with beds for up to 40 people. Although, like most other bunkhouses on the Dales Way, it's usually reserved exclusively for the use of groups, at least here they'll consider allowing individuals to use it, particularly out of season, for £20pp. With TV, internet access, lovely hot showers and a large kitchen (bring your own supplies for there's little stored here save for condiments), it's worth it. Even dogs are allowed too, by prior arrangement.

From here it's a simple matter of traversing field after field, ascending slowly, crossing the **watershed** and reaching **Breadpiece Barn**, one of the few barns on the Way to have been honoured with a name. Thereafter dodging both bog and bull you make your way to isolated **Cam Houses**, where a final deci-sion needs to be made: do you want to stick to the official, traditional Dales Way Route? Or would you rather spice things up with a stroll on the Alternative (High Level) Route, which as the name suggests is higher. If the latter, it's time you turned to p126; while to stick to the main trail, read on.

One of the hardest things about the regular route is finding where it starts from Cam Houses: if you find yourself heading on the main drive straight up the hill, suffice to say, you've gone wrong. Instead, you need to go through the series of gates by the side of the main barn. Locate this trail correctly and it's not long before you find yourself striding through **Cam Woodland**, though this corner of the pine plantation is now largely felled. From here it's a mere skip to join the **Pennine Way** and the **Cam High Road**; the cairn that marks the mile-long union of the two, incidentally, also marks **the high point of the entire**

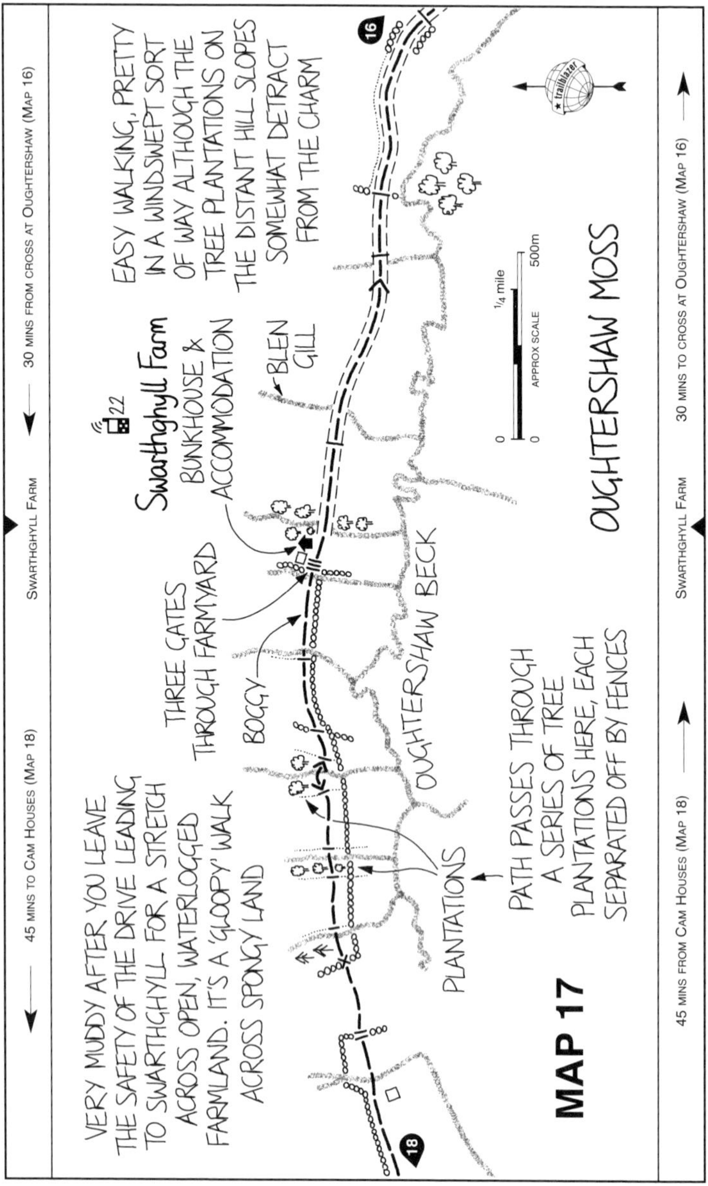

← 45 MINS TO CAM HOUSES (MAP 18)   SWARTHGHYLL FARM ▶   30 MINS FROM CROSS AT OUGHTERSHAW (MAP 16) →

45 MINS FROM CAM HOUSES (MAP 18) →   ◀ SWARTHGHYLL FARM   30 MINS TO CROSS AT OUGHTERSHAW (MAP 16) →

EASY WALKING, PRETTY IN A WINDSWEPT SORT OF WAY ALTHOUGH THE TREE PLANTATIONS ON THE DISTANT HILL SLOPES SOMEWHAT DETRACT FROM THE CHARM

Swarthghyll Farm
BUNKHOUSE & ACCOMMODATION
☐22

BLEN GILL

OUGHTERSHAW MOSS

THREE GATES THROUGH FARMYARD

BOGGY

OUGHTERSHAW BECK

PATH PASSES THROUGH A SERIES OF TREE PLANTATIONS HERE, EACH SEPARATED OFF BY FENCES

PLANTATIONS

VERY MUDDY AFTER YOU LEAVE THE SAFETY OF THE DRIVE LEADING TO SWARTHGHYLL FOR A STRETCH ACROSS OPEN, WATERLOGGED FARMLAND. IT'S A 'GLOOPY' WALK ACROSS SPONGY LAND

MAP 17

¼ mile
APPROX SCALE
500m

Dales Way. Cam High Road is actually an old Roman Road (you can probably tell this by how straight it is) that once linked Ingleton with the fort at Bainbridge.

The descent from here is steady and easy, allowing you to peruse the messages that are doubtless coming into your mobile phone after you've been with-

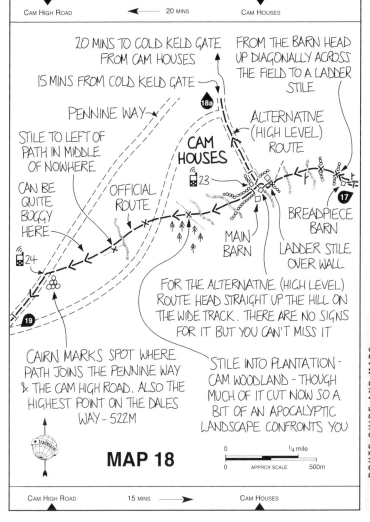

CAM HIGH ROAD   ← 20 MINS   CAM HOUSES

20 MINS TO COLD KELD GATE
FROM CAM HOUSES

15 MINS FROM COLD KELD GATE

PENNINE WAY

STILE TO LEFT OF
PATH IN MIDDLE
OF NOWHERE

CAN BE
QUITE
BOGGY
HERE

OFFICIAL
ROUTE

FROM THE BARN HEAD
UP DIAGONALLY ACROSS
THE FIELD TO A LADDER
STILE

18a

ALTERNATIVE
(HIGH LEVEL)
ROUTE

CAM
HOUSES

23

17

BREADPIECE
BARN

MAIN
BARN

LADDER STILE
OVER WALL

24

19

FOR THE ALTERNATIVE (HIGH LEVEL)
ROUTE HEAD STRAIGHT UP THE HILL ON
THE WIDE TRACK. THERE ARE NO SIGNS
FOR IT BUT YOU CAN'T MISS IT

CAIRN MARKS SPOT WHERE
PATH JOINS THE PENNINE WAY
& THE CAM HIGH ROAD. ALSO THE
HIGHEST POINT ON THE DALES
WAY - 522M

STILE INTO PLANTATION -
CAM WOODLAND - THOUGH
MUCH OF IT CUT NOW SO A
BIT OF AN APOCALYPTIC
LANDSCAPE CONFRONTS YOU

★ trailblazer

MAP 18

0   1/4 mile

0   APPROX SCALE   500m

CAM HIGH ROAD   15 MINS →   CAM HOUSES

out a signal for a day or more. Do look up temporarily, at least, to enjoy the views, not least the staggering sight of the Ribblehead Viaduct across the valley from the junction known as **Cam End**, where the Pennine Way diverts off left.

Unless you're staying at Station Inn at Ribblehead (see p130), you'll have to content yourself with this distant view of the viaduct right now. But don't despair – before the day is out you'll be walking under a second, just as mighty, viaduct and within sight of another, while within 48 hours you will be walking

---

❏ **The Settle to Carlisle Railway Line and the viaducts on the Dales Way**
Guaranteed to fill the memory banks of both cranium and camera, the huge viaducts that one passes by, under and alongside during the walk are the most distinguishing features of the latter half of the Dales Way. As one gazes in wonder at their sheer size and grandeur, one can only imagine the levels of cooperation and teamwork that must have been required to get these huge projects completed. Ironic, then, that without man's more petty, self-serving instincts, these monolithic wonders of the Industrial Age might never have been required at all!

For behind the viaducts' construction is a disagreement between the two main rail companies in the region in the middle of the 19th century, the London & North Western Railway (LNWR) and the Midland Railway. The former had control of the main line between London and Scotland. The latter wanted access to it but their own network only went as far as Ingleton. From Ingleton, the line did continue to Low Gill and a union with the main London–Scotland line – but this section was under the ownership of LNWR, who were loath to allow Midland Railway trains on their tracks. Indeed, the relationship between Midland and LNWR were in such a parlous state that the two networks even built their own stations at Ingleton, a mile apart from each other, and passengers were forced to walk between the two in order to continue their journey.

So the Midland Railway decided to build its own railway – and the idea of the Settle–Carlisle line was born. Work began on the line in 1870 and during the course of its construction over 6000 navvies were employed, each labouring on some of the toughest terrain in England and, as you may have already experienced, under some of the worst weather conditions the British Isles could throw at them!

Camps for the workers were set up right by the course of this new railway, with names like Jericho and Sebastapol – the Crimean War of the 1850s still being fresh in people's minds at this time. These unofficial 'townships' came complete with schools, post offices and chapels, with scripture readers employed by the Midland Railway to warn workers against the demon drink. The remains of one of these camps, **Batty Green**, where over 2000 lived and worked, can be seen by the arches of the Ribblehead Viaduct.

An estimated 100 workers were killed during the construction of the 73-mile (117.5km) Settle and Carlisle (as the Settle to Carlisle Railway is sometimes called). Nor was it just industrial accidents that one had to watch out for: a plaque in the church at Chapel-le-Dale near Ribblehead is dedicated to the 80 souls who lost their lives in a smallpox outbreak at Batty Green; in total there are over 200 burials of men, women and children in the church graveyard that date back to this time.

The railway was eventually opened to goods traffic in the summer of 1875 and passenger services followed the next year. For the first few decades the line was a success, though after the Second World War it appeared to be running out of steam, its greater gradients making it slower and thus less competitive than rival lines.

under two more! Incidentally, the stream at the bottom of the descent, running parallel to the B6255, is **Gayle Beck**, which is a major tributary of the Ribble River. This in turn flows west to Preston and the Irish Sea, whereas up to now every river encountered on the route has eventually found its way east to the North Sea – incontrovertible proof that you have now crossed the watershed of England! For the Alternative (High Level) Route see p126 and for the continuation of the main route see p130.

The Beeching Report of 1963 recommended its closure and by 1970 there were only two passenger services a day using the line. However, in the 1980s, as other lines became clogged with traffic, the line enjoyed an upturn in fortunes. This coincided with campaigns, mainly from railway enthusiasts, to keep the line open. Today, with eight of the original stations that were shut in 1970 now reopened, the line is fully operational once more with at least five passenger services in each direction each day; see 🖥 www.settle-carlisle.co.uk for a timetable.

The viaducts
Central to the railway's construction were, of course, the viaducts necessary to enable the line to cross such undulating terrain. In total there are 22 viaducts, each one built in just four years between 1870 and 1874. The most famous of these is the **Ribblehead Viaduct**, also known, more correctly, as the **Batty Moss Viaduct**. With a 400m span, it's the longest on the railway and rises 32 metres above the mire of Batty Moss.

Linking Ribblehead with the neighbouring viaduct at Dent Head is **Blea Moor Tunnel**, over 1½ miles (2.4km) long and the longest of the 14 tunnels on the line. As for **Dent Head Viaduct**, it was actually built above a marble quarry, from which the massive blocks used in its construction were hewn. At 182 metres long, Dent Head's span may be less than half of Ribblehead's but it *can* match its neighbour's 30m+ height – something you'll appreciate as you walk underneath it on entering Dentdale.

Even higher, **Arten Gill Viaduct**, to the north of Dent Head, reaches a height of 35m and is visible from the path, particularly when descending past Dent Station on the Alternative (High Level) Route (see pp126-9). If you're on the regular route, look east near where the road and path cross the Dee at a place called **Stone House**.

So what are the other viaducts on the Dales Way?
The other two enormous viaducts visited on the Dales Way (and in both cases you walk right underneath them) are part of the original Ingleton to Lowgill line that roughly follows the course of the Lune River and was owned by LNWR. In other words, it's the 19-mile (30.5km) line that connected the Midland network (that stopped at Ingleton) with the main line running between London and Scotland. As such, these viaducts are actually older than those mentioned above. The **Lune Viaduct**, for example, more properly called the **Waterside Viaduct**, was built between 1857 and 1861; that at **Lowgill**, as you leave the Dales National Park, in 1859. The lovely **iron bridge across the Rawthey River** (see Map 26, p142) that you pass after the mill at Birks is part of the same line.

Due to the disagreement between LNWR and Midland and the subsequent building of the Carlisle and Settle Line (see above), this line remained a minor branch line before eventually closing in 1967.

Alternative (High Level) Route
Map 18, p123; Maps 18a-b, p128; Map 18c, p129; Map 21, p133

For those who crave both solitude and the opportunity to take a trail that one friend rightly describes as 'viewtastic', the Alternative (High Level) Route is a terrific option. The only drawbacks that I can think of are: i) you don't get the spectacular view of Ribblehead Viaduct that you do on the official trail (though you do get several, oblique views of the other viaducts); ii) if you're staying in Cowgill at the Sportsman's Inn or the neighbouring campsite, you'll have to walk back up the hill for 20 minutes (though there is a second campsite in Lea Yeat); and iii) this high-level trail is very exposed and there's little shelter en route – unless, perhaps, you're willing to hunker down behind a drystone wall or beneath a particularly obliging cow. That said, there are a couple of opportunities to rejoin the main route should the weather turn against you: at one point the trail drops to the B6255 and follows the Dent Road, thus passing within waving distance of the official route, just a 2-minute walk away. Then, further on, after the path has rounded **Wold Fell** there's the chance to drop down **Arten Gill**, underneath its magnificent **viaduct** and on to **Stone House** in Upper Dentdale.

Distance-wise, if you come off the High Level trail before Wold Fell and rejoin the official path on the Dent Road, you've actually shortened your walk by 1¾ miles compared to the official trail, ie **16 miles (24.5km)**, rather than 17¾ miles (28.5km) that you would have clocked up if you'd stayed on the official trail all the way to Lea Yeat. Stay on the Alternative (High Level) Route until Arten Gill, and you've still shortened your walk when compared to the official trail, though only by half a mile now, the distance now being **17¼ miles (27.7km)** to Lea Yeat. While if you stay on to the very end and drop down to Lea Yeat via Dent Station, you've actually walked three-quarters of a mile *more* than if you took the official trail, a magnificent **18½ miles (29.8km)** to Lea Yeat – and you've probably got to walk at least another three-quarters of a mile (1.2km) to get to your accommodation too! But trust us, if your pack's light and the weather's right, you'll think it's worth it. Expect the walk from Cam Houses to Lea Yeat Bridge to take about 3 hours 25 minutes.

From Cam Houses the path initially follows the farmhouse road out and up the slope, leaving it to head for the same Roman road, **Cam High Road**, that you would have joined if you'd stuck to the official trail; though this time you'll head north-east along it rather than south. This you leave after passing through the monumental gateposts at **Cold Keld Gate**, the path now following the **Pennine Bridleway** as it describes an almost hairpin bend to head virtually due west, passing the high point on the trail at 574m soon after. The terrain is cold, windswept, empty and landmarks are few; the path, however, is fairly clearly scoured into the ground.

Passing through a gate in a wall known as **Gavel Gap**, you join up with the Ribble Way which starts here (the source of the Ribble being nearby) to enjoy a steady descent along the line of **Jam Sike** and then **Long Gill** (the first being a tributary of the second), before leaving the waters altogether for the clear path leading down to **Newby Head** and the junction of the **B6255** with the Dent Road. You're on the tarmac for less than three minutes, however, before you leave it again through a gate to head up **Wold Fell**; don't forget to look around you as you approach the summit for the three highest peaks of the Dales – Pen-y-ghent (694m), Ingleborough (723m) and, largest of the lot, Whernside (736m).

From the top you drop round to reach **Arten Gill**; the path down from here to Stone House is straightforward and walking under the viaduct is always a thrill, but if time and weather are on your side I suggest staying on the trail, which now follows an old drover's track known as **Galloway Gate**. This contours round **Great Knoutberry** (aka **Widdale Fell**), with the fantastic prospect

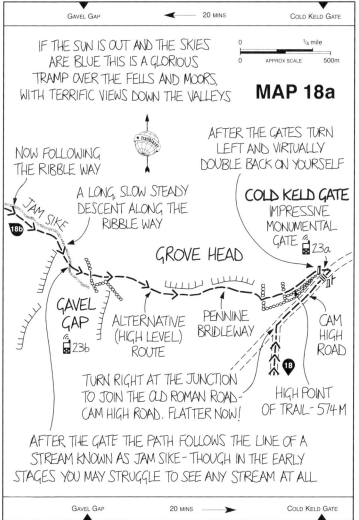

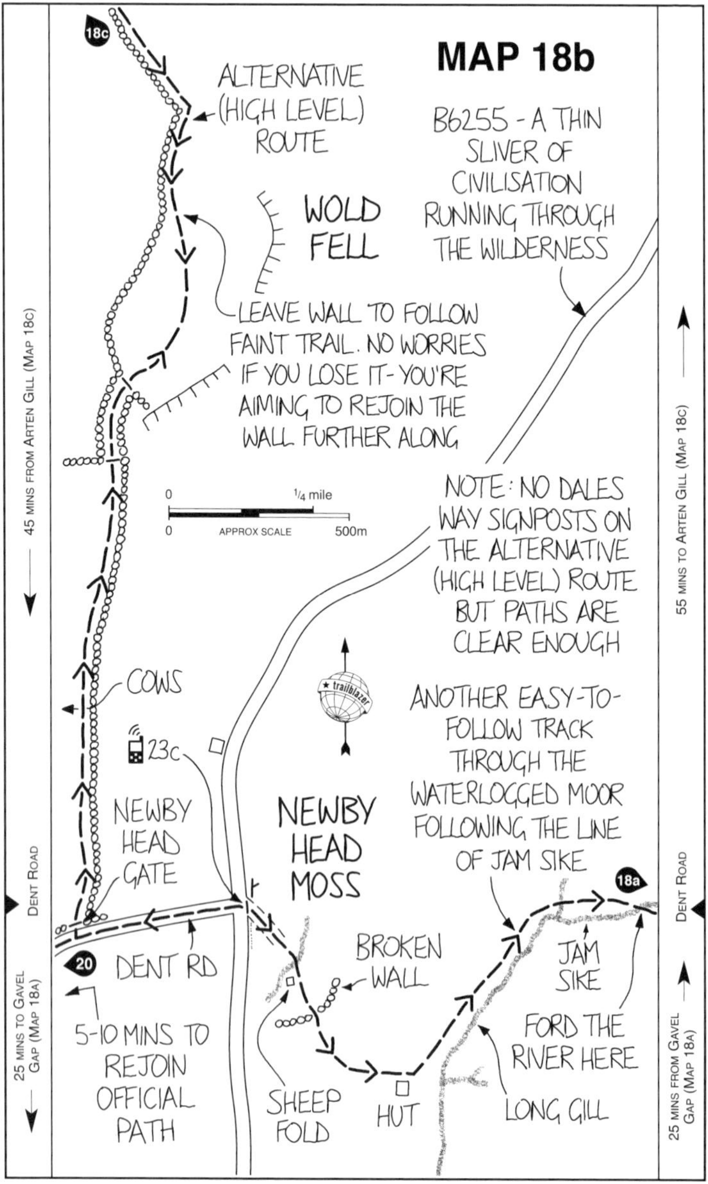

MAP 18b

18c

ALTERNATIVE (HIGH LEVEL) ROUTE

WOLD FELL

B6255 - A THIN SLIVER OF CIVILISATION RUNNING THROUGH THE WILDERNESS

LEAVE WALL TO FOLLOW FAINT TRAIL. NO WORRIES IF YOU LOSE IT - YOU'RE AIMING TO REJOIN THE WALL FURTHER ALONG

0   ¼ mile
0   APPROX SCALE   500m

NOTE: NO DALES WAY SIGNPOSTS ON THE ALTERNATIVE (HIGH LEVEL) ROUTE BUT PATHS ARE CLEAR ENOUGH

COWS

23c

★ trailblazer

ANOTHER EASY-TO-FOLLOW TRACK THROUGH THE WATERLOGGED MOOR FOLLOWING THE LINE OF JAM SIKE

NEWBY HEAD GATE

NEWBY HEAD MOSS

18a

JAM SIKE

20 DENT RD

BROKEN WALL

FORD THE RIVER HERE

5-10 MINS TO REJOIN OFFICIAL PATH

SHEEP FOLD

HUT

LONG GILL

45 MINS FROM ARTEN GILL (MAP 18C)

DENT ROAD

25 MINS TO GAVEL GAP (MAP 18A)

55 MINS TO ARTEN GILL (MAP 18C)

DENT ROAD

25 MINS FROM GAVEL GAP (MAP 18A)

ROUTE GUIDE AND MAPS

of Dentdale stretching below you and views north into neighbouring **Garsdale**.
The track – and your time on the Pennine Bridleway – ends by **Monkey Beck**
and **Coal Road** that leads down, down, down to **Dent Station** (Map 21),
England's highest, and beyond to **Lea Yeat** and a reunion with the official trail.

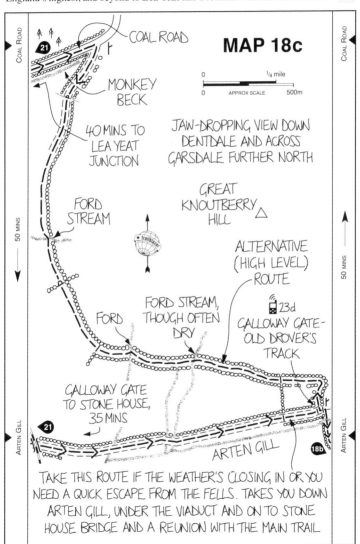

COAL ROAD

COAL ROAD

21

COAL ROAD

MAP 18c

0   ¼ mile

0   APPROX SCALE   500m

MONKEY
BECK

40 MINS TO
LEA YEAT
JUNCTION

JAW-DROPPING VIEW DOWN
DENTDALE AND ACROSS
GARSDALE FURTHER NORTH

FORD
STREAM

GREAT
KNOUTBERRY △
HILL

50 MINS

★ trailblazer

50 MINS

ALTERNATIVE
(HIGH LEVEL)
ROUTE

FORD STREAM,
THOUGH OFTEN
DRY

23d
CALLOWAY GATE-
OLD DROVER'S
TRACK

FORD

CALLOWAY GATE
TO STONE HOUSE,
35 MINS

ARTEN GILL

21

ARTEN GILL

ARTEN GILL

18b

TAKE THIS ROUTE IF THE WEATHER'S CLOSING IN OR YOU
NEED A QUICK ESCAPE FROM THE FELLS. TAKES YOU DOWN
ARTEN GILL, UNDER THE VIADUCT AND ON TO STONE
HOUSE BRIDGE AND A REUNION WITH THE MAIN TRAIL

FAR GEARSTONES & RIBBLEHEAD
[Map 19]

With so few amenities on the way today, many people will happily walk the mile and more along the B6255 from the path at Far Gearstones to *The Station Inn* (☎ 01524 241274, 🖳 www.thestationinn.net; 2T/4D; en suite; 🐾; WI-FI; **B&B** rates from £40-45pp, £60 sgl occ). In addition there are **bunkhouses** (1 x 11-bed, 1 x 8-bed, 2 x 6-bed; these provide good value too, with a bunk in a bunkhouse just £12.50pp). Food noon-2.30pm & 6-9pm, weekends & bank hols noon-9pm). It's not a bad place, though not outstanding, with **food** including the slightly odd hot beef in gravy baguette for £5.95 (gravy in a baguette apparently being quite the local delicacy around here). The best thing, of course, is the pub's location, right next to Ribblehead station and just a few hundred metres from the viaduct itself. There's **camping** in the

adjacent field for free but no facilities other than a simple water tap at the back when the pub is shut.

Well before you reach the station, on the road is the *Gearstones Outdoor Centre* (☎ 01924 499837, 🖳 gearstones.com; WI-FI). However, though it seems to allow ghosts to stay (sightings of a 'blue lady' are frequent), apparently it doesn't allow individual walkers to do so for, once again, it is for **groups only** (minimum £240 per night).

Do I need to tell you there's a **train service** at Ribblehead? Northern's services between Leeds and Appleby call here; some services also stop at Dent Station (see box p45). There's also the Sunday/bank holiday 830 **bus** service running between Ingleton and Richmond via Far Gearstones and Ribblehead Station. See public transport map and table pp47-50 for details.

(Main route continued from p125)　Back on the trail at **Far Gearstones**, the path picks its way across the road and up **Blea Moor**, opposite, bending round **Winshaw** (house) to head north-east for a couple of miles across often saturated ground to Dent Road, which you then follow downhill under **Dent Head Viaduct** (see box p125) and for a couple of miles (the longest stretch of road walking on the entire Dales Way) to Cowgill, Cumbria – and the end of this stage.

COWGILL & LEA YEAT
[Map 21, p133; Map 22, p135]

Often pronounced "Ca'gil" by the locals – although, given the preponderance of precipitation in these parts, perhaps it would be more appropriate if it was pronounced "Cagoule" – Cowgill and its even tinier neighbour Lea Yeat are little more than a few houses, a church, a couple of campsites and a pub, all stretched over a couple of miles of tarmac running down **Dentdale** (🖳 www.dentdale.com).

Above Lea Yeat is Dent railway station, the highest mainline station in England, a sweaty 15-minute ascent up from the main/only junction in Lea Yeat (and a good four miles from the village which it purports to serve).

For accommodation, *Cow Dub Farm* (☎ 01539 625278) charges just £5pp to **camp** in their sheep field across the road

from the farmhouse and the next-door pub. Dogs are allowed as long as they are kept on a lead. There is no shower, just a toilet and water trough. Or you can pay an extra pound and stay at *Ewegales Camping* (Map 22; ☎ 01539 625440; 🐾) at the other end of Cowgill (after Lea Yeat), which *does* have simple shower facilities.

The Sportsman's Inn (☎ 01539 625282, 🖳 www.thesportsmansinn.com; 2D/2T, private facilities; 🐾; ⓛ) is a bit of a landmark on the Dales Way if only because it's the only place to eat for miles around – and as such, sees most of the people on the trail at some time or other. Dogs aren't allowed in the inn, though. Still, you can't fault the food, with all mains both over sized and underpriced and no dish more than a tenner. As the kitchen has limited opening times ... *(continued on p134)*

ROUTE GUIDE AND MAPS

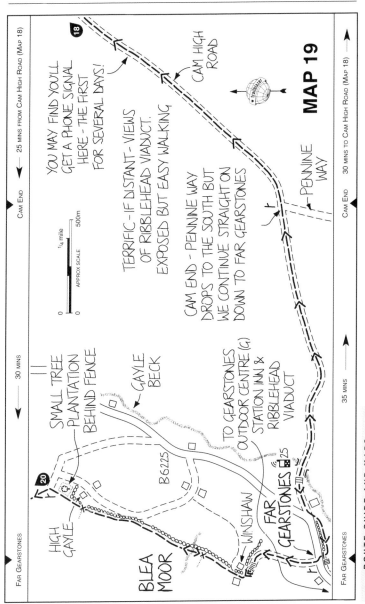

CAM END — 25 MINS FROM CAM HIGH ROAD (MAP 18)

YOU MAY FIND YOU'LL GET A PHONE SIGNAL HERE – THE FIRST FOR SEVERAL DAYS!

CAM HIGH ROAD

MAP 19

TERRIFIC – IF DISTANT – VIEWS OF RIBBLEHEAD VIADUCT. EXPOSED BUT EASY WALKING.

CAM END – PENNINE WAY DROPS TO THE SOUTH BUT WE CONTINUE STRAIGHT ON DOWN TO FAR GEARSTONES

PENNINE WAY

CAM END — 30 MINS TO CAM HIGH ROAD (MAP 18)

FAR GEARSTONES ◄ ——— 30 MINS ———

APPROX SCALE
¼ mile
0   500m

SMALL TREE PLANTATION BEHIND FENCE

GAYLE BECK

——— 35 MINS ———

TO GEARSTONES OUTDOOR CENTRE (¼) STATION INN & RIBBLEHEAD VIADUCT

25

HIGH GAYLE

B6225

20

BLEA MOOR

WINSHAW

FAR GEARSTONES

FAR GEARSTONES

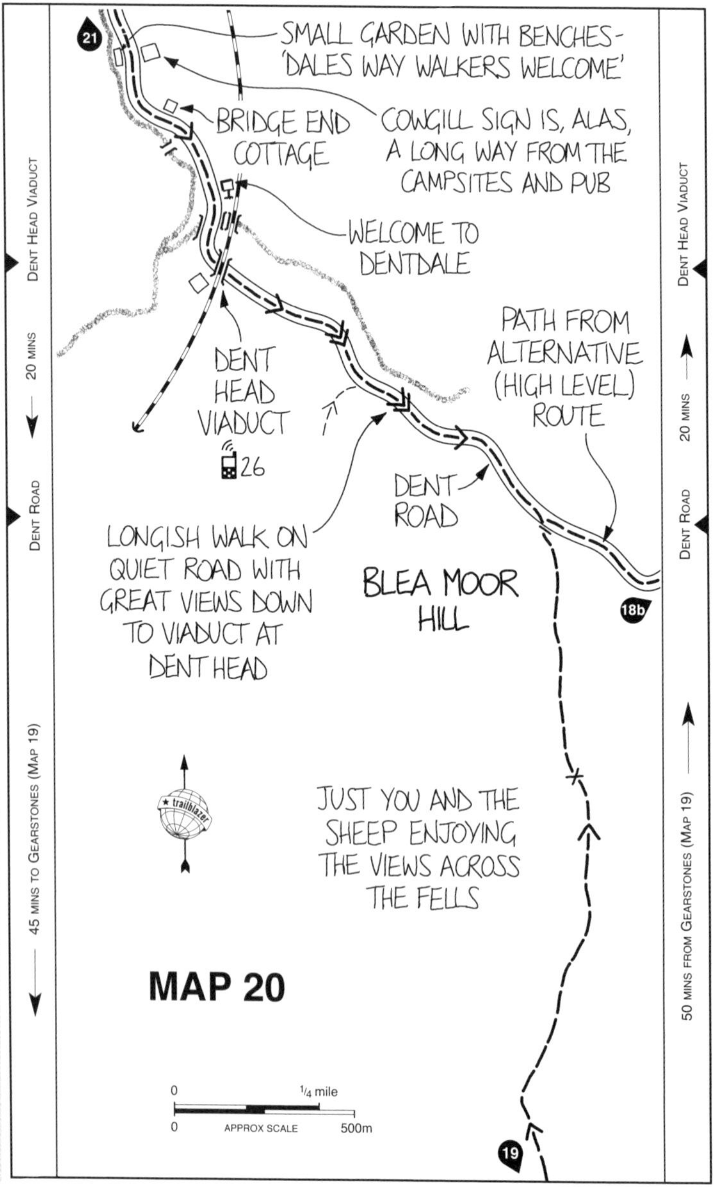

21

SMALL GARDEN WITH BENCHES-
'DALES WAY WALKERS WELCOME'

BRIDGE END
COTTAGE

COWGILL SIGN IS, ALAS,
A LONG WAY FROM THE
CAMPSITES AND PUB

WELCOME TO
DENTDALE

DENT
HEAD
VIADUCT
📱 26

PATH FROM
ALTERNATIVE
(HIGH LEVEL)
ROUTE

DENT
ROAD

LONGISH WALK ON
QUIET ROAD WITH
GREAT VIEWS DOWN
TO VIADUCT AT
DENT HEAD

BLEA MOOR
HILL

18b

JUST YOU AND THE
SHEEP ENJOYING
THE VIEWS ACROSS
THE FELLS

★ trailblazer

MAP 20

0   ¼ mile
0   APPROX SCALE   500m

19

DENT HEAD VIADUCT

20 MINS

DENT ROAD

45 MINS TO GEARSTONES (MAP 19)

DENT HEAD VIADUCT

20 MINS

DENT ROAD

50 MINS FROM GEARSTONES (MAP 19)

ROUTE GUIDE AND MAPS

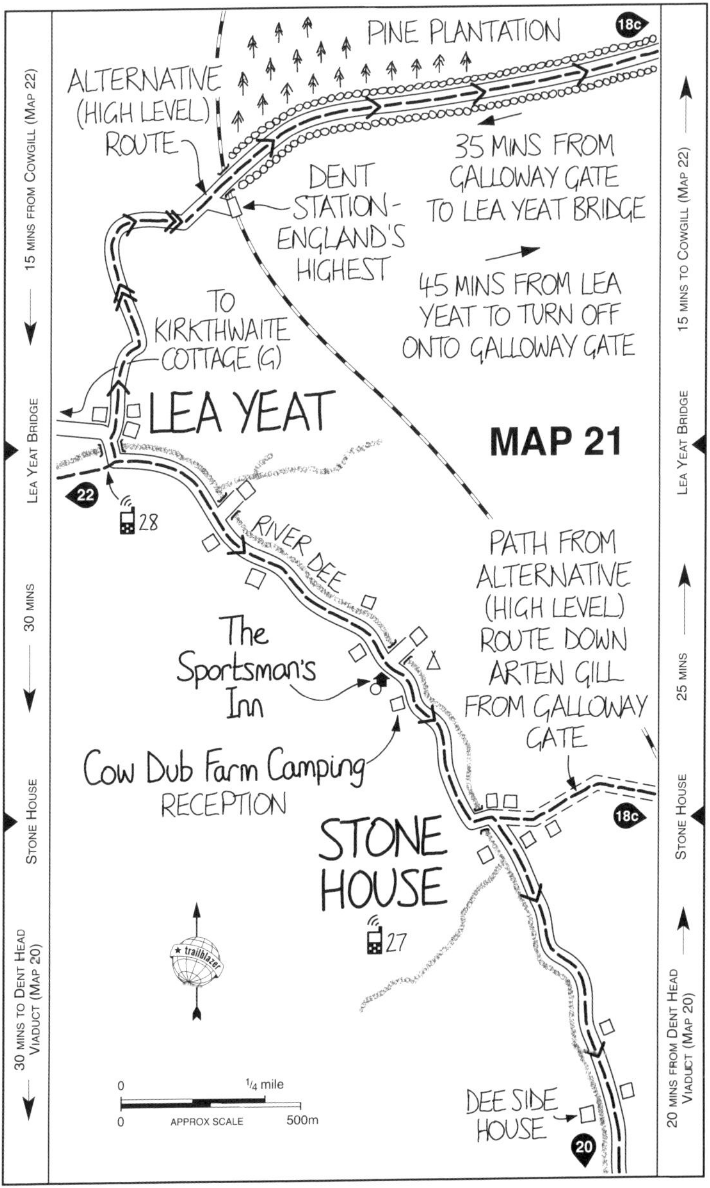

PINE PLANTATION

18c

ALTERNATIVE
(HIGH LEVEL)
ROUTE

DENT
STATION-
ENGLAND'S
HIGHEST

35 MINS FROM
GALLOWAY GATE
TO LEA YEAT BRIDGE

45 MINS FROM LEA
YEAT TO TURN OFF
ONTO GALLOWAY GATE

TO
KIRKTHWAITE
COTTAGE (G)

LEA YEAT

MAP 21

22 📱28

RIVER DEE

The
Sportsman's
Inn

PATH FROM
ALTERNATIVE
(HIGH LEVEL)
ROUTE DOWN
ARTEN GILL
FROM GALLOWAY
GATE

Cow Dub Farm Camping
RECEPTION

STONE
HOUSE

18c

📱27

★ trailblazer

DEE SIDE
HOUSE

20

0 .... 1/4 mile
0 .... 500m
APPROX SCALE

15 MINS FROM COWGILL (MAP 22)

LEA YEAT BRIDGE

30 MINS

STONE HOUSE

30 MINS TO DENT HEAD
VIADUCT (MAP 20)

15 MINS TO COWGILL (MAP 22)

LEA YEAT BRIDGE

25 MINS

STONE HOUSE

20 MINS FROM DENT HEAD
VIADUCT (MAP 20)

ROUTE GUIDE AND MAPS

(continued from p130) ... (Tue-Fri noon-2pm, Sat & Sun noon-8.30pm, Mon-Fri 7-9pm) make sure you time your visit. The publican's trademark gruffness seems to be all part of the character of the place. B&B room rates are £40pp (sgl occ £60), which is very reasonable given the lack of competition around.

Down in **Lea Yeat**, *Kirkthwaite Cottage* (☎ 01539 625402, 🖳 www.kirkth waitecottage.co.uk; 1S/2D/1T; WI-FI) was, once upon a time, the local school. Now, it's usually used as a self-catering cottage sleeping 2-7 people that's rented out for the

week but *very occasionally* they allow people to stay for just one night if it's available. The price of £50pp includes a self-catering breakfast. There is a pub a 20-minute stroll away for an evening meal.

The S1 **bus** runs on Saturday between Dent Station and Kendal. On Wednesday the W2 (Cowgill to Kendal) needs to be booked in advance with the operator, Woofs of Sedbergh; for details see pp47-50.

Dent Railway Station is a stop on Northern's Leeds to Appleby service (see box p45).

STAGE 4: COWGILL TO MILLTHROP (FOR SEDBERGH)
[MAPS 22-26]

This is a deliberately short stage of just **10½ miles (16.9km; 3½hrs)**, designed to allow you time to enjoy two of the loveliest settlements on the Dales Way – or rather, just off it, for one lies a couple of minutes off the path and the other one is a full 10 minutes from it (ie Dent is 200m from the path, Sedbergh is half a mile/800m away – both of which you'll have to add to the above mile count to get the true distance of this stage). Given your exertions of the previous stage (not to mention the 16-miler on the next one), it really is time to take it easy and revel in the local tearooms and taverns – establishments in which both Dent and Sedbergh excel.

The walking is straightforward and, unless encounters with cows intervene (for the first time on the walk there are as many bovines as ovines on this stage), you should find yourself dancing into Dent by lunchtime and strolling smugly into Sedbergh for afternoon tea. If you *do* want to push on further, Patton Bridge, just past Grayrigg, has accommodation, though it's more than 10 miles from Sedbergh and you may need to arrange with them where you're going to eat that night for (save the campsite there) none offers meals and there are no pubs or shops nearby; another reason, I think, for taking it easy today, putting your feet up – and saving the sweaty stuff for tomorrow.

The route

Depending where you stayed in Cowgill, your first action of the day will probably be to continue along the same road that you finished on yesterday, swapping road for river only by the bridge at **Lea Yeat** where the trail diverts off the tarmac. Though you may walk in a different Dale, the trail soon follows a familiar pattern to what's gone before, sticking fast to the river through fields of sheep and cattle.

After Ewegales Farm and its campsite, however, things take an unexpected turn, with road and river branching off to your right while you climb through fields towards **Little Town** – which is certainly little, but ain't no town. Instead, it's a simple listed farmhouse set in what was until recently a felled

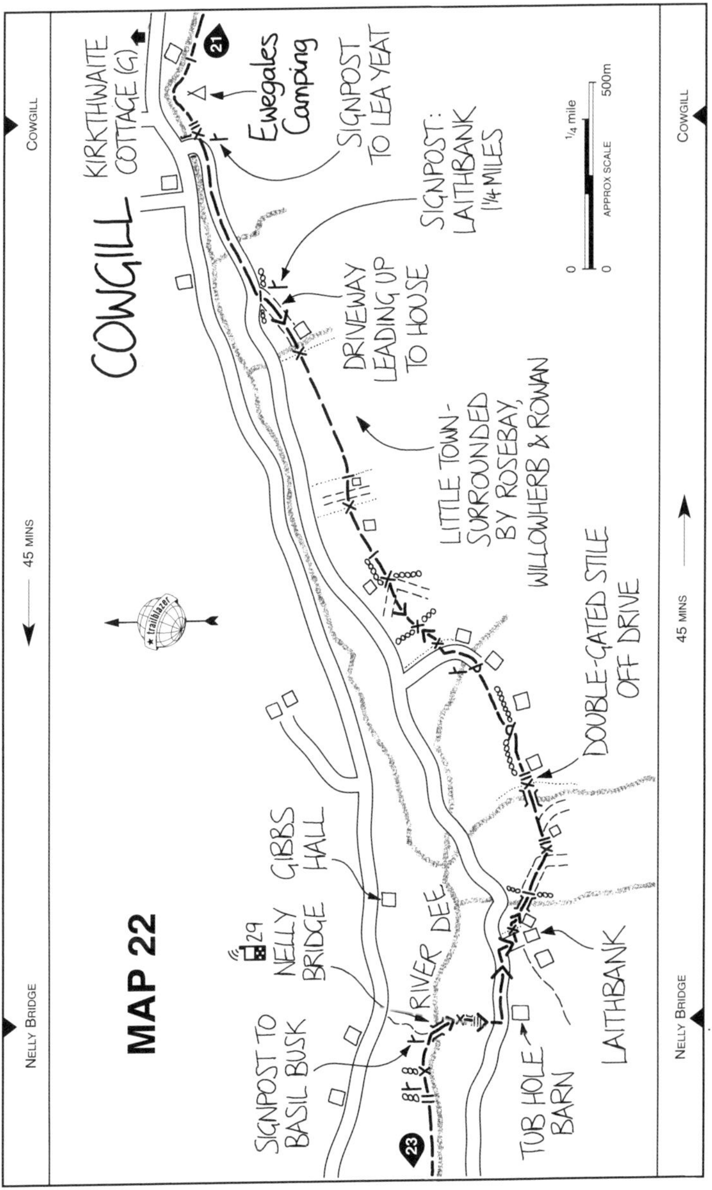
MAP 22
COWGILL
NELLY BRIDGE
45 MINS
NELLY BRIDGE
45 MINS
COWGILL
21
23
KIRKTHWAITE COTTAGE (G)
Ewegales Camping
SIGNPOST TO LEA YEAT
SIGNPOST: LAITHBANK 1¼ MILES
DRIVEWAY LEADING UP TO HOUSE
LITTLE TOWN - SURROUNDED BY ROSEBAY, WILLOWHERB & ROWAN
DOUBLE-GATED STILE OFF DRIVE
LAITHBANK
TUB HOLE BARN
RIVER DEE
GIBBS HALL
29
NELLY BRIDGE
SIGNPOST TO BASIL BUSK
trailblazer
APPROX SCALE
0
¼ mile
0
500m

tree plantation but now feels more like a nature reserve for wildflowers, with rosebay willow herb particularly prominent. Follow the waymarks and maps carefully on this section for there are lots of fields and farms to cross – though as long you find yourself contouring the valley side in a westerly direction, you shouldn't be too far off the trail. And besides, it's not long before the Dales Way loses its nerve and once again heads to the security of the riverbank, initially reuniting with the River Dee at **Nelly Bridge** before forsaking it at **Tommy Bridge** for a second waterway, **Deepdale Beck**, which you join at **Mill Bridge**. Beck and river unite soon afterwards and flow together beneath **Church Bridge**, with lovely Dent just a minute away.

DENT   [Map 23]

Dent is a dreamy little place. A cobbled village of narrow, twisting streets, there's nothing of any major interest to compel you to take the two-minute diversion off the trail to get there – but, in all honesty, you'd be mad to miss it.

Do call in and you'll notice that for the first time the brochures and bus timetables tend to focus on the Lakes now, and the local paper on offer is probably the *Westmoreland Gazette* too. It's a reminder that, while Dent was actually part of Yorkshire until 1974 (and though you're still in the Yorkshire Dales National Park),

you're no longer *actually* in Yorkshire; and Dent, lying west of the Pennines, feels both geographically and in spirit more a part of Cumbria too.

Given its tiny size and isolation, Dent boasts an impressive history. Settled by the Vikings in the 10th century, Dent's main claim to fame is as the birthplace of celebrated geologist Adam Sedgwick, born in 1785, the man responsible for proposing the Devonian and Cambrian periods on the geological timescale. Today, a big lump of rock in the village centre, across from The George and Dragon pub, celebrates this

---

❏ The terrible knitters of Dent

For over 300 years, from the 16th to the 19th centuries, the people who lived and worked in the Yorkshire Dales became renowned for their talent for working with wool. The knitting industry here had, at its root, a school that was set up in York in 1590 to teach the children of the poor of the city to knit as a way of supplementing the household income. It wasn't a success and soon closed but a second school, based in Richmond, on the eastern edge of the Dales, did manage to thrive, and from there the craft spread throughout the rural districts.

Other knitting schools opened in various parts of the Dales, including four at Dent alone. The village's reputation as a centre for the knitting industry soon grew, and the people were dubbed the 'terrible knitters of Dent' – 'terrible' in this instance being used to mean something like 'furious' or 'obsessive' and refers to the sheer speed and skill with which they worked their needles and the fact that they pretty much knitted the whole time, whether at home, outdoors, sitting, walking... even at church! The whole family would join in too – fathers, mothers, grandmothers (of course), grandfathers and children.

Yet despite their fine reputations, the knitters made little money from their knitwear, and had to work long hours in order to earn enough to survive, sometimes working in very dark, cramped conditions in smoky, cold, dimly-lit rooms. Once the candles had burnt out or the hearth had been extinguished, the knitters would still carry on, knitting under their blankets to keep themselves warm.

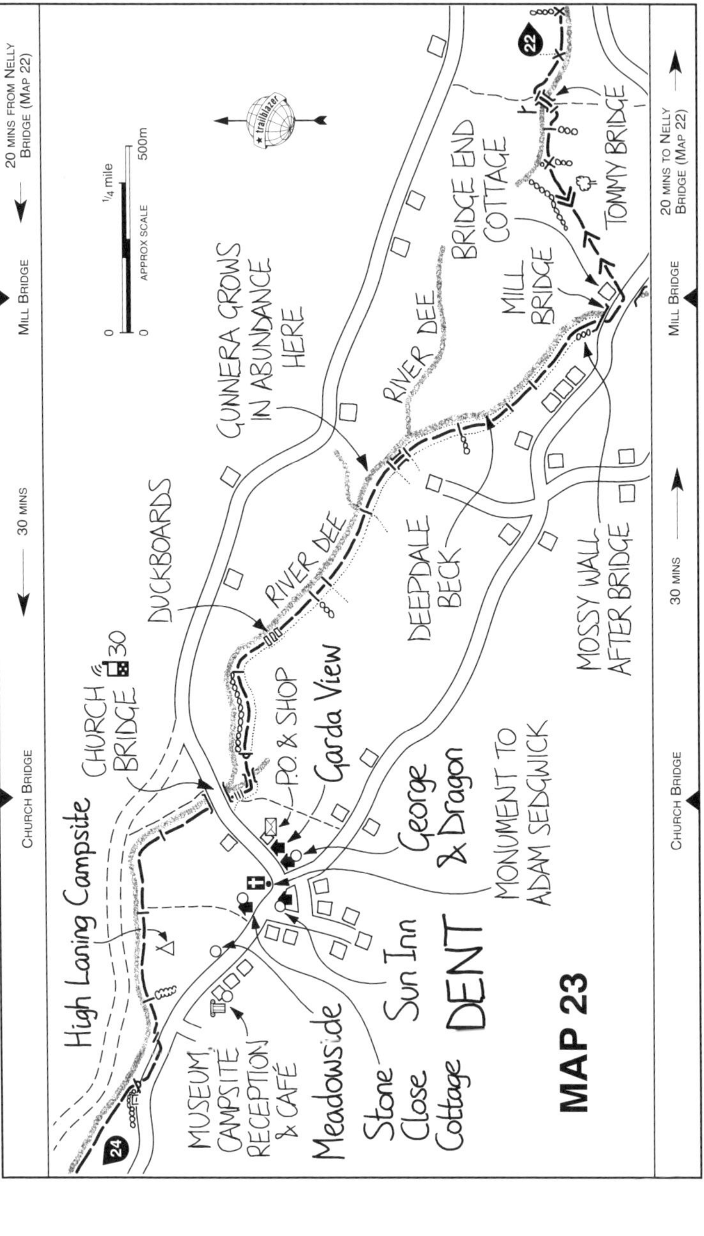

MAP 23

20 MINS FROM NELLY
BRIDGE (MAP 22)

MILL BRIDGE

CHURCH BRIDGE

30 MINS

¼ mile

500m

0

0

APPROX SCALE

GUNNERA GROWS
IN ABUNDANCE
HERE

DUCKBOARDS

CHURCH
BRIDGE

RIVER DEE

PO & SHOP

Garda View

George
& Dragon

MONUMENT TO
ADAM SEDGWICK

DEEPDALE
BECK

RIVER DEE

MOSSY WALL
AFTER BRIDGE

BRIDGE END
COTTAGE

MILL
BRIDGE

TOMMY BRIDGE

20 MINS TO NELLY
BRIDGE (MAP 22)

MILL BRIDGE

CHURCH BRIDGE

30 MINS

High Laning Campsite

MUSEUM,
CAMPSITE
RECEPTION
& CAFÉ

Meadowside

Stone
Close
Cottage

Sun Inn

DENT

fact. For around 500 years, from the 16th to the 20th centuries, Dent was also famous for its 'terrible knitters' (see box p136), about whom you can find out more at the **Dent Village Museum and Heritage Centre** (☎ 01539 625800, 🖳 www.museumsintheyorkshiredales.co.uk; daily 11am-4pm), a real hotch-potch of a collection with a few animated mannequins scattered hereabouts to amuse the adults and scare the children.

Today, with the knitting industry all but expired the town depends on tourism for its survival and, for the past few years, has held the **Dent Music and Beer Festival** at the end of June which helps bring in the hordes; see p14 for details.

Services

What few services Dent has to offer are concentrated on its **Village Store** (Mon, Wed, Thur & Fri 8.30am-5pm, Tue 8.30am-1pm, Sat & Sun from 9am), where you'll find a part-time **post office** (Tue & Thur 9am-1pm). The store also offers a **cashback** service – useful, as there's no ATM here; up to £50 is available for those spending a minimum of £10 (60p bank charge). The store also offers hot drinks and snacks to take away.

Transport

[See public transport map & table pp45-50] Dent is served by several infrequent buses, ie the S1 (Sat only), S2 (Sun only) and the W2 (Wed only); these run between Cowgill, Dent Village, Dent Station and Sedbergh/Kendal. The S3 (Tue only) goes to Sedbergh & Hawes via Dent and the S4 (Fri only) runs between Kirkby Stephen and Sedbergh via Dent.

Dent Railway Station (Map 21) is 4½ miles from Dent village, near Lea Yeat.

Where to stay

Dent's **campsite** is at the far end of the village; *High Laning Caravan & Camping Park* (☎ 015396 25239, 🖳 www.highlaning.com; walkers £9, 🐾 £1) is part of the same complex as the museum.

Next door to the Village Store is the only **B&B** in the village that isn't also a

tearoom or a pub. *Garda View B&B* (☎ 015396 25209; 1D en suite, 1D/1T share facilities; WI-FI). Recently refurbished, there is now a separate lounge for guests, B&B rates are £30pp (sgl occ from £40). However, my favourite accommodation in Dent is at *The Sun Inn* (☎ 015396 25208, 🖳 www.suninndent.co.uk; 1D en suite, 1T/1D/1Tr share facilities; WI-FI), largely because I haven't seen prices as cheap as this for several years on any long-distance trail, with rooms including breakfast just £21pp, or £32.50pp to £37.50 for the en suite room; even single occupancy is only £30! However, do note that there's a minimum stay of two nights over a weekend. The other pub, *The George and Dragon* (☎ 015396 25256, 🖳 www.thegeorgeanddragondent.co.uk; 1S/2T/4D/1Tr/1Qd; all en suite; 🍴; 🐾 £10; WI-FI though it's better in the pub than in the rooms), is the smartest place to stop in the village. B&B rates are £45pp (£65 sgl occ, £110/130 for three/four sharing), though note that rates are said to be cheaper on various websites (eg Laterooms).

Finally, *Stone Close Cottage* (☎ 015396-25231, 🖳 www.stoneclose.co.uk; 1T en suite, 1D/1Tr with shared bathroom; 🍴; WI-FI; Ⓛ) is a cosy snug and guests are allowed to use the tearoom in the evenings – a nice place to relax and play one of their board games. Rates are £35pp, £45pp for the en suite (£50-70 sgl occ) – though you need to add another £2.50pp if you want to upgrade from a simple breakfast (porridge, fruit etc) to a full English.

Where to eat and drink

There are three decent cafés in Dent. Busy *Stone Close Cottage* (see Where to stay; Wed-Sun 10am-5pm), on Dent's Main St, has a lovely old flagstone floor and fireplace, as well as more modern features such as WI-FI. Dog and walker friendly, it can get a little cramped so you may be asked to leave your bags outside the toilet in the vestibule. Offering a fine array of teas, they are also rightly proud of their range and variety of cakes, and also serve up several versions of cheese on toast (£5.75-6.75), including buck rarebit with bacon.

Down the road and the hill, after Main St has turned into The Laning, *Meadowside Café* (☎ 01539 625329, 💻 www.meadow sidecafe.co.uk; Mon 10am-5pm, Tue & Thur-Sun 10am-4pm; WI-FI) does a great bacon & egg sandwich for £3.50, with meat from the butcher's in Sedbergh. Dog and walker friendly, it's a lovely place to hunker down by the wood-burning stove if it's bucketing down outside.

Still further down the hill, and again both dog friendly and with WI-FI, is the *café*

at the **Museum** (see opposite; daily 11am-4pm).

For evening meals, *The George and Dragon* (see Where to stay; daily noon-2pm & 6-8.30pm) does the best food, tasty no-nonsense pub grub including a trio of local Cumberland sausages with mash and gravy (£12.25). *The Sun Inn* (see Where to stay; food Mon-Fri noon-2pm & 6.30-8.30pm, Sat & Sun noon-8.30pm) also does standard pub grub to accompany their real ales.

Back on the trail, much of the next three miles are as flat as the proverbial pancake and continue the riparian theme, shadowing the river wherever it meanders. So far, so familiar – but at the same time, things are subtly changing too. For near where you rejoin the road you cross the geological feature known as the **Dent Fault**. And though the geology described by the system is happening way below ground (see box p140), there are subtle changes above ground too. The buildings are still made from the local stone, but that stone is now largely

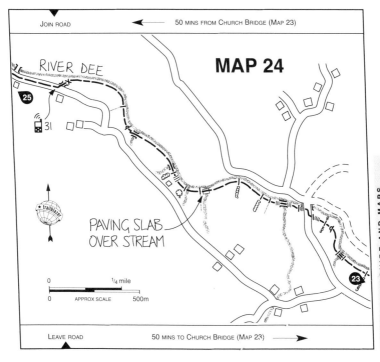

❏ The Dent Fault System

In between Dent and Brackensgill one crosses over an important geological boundary known as the Dent Fault (or, more correctly, the Dent Fault System). This fault in the Earth's crust defines the north-western limit of what is known as the **Askrigg Block** – a huge block of granite that lies deep underground underneath pretty much all of the Yorkshire Dales. Indeed, so deep underground is it that proof of its existence only arrived recently when bore samples from a deep-drilling rig near Semerwater were examined.

But though it lies deep underground, the Askrigg Block has important consequences for the land above it. As granite is a very hard rock, so the land that lies upon the Askrigg Block, which was mainly laid down during the Carboniferous period (around 350-300 million years ago), has enjoyed relative stability and has been subjected to less pressure to buckle, shift and crumple when compared to similarly aged rock elsewhere. As a result, the distinctive, horizontal limestone terraces and scars of the Dales (think of Loup Scar, outside Burnsall, which is a classic example) have been able to form and survive. Alight from the Askrigg Block, however, by, for example, crossing over the Dent Fault System (though there is no actual vertical jump on the path to suggest you are doing this), and you enter the Howgill Fells, their characteristic smooth-topped hills comprised of much older Silurian and Ordovician (anywhere from 485 million to 419 million years ago) slate and gritstones.

---

slate, rather than the limestone, sandstone and gritstone of the Dales. It is another minor, yet significant sign that you are leaving the Dales behind now, and heading for the Lake District, which traditionally uses a lot of slate in its buildings.

There's more evidence that you are leaving the Dales in a couple of miles, but first you must cross the sturdy **Brackensgill Bridge** and leave the river to head up an old farm track, passing the lovely old wooden back door of **Gate Manor** on the way, to **Gap Wood**. It's a smashing stretch, this, with terrific views beyond the wood over the lush pastures of Dentdale. It's also your last chance to glimpse a 'proper' Dales landscape for it's not long before you're savouring the views across to Sedbergh while descending to photogenic **Millthrop**, with the smooth undulations of the Howgills a spectacular backdrop. The trail itself heads off west after 18th-century Millthrop Bridge, though most people opt to take the 10-minute road walk into town. If here at the right time on a Wednesday you could take the W2 bus service to Sedbergh; see pp47-50.

SEDBERGH   see map p145

Sedbergh is both dominated by and synonymous with the ancient and highly regarded school (see box opposite) that sits to the south-west of the town centre. Refreshingly, there seems to be little of the 'town-and-gown' friction that afflicts other major seats of learning in the UK – but then, as the school has been there since 1525, they have had a long time to get used

to each other! Sedbergh's other claim to fame is that it describes itself as 'England's Book Town'; don't come expecting a northern version of Hay-on-Wye, though there are about half-a-dozen book stores on the main street.

The town, like so many others on the trail, doesn't actually lie on the path but 10 minutes from it. Furthermore, the road that

❑ Sedbergh School

Sedbergh School (🖥 www.sedberghschool.org) is today a co-educational boarding school, comprising a junior school for pupils aged 4-13, which opened in 2002, and a senior school which has admitted girls since 2001. It was founded by Roger Lupton, who was born at nearby Cautley. In 1525 Lupton, then provost at Eton, provided for a chantry school close to his hometown. He also provided various scholarships to the brightest pupils to enable them to study at St John's College, Cambridge, and to this day the college appoints the school's headmasters.

Today there are over 500 pupils attending Sedbergh, paying the £7650 tuition fees (or £10,000-plus if boarding) per term. For that money your son or daughter gets to study at a school that is renowned not only for its academic achievements but its sporting ones too, particularly on the rugby field where past alumni have included ex-England captain, Will Carling, and World Cup winner, Will Greenwood. Thankfully, the school doesn't ignore the glories of its surroundings but celebrates them. Indeed, the school song, *Winder*, is named after the nearby fell that overlooks Sedbergh and tradition dictates that all pupils must climb it at least once during their school career.

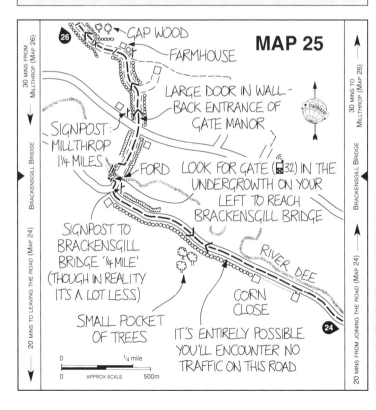

MAP 25

26

GAP WOOD

FARMHOUSE

LARGE DOOR IN WALL –
BACK ENTRANCE OF
GATE MANOR

★ trailblazer

SIGNPOST:
MILLTHROP
1¼ MILES

FORD

LOOK FOR GATE (📱32) IN THE
UNDERGROWTH ON YOUR
LEFT TO REACH
BRACKENSGILL BRIDGE

SIGNPOST TO
BRACKENSGILL
BRIDGE '¼ MILE'
(THOUGH IN REALITY
IT'S A LOT LESS)

SMALL POCKET
OF TREES

RIVER DEE

CORN
CLOSE

IT'S ENTIRELY POSSIBLE
YOU'LL ENCOUNTER NO
TRAFFIC ON THIS ROAD

24

0   ¼ mile
0   APPROX SCALE   500m

30 MINS FROM MILLTHROP (MAP 26)

BRACKENSGILL BRIDGE

20 MINS TO LEAVING THE ROAD (MAP 24)

30 MINS TO MILLTHROP (MAP 26)

BRACKENSGILL BRIDGE

20 MINS FROM JOINING THE ROAD (MAP 24)

ROUTE GUIDE AND MAPS

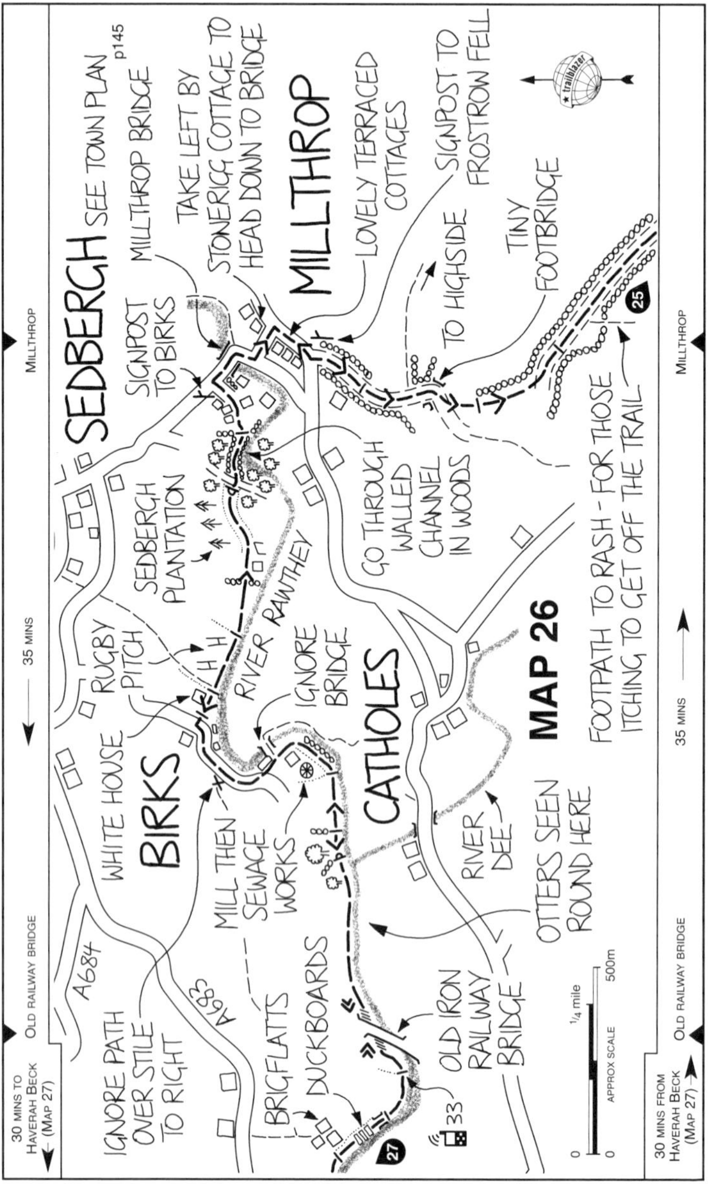

MAP 26

SEDBERGH SEE TOWN PLAN p145

MILLTHROP

MILLTHROP BRIDGE

TAKE LEFT BY STONERIGG COTTAGE TO HEAD DOWN TO BRIDGE

SIGNPOST TO BIRKS

LOVELY TERRACED COTTAGES

SIGNPOST TO FROSTROW FELL

TO HIGHSIDE

TINY FOOTBRIDGE

25

SEDBERGH PLANTATION

RIVER RAWTHEY

GO THROUGH WALLED CHANNEL IN WOODS

BIRKS

WHITE HOUSE

RUGBY PITCH

IGNORE BRIDGE

CATHOLES

FOOTPATH TO RASH – FOR THOSE ITCHING TO GET OFF THE TRAIL

A684

IGNORE PATH OVER STILE TO RIGHT

A683

MILL THEN SEWAGE WORKS

RIVER DEE

OTTERS SEEN ROUND HERE

BRIGFLATTS

DUCKBOARDS

OLD IRON RAILWAY BRIDGE

33

27

MILLTHROP

35 MINS

30 MINS TO HAVERAH BECK (MAP 27)

OLD RAILWAY BRIDGE

MILLTHROP

35 MINS

30 MINS FROM HAVERAH BECK (MAP 27)

OLD RAILWAY BRIDGE

APPROX SCALE

¼ mile

500m

0

0

you take is sometimes pavement-less and not particularly pleasant. But Sedbergh is the last town before Bowness within walking distance of the trail that offers a decent selection of amenities and it's a lovely place to while away an afternoon, resting your bunions, blisters, corns and callouses in one of the town's lovely cafés while watching the world go by.

Services

Sedbergh has the last **tourist information centre** (🖥 www.sedbergh.org.uk; Mon-Sat 10am-4pm, Sun noon-4pm) before the end of the trail as well as a **post office** (Mon-Fri 9am-5.30pm, Sat 9am-12.30pm).

For **provisions** your best bet is the large Spar (daily 7am-10pm), built on the old cattle market to the west of town. There's no **outdoor shop** as such but the curiously named Sleepy Elephant (Mon-Sat 10am-5pm, Sun 1-5pm) has a small selection of trekking clothes and equipment amongst its books. There's also a Boots the **chemist** (Mon-Fri 9am-5.30pm, Sat 9am-1pm) across the road.

For money there are a couple of banks with **cashpoints** on Main St, and an ATM outside the Spar too.

Transport

[See public transport map & table pp47-50] It may be one of the largest towns in the Howgills but don't expect Sedbergh to have a frequent **bus** service to anywhere else. Local company Woofs operates the S1 (Sat only), S2 (Sun only) and the W2 (Wed only); these run between Cowgill, Dent Village, Dent Station and Sedbergh/Kendal. The S3 (Tue only) goes to Hawes via Dent and the S4 (Fri only) runs to Kirkby Stephen via Dent.

Stagecoach operate a 502 service (term time Mon-Fri) to Kirkby Stephen.

Where to stay

There is **no campsite** within 2½ miles (4km) of Sedbergh and, frustratingly, the 36-bed *Howgills Bunk Barn* (🕿 015396 21990, 🖥 www.howgillsbunkbarn.co.uk; WI-FI; 🐾 £16), 600m east of town on Castlehaw Farm, is, once again, for **groups**

only. Occasionally they'll let individuals stay from Mondays to Thursdays if they don't have anyone else in but at £32 for a bed in a dorm and no breakfast, it's not a cheap option.

Instead, you're better off staying in a **B&B,** and thankfully there are several great ones in Sedbergh. The first place you come to when leaving the trail is the flower-fronted, green-doored 18th-century cottage, *Yew Tree* (🕿 015396 21600; 1D/1T, shared bathroom; 🕳; 🐾), on Loftus Hill, run by a South African lady with a reputation for helpfulness and efficiency. Rates here are £29pp (£38 sgl occ).

Round on Back Lane, at No 15, *Wheelwright Cottage* (🕿 015396 20251; 1T/1D, shared bathroom; 🕳; 🐾; WI-FI) is run by the characterful Susie, who takes a no-nonsense approach both to her business and her guests – as you'd expect from someone who was born in Australia but has lived for the last 60 years in Yorkshire (without, curiously, ever losing her Aussie accent). But that doesn't mean this isn't a lovely, cosy, friendly place. There are no TVs in the bedrooms but more-than-adequate compensation is provided by the jar of cookies that form part of the in-room tea-tray (and there's a small TV in the lounge if you find you can't live without one). Located just a stroll away from the centre of town but on a quiet road overlooking the school playing fields, dogs are more than welcome here – which, as Susie points out, means rather more than just being 'allowed'. Rates are £29pp (sgl occ £38).

There are several options on and near Sedbergh's high street, and its continuation, Station Rd. *No 10 Main St*, (🕿 015396 21808; 1D/1Tr, en suite; WI-FI) is a simple place decked out largely in red, black and white (which reflects the owner's favourite football team), with room rates at £34pp (sgl occ £48, £85 for three sharing).

Continuing west onto Station Rd, *Daleslea* (🕿 015396 21789, 🖥 www.dales lea.co.uk; 1D/1Tr/1Qd; all en suite; 🕳; WI-FI) is another very friendly option, a large Victorian semi-detached townhouse just a small stroll into the centre, with very large rooms priced at £33.50-42.50pp, or £50 single occupancy, for B&B. Nearby, up the hill on Highfield Rd at No 7, ***Summerhill*** (☎ 015396 20360, 💻 www.summerhillsedbergh.com; 1D en suite, 1D/1T private facilities unless both rooms are booked by a group or family; ☛; 🐕; WI-FI; Ⓛ) is a very clean and efficiently run B&B as you'd expect, given that the owner is a trainer and coach. It's a good little place with some nice touches, including a welcome slice of cake on arrival and fresh, organic, home-grown food, much of it locally sourced, for breakfast. Rates are £45-60pp (sgl occ £81-118).

Back on Station Rd but still further west, several hundred metres this time past the Spar and the garage, ***Holmecroft*** (☎ 015396 20754, 💻 www.holmecroftbandb.co.uk; 1S/1D/1T, shared facilities; WI-FI) is run by hospitable and amiable Susan. The B&B is far enough out of town to enjoy pretty unrestricted views of the surrounding Howgills and Middleton Fells. B&B costs from £34pp (£46 for single occupancy of the double room).

At the time of writing the Bull Hotel was closed due to flood damage (though it is being repaired) so there is only one pub offering accommodation: ***The Dalesman Country Inn*** (☎ 015396 21183, 💻 www.thedalesman.co.uk; 1S/3D or T/1D plus a self-contained cottage, all en suite; ☛; WI-FI), on Main St, is a smart, swanky affair with prices that reflect this (£42.50-80pp, sgl £40); the self-catering cottage, which consists of a double and a single plus a bed settee, £60pp for two sharing plus £25 for each extra person. All rates include breakfast.

Where to eat and drink

My favourite café is ***Three Hares*** (☎ 015396 21058, 💻 www.threeharescafe.co.uk; Mon-Thur 8.30am-5pm, Fri & Sat 8.30am-11pm, Sun 10.30am-4pm; WI-FI), on Main St, which is dog friendly and they bake pretty much everything they sell themselves, so turn up in the morning and you'll be welcomed by the smell of freshly baked bread or cinnamon. The Hares' closest rival is ***Smatt's Duo*** (☎ 015396 20552, 💻 www.smattsduo.co.uk; Wed-Mon 9am-6pm; WI-FI); it is also dog friendly and does a good line in paninis (from £5.50 for cheese and marmite) and create-your-own-omelettes (from £5.95) as well as a range of hot meals.

Café Nova is a quasi-Italian place (Tue-Fri 10am-6pm, Sat & Sun 9am-6pm; WI-FI) by the post office, dog friendly and selling a range of Italian and English dishes including pizza baguettes (£4.95).

The cheapest café in town is the one attached to the brilliantly named chippy, the ***Haddock Paddock*** (Mon & Thur 5-7.30pm, Wed, Fri & Sat 11.30am-1.30pm & 5-7.30pm), where you can get a bacon bap for just £1.90, or add 60p and get a cup of tea too! While for quick food-on-the-go, ***On a Roll*** (Mon-Sat 8am-2.30pm) is a takeaway sandwich place where each baguette is filled in front of you.

In the evenings ***The Red Lion*** (☎ 015396 20433; food noon-3pm & 6-8.30pm or 9pm at weekends, Sun noon-7pm) has the best reputation amongst the pubs for food; the menu is pretty standard pub fare but the quality is very good.

The food at ***The Dalesman*** (see Where to stay; food served daily noon-9pm) has a variable reputation, though the belly pork (£18.50) was fine when I tried it and they do have a decent selection of real ales. Sadly neither of these pubs allows dogs inside so I hope the weather is fine if you are here with a dog so you can sit outside.

Or, of course, you could grab a meal from one of the takeaways such as the ***Haddock Paddock*** (see above), the Chinese ***Happy Valley*** (☎ 015396 21277; Sun, Mon, Wed & Thur 5-11pm, Fri & Sat to 11.30pm), and the local Indian restaurant, ***Aamilah's*** (☎ 015396 20000; mains £8-11.50), which also has a takeaway service, though if you're dining in the restaurant do note that it's not licensed – so bring your own booze.

Sedbergh

To Howgills Bunk Barn (G), 300m

Castlehaw La

Vicarage La

New St

Tourist information

Back La

Joss La

On a Roll

Boots

Toilets

The Haddock

Three Paddock

Hares

Wheelwright Cottage

Bainbridge Rd

Bull Hotel

Main St

Sleepy Elephant

Smatt's Duo

A684

Loftus Hill

Yew Tree

26

Busk La

Fairholme

Aamilah's

Café Nova

The PO

The Dalesman

Happy Valley

The Red Lion

Howgill La

Highfield Rd

Number 10 Main St

★ Trailblazer

To Dales Way

26

Summerhill

Daleslea

A684

Station Rd

Spar £

Guldrey La

Busk La

26

Holmecroft

0   50   100m

STAGE 5: MILLTHROP (FOR SEDBERGH) TO BURNESIDE (FOR KENDAL)

MAPS 26-32

On paper this looks like the most unpromising day on the trail. A quick glance at a map will show you that on this stage you leave one national park without covering quite enough ground to reach the next one. You'll also notice that en route you'll have to contend with both the M6 motorway and a couple of busy A roads. Furthermore, there are no towns or villages en route so opportunities for refreshments are few. It is also, by necessity, quite a long stage at **16 miles (25.7km; 6¾hrs)** – not forgetting the extra half mile/800m to get you to the trail from Sedbergh at the start of the day – with only the occasional B&B providing you with an opportunity to break the stage into two halves.

But if there's one lesson learnt about the Dales Way by now, it's that it does provide ample rewards in return for all the efforts it demands. And once again on this stage it's not the natural landscape that sticks in the mind so much as the mighty constructions that man has placed upon it. Less than two miles from Millthrop Bridge, for example, the trail takes you by an old and impressive iron

---

❑ The Howgills

It can't be easy for a range of hills that soar almost 700 metres high to be overlooked. But that's exactly what has happened to the Howgills, a triangular area of fells bounded by the Lune and Rawthey rivers, with the towns of Sedbergh, Kirkby Stephen and Tebay the three corners (approximately) of that triangle.

But I think it's fair to say that most trekkers, unless they live in the area, won't have heard of them. There aren't many guidebooks or other publications about them (Alfred Wainwright's *Walks on the Howgill Fells*, published way back in 1972, is probably the most famous). And, up until now, despite the Howgills' undoubted beauty, they've been largely ignored by the authorities too – though the recent extensions to the Dales National Park has rectified this, and pretty much all of the Howgills now fall within the boundaries of the enlarged park.

It really is curious how little-known and seldom visited the Howgills are, for their landscape and character seem so inviting to anyone who likes hiking in high places. For one thing, the paths are certainly very quiet, particularly when compared to the Lakes and the Dales which definitely receive the lion's share of walkers. As a result, you may well have the place to yourself, with only sheep and the occasional wild pony for company. The Howgills – the name, incidentally, comes from the old Norse words for hill ('haugr') and valley ('gil') – are renowned for having few walls and fences, too, so there are few stiles and gates to negotiate, thus enabling you to enjoy some great views across to the neighbouring Yorkshire Dales, Northern Pennines and the Eastern Lake District. Nor are the Howgills bereft of their own attractions, including **Cautley Spout**, at 180m one of England's highest (cascade) waterfalls.

Plus, of course, there are the Howgills' distinguishing, smooth summits; hilltops that over the years have been compared by various people to a herd of sleeping elephants (Alfred Wainwright's description), the backs of hippos, a basket of labrador puppies, and the smooth, unwrinkled bottoms of babies. The highest of these summits is **Calf** at 676m, with Calders only just behind at 674m and Great Dummacks a further 11m shorter at 663m.

railway bridge, while further on you'll find yourself shuffling open-mouthed in amazement beneath two huge old Victorian viaducts that served the same railway. Throughout this stage there's plenty of good walking too, much of it through lush farmland via the little-visited valley of Lunesdale, on the edge of the impressive Howgill Fells, with good views aplenty looking west towards the jagged tops of the Lake District. And if 16 miles is too ambitious for a single day there a few accommodation opportunities scattered along – or just off – the trail too.

The route

For the initial part of this stage you'll be largely walking through grounds owned by Sedbergh School – which, considering the large amount of prime real-estate you go through, gives you some idea of how much money must be sloshing around the top-tier educational establishments in this country! Eventually, however, you leave the outer reaches of the town to join the lane leading down to Birks and a ramble along the Rawthey. Soon you're scaling an embankment that leads to a 19th-century **iron railway bridge** – now closed to human traffic, though it carries a gas pipeline on part of its structure.

A little way further on, and hidden by a fence to the right of the trail, is Brigflatts, a place of monumental importance to the Quaker faith (see box p86).

It's not long before you're forsaking one river for another, as you bid farewell to Rawthey in favour of the Lune. The Lune actually marks the western boundary of the national park in this region (and once upon a time the county boundary too between Yorkshire and the defunct county of Westmoreland).

The trail takes a more northerly course now, as if determined to stay within the national park boundaries, and for much of the next hour you adhere closely to the riverbank, drifting away only at the first of the great Victorian viaducts on this stage, the **Lune or Waterside Viaduct** (see box p125), to climb to **Low Branthwaite**. From here you can take the path to *Ash Hining Farm* (☎ 01539-620957, 🖳 www.ashhiningfarm.co.uk; 2D/2T, en suite; ☞; WI-FI; (Ⓛ)), an award-winning B&B set on a 17th-century working farm, the guest lounge boasting exposed beams, an open fire and terrific views down the Lune Valley and over the Howgills – and all very reasonable value at £35pp (£40 single occupancy). The farm is off Howgill Lane; take the lane to the junction, and from there turn right – it's about half a mile from the path. For dinner they offer lifts to and from Sedbergh.

A little further on is the excellent B&B and campsite at *Bramaskew Farm* (01539 621529; 🖳 www.drawellcottage.co.uk/farmhouse-bed-and-breakfast.htm; 1D/1D or T, en suite; WI-FI; (Ⓛ) a dairy and sheep farm which received several very good reviews from fellow walkers. Rates are £34pp (£37 sgl occ) in the B&B, with evening meals (if arranged in advance) from £13pp. They also offer **camping** for £6pp; this includes use of their shower and toilet in the downstairs utility room.

With cattle studying your progress for much of the way, the path now eases back down to the river and the gorgeous late medieval **Crook of Lune Bridge**, built perhaps as early as the 16th century. *(continued on p150)*

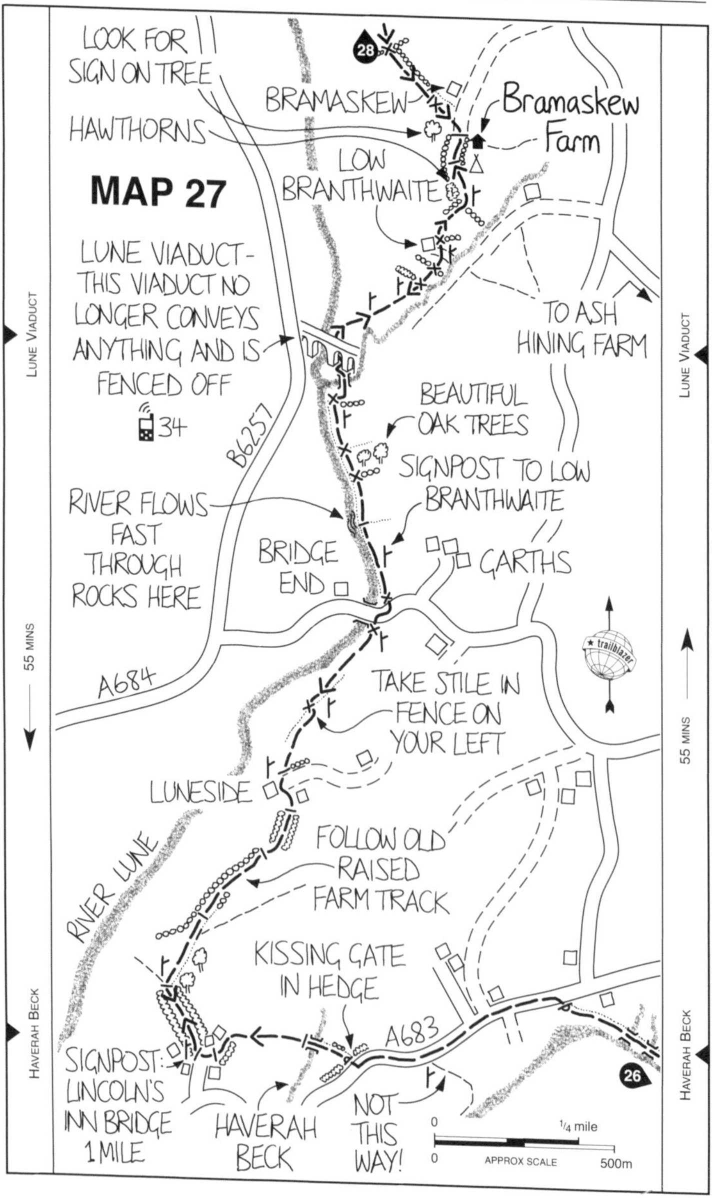

LOOK FOR SIGN ON TREE

BRAMASKEW

Bramaskew Farm

HAWTHORNS

MAP 27

LOW BRANTHWAITE

LUNE VIADUCT — THIS VIADUCT NO LONGER CONVEYS ANYTHING AND IS FENCED OFF

📶 34

TO ASH HINING FARM

LUNE VIADUCT

B6257

BEAUTIFUL OAK TREES

SIGNPOST TO LOW BRANTHWAITE

RIVER FLOWS FAST THROUGH ROCKS HERE

BRIDGE END

GARTHS

A684

TAKE STILE IN FENCE ON YOUR LEFT

LUNESIDE

FOLLOW OLD RAISED FARM TRACK

RIVER LUNE

KISSING GATE IN HEDGE

A683

26

SIGNPOST: LINCOLN'S INN BRIDGE 1 MILE

HAVERAH BECK

NOT THIS WAY!

trailblazer

0   1/4 mile
0   APPROX SCALE   500m

55 MINS

55 MINS

LUNE VIADUCT

HAVERAH BECK

ROUTE GUIDE AND MAPS

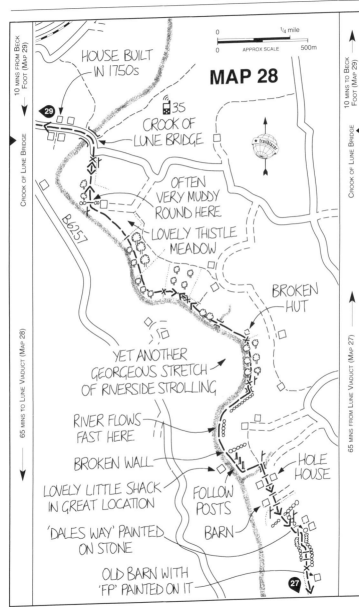

MAP 28

HOUSE BUILT IN 1750s

📱35
CROOK OF LUNE BRIDGE

OFTEN VERY MUDDY ROUND HERE

LOVELY THISTLE MEADOW

BROKEN HUT

YET ANOTHER GEORGEOUS STRETCH OF RIVERSIDE STROLLING

RIVER FLOWS FAST HERE

BROKEN WALL

LOVELY LITTLE SHACK IN GREAT LOCATION

'DALES WAY' PAINTED ON STONE

OLD BARN WITH 'FP' PAINTED ON IT

FOLLOW POSTS

BARN

HOLE HOUSE

0 ———— ¼ mile
0 ———— 500m
APPROX SCALE

★ trailblazer

B6257

10 MINS FROM BECK FOOT (MAP 29)

CROOK OF LUNE BRIDGE

65 MINS TO LUNE VIADUCT (MAP 28)

10 MINS TO BECK FOOT (MAP 29)

CROOK OF LUNE BRIDGE

65 MINS FROM LUNE VIADUCT (MAP 27)

ROUTE GUIDE AND MAPS

(continued from p147) Cross the bridge to climb to the second magnificent viaduct, the 11-arch **Lowgill Viaduct** which soars 27m above the road. In passing under here, you finally leave the confines of the Yorkshire Dales National Park, which you've been in for all but the first five miles of your walk so far.

To celebrate, if anybody's home do call in at *Half Island House* (irregular opening hours), a lovely surprise. Though sitting well within earshot of the thundering M6, the streams that cascade around the house make the traffic all but inaudible, and it's a lovely place to stick your feet up for half an hour and enjoy both the food – including home-baked scone, jam and cream for just £1.50 – and the company of the slightly eccentric, pith-helmet-wearing owner.

The next stretch of the trail from here to Burneside is, in all honesty, my least favourite part of the whole walk. This is partly to do with the fact that one must negotiate both the M6 and the A6, and while the traversing of neither is in any way difficult – there is a footbridge across the former, and the latter, while fast, is quiet enough to allow plenty of opportunities to cross safely – their noisy presence is a interruption to one's enjoyment of the scenery around here. It's also partly to do with the cattle which for some reason took a particular dislike to Daisy the Dog – and, for once, it was no fault of her own. (Remember if you have a canine companion with you, give all cattle a wide berth and keep him or her on a short lead – unless the bellicose bovines behave aggressively towards you, in which case drop the lead, head to safety, and call your dog to you as quickly as you can.)

The scenery, too, while pleasant enough, does lack the pizzazz of earlier stages; just as the scenery improved markedly once you entered the park near Bolton Abbey all those miles ago, so it deteriorates – slightly but noticeably – now.

Given that you've already walked over seven miles on this stage, you may find this latter section a bit of a trudge. Thankfully, you can break it up by stopping at the exquisite *Moresdale Barn B&B* (☎ 01539-824463; 1D/1T; share facilities; WI-FI; Ⓛ) at **Lambrigg**, the gardens of which the Dales Way passes right through. A thoroughly comfortable and modern conversion of an 1860s' barn, it boasts majestic views from its large windows. Tea and cakes are offered on your arrival and the price includes a lift into Kendal for your evening meal. B&B costs £40pp or £45 for single occupancy.

The next accommodation is a further two miles away at least so you have no choice but to press on, through the fields and across the railway, with **Grayrigg** in the distance, its church tower one of the major landmarks in this area. More fields need to be crossed and cattle dodged as you swerve your way through the pastoral landscape to the A685 and *Grayrigg Foot Campsite* (☎ 01539 824655; 🐾) charging £5pp.   *(continued on p154)*

❏ **Important note – walking times**
Unless otherwise specified, all times in this book refer only to the time spent walking. You will need to add 20-30% to allow for rests, photography, checking the map, drinking water etc. When planning the day's hike count on 5-7 hours' actual walking.

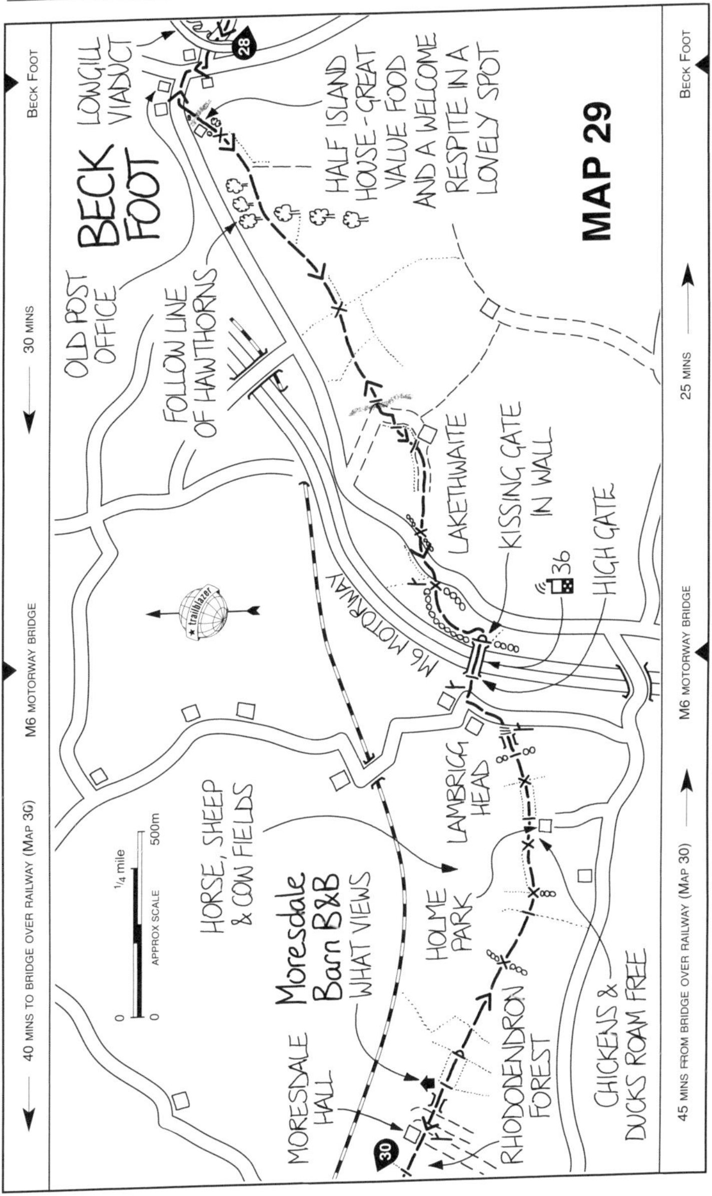

MAP 29

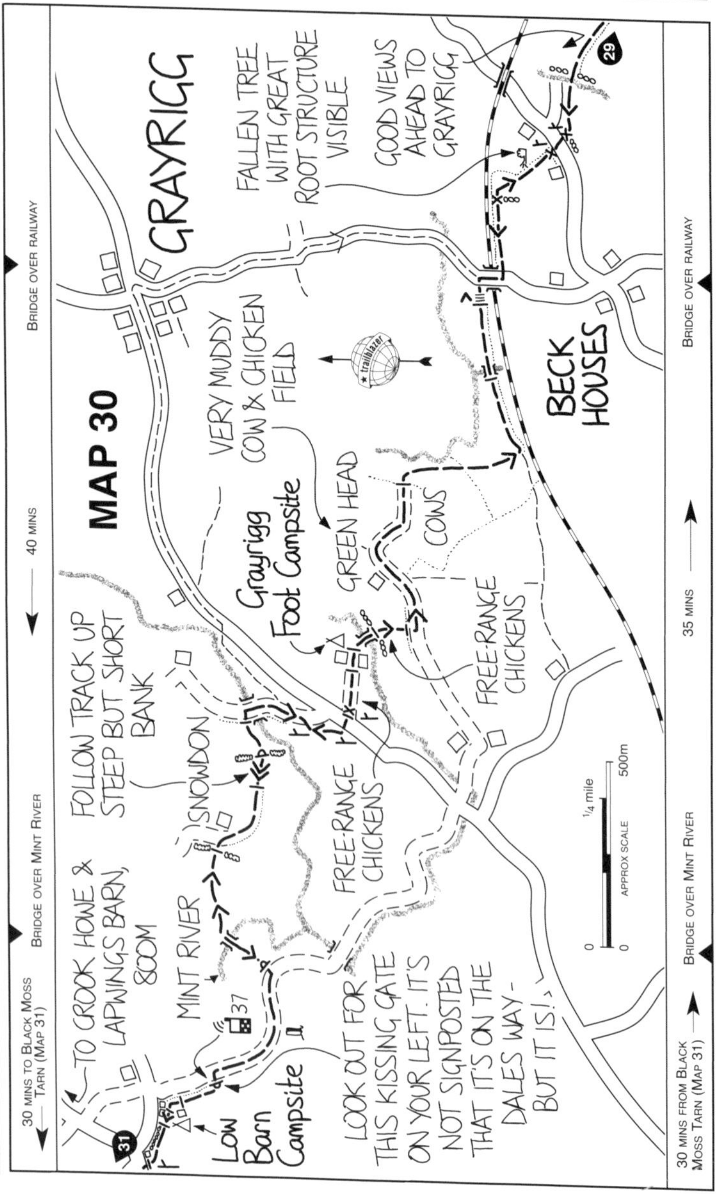

MAP 30

GRAYRIGG

FALLEN TREE WITH GREAT ROOT STRUCTURE VISIBLE

GOOD VIEWS AHEAD TO GRAYRIGG

29

BRIDGE OVER RAILWAY

40 MINS

VERY MUDDY COW & CHICKEN FIELD

Grayrigg Foot Campsite

GREEN HEAD

COWS

FREE-RANGE CHICKENS

BECK HOUSES

BRIDGE OVER RAILWAY

35 MINS

FOLLOW TRACK UP STEEP BUT SHORT BANK

SNOWDON

FREE-RANGE CHICKENS

MINT RIVER

37

TO CROOK HOWE & LAPWINGS BARN, 800M

30 MINS TO BLACK MOSS TARN (MAP 31)

BRIDGE OVER MINT RIVER

Low Barn Campsite

31

LOOK OUT FOR THIS KISSING GATE ON YOUR LEFT. IT'S NOT SIGNPOSTED THAT IT'S ON THE DALES WAY - BUT IT IS!

1/4 mile

500m

0

0

APPROX SCALE

BRIDGE OVER MINT RIVER

35 MINS

30 MINS FROM BLACK MOSS TARN (MAP 31)

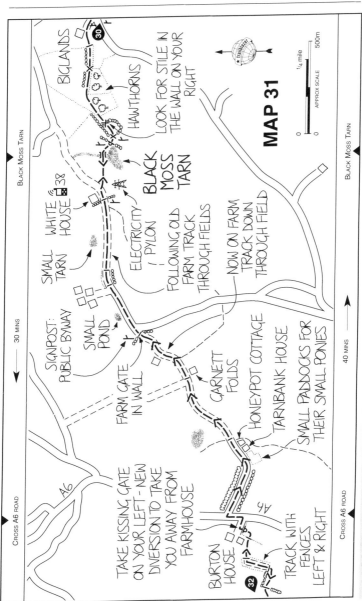

MAP 31

BLACK MOSS TARN

BLACK MOSS TARN

CROSS A6 ROAD

CROSS A6 ROAD

30 MINS

40 MINS

APPROX SCALE

¼ mile

500m

BIGLANDS

LOOK FOR STILE IN THE WALL ON YOUR RIGHT

HAWTHORNS

WHITE HOUSE 38

SMALL TARN

SIGNPOST: PUBLIC BYWAY

SMALL POND

FARM GATE IN WALL

ELECTRICITY PYLON

FOLLOWING OLD FARM TRACK THROUGH FIELDS

NOW ON FARM TRACK DOWN THROUGH FIELD

GARNETT FOLDS

HONEYPOT COTTAGE

TARNBANK HOUSE

SMALL PADDOCKS FOR THEIR SMALL PONIES

A6

TAKE KISSING GATE ON YOUR LEFT - NEW DIVERSION TO TAKE YOU AWAY FROM FARMHOUSE

BURTON HOUSE

TRACK WITH FENCES LEFT & RIGHT

ROUTE GUIDE AND MAPS

(continued from p150) There's a simple wash house outside with a wash basin and a toilet but remember, of course, you'll have to bring your own food or be prepared to catch a taxi to Kendal for about a tenner (the owners have tea and cake for campers but little else).

Across the road the path continues over the River Mint and up to a second campsite in a walled garden; ***Low Barn Campsite*** (☎ 01539 824892, 🖂 moon feather7@gmail.com; 🐾) charges £8pp, or £12pp if you want to sleep in their 3-bed caravan – which could prove a lifesaver if the weather closes in. If arranged in advance they also do dinners for just £8 (usually homemade lasagne or shepherds pie with veg), and a bacon & egg butty and hot drink for breakfast for £4. It's a great place with very friendly owners but there is no shower – just a sink and toilet for campers.

A little further along the trail, you come to a quiet lane, with **Biglands Farm** opposite. Half a mile from the trail are two B&Bs either side of Whinfell Tarn. Both offer an evening meal as part of the package if booked in advance – essential, as there's no pub or restaurant for miles around. On the western side is ***Crook Howe*** (☎ 01539 824448, 🖂 www.crookhowe.co.uk; 1Tr/1Qd, both en suite; 🍽; WI-FI; B&B £40pp, £55 sgl occ; dinner £20pp). To reach it, come off the trail opposite Biglands Farm, turning right down the hill to **Patton Bridge** then take the first left; there's a sign in the wall for Crook Howe, approximately 10 minutes away.

The second option, to the east of the tarn, is ***Lapwings Barn*** (☎ 01539 824373, 🖂 www.lapwingsbarn.co.uk; 2D or T, en suite; 🍽; WI-FI). From the bridge keep on the road past Borrans Farm, taking the left-hand fork for about 600m. Rates are from £39pp (sgl occ from £55); a 3-course dinner is £22pp. The owners also offer pick up and drop off to Dales Way if pre-arranged.

Those sticking with the trail have the joys of **Black Moss Tarn** to look forward to, though it's really little more than an oversized pond with delusions of grandeur than an actual tarn; still, it's a smashing place to stop and recover for five minutes if you can find a dry patch of grass on which to sit. Thereafter, there's some pleasant enough rural rambling leading down to and beyond the A6, though the undulating terrain and sheer number of stiles will sap any last vestiges of energy and enthusiasm that you may have managed to save. It's with some relief, therefore, that you finally hit the road leading into Burneside – though it's important not to lose concentration on this final stretch for the road is fast and the pavement non-existent.

BURNESIDE [Map 32]

It may sound a bit harsh but the main attraction of Burneside for most Dales Way walkers is the chance it offers to leave it immediately and head to Kendal, just one stop and four minutes away on the Trans-Pennine line. (Staveley and Windermere, a mile outside Bowness, are also on this line.) For while Burneside does have the odd facility for those who want to stay near the trail, including a **food store** (Mon-Sat 6.30am-9pm, Sun 7.30am-8.30pm) with a **cash machine** inside (fee £1.99) and a part-time **post office** (Mon, Wed & Fri 9am-1.45pm) in the church, you'll find so much more in its bigger neighbour two miles (3km) to the south (see p156).

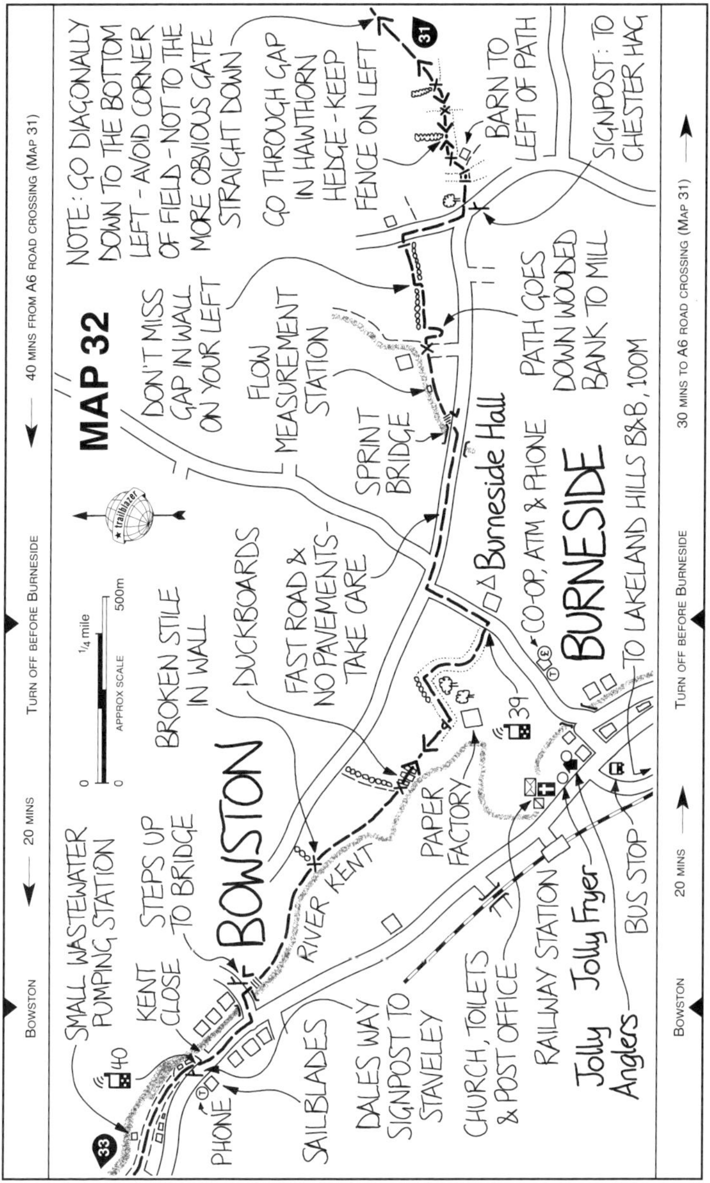

MAP 32

⬅ 40 MINS FROM A6 ROAD CROSSING (MAP 31)

30 MINS TO A6 ROAD CROSSING (MAP 31) ➡

TURN OFF BEFORE BURNESIDE

TURN OFF BEFORE BURNESIDE

⬅ 20 MINS | 20 MINS ➡

BOWSTON | BOWSTON

NOTE: GO DIAGONALLY DOWN TO THE BOTTOM LEFT - AVOID CORNER OF FIELD - NOT TO THE MORE OBVIOUS GATE STRAIGHT DOWN

GO THROUGH GAP IN HAWTHORN HEDGE - KEEP FENCE ON LEFT

BARN TO LEFT OF PATH

SIGNPOST : TO CHESTER HA\C\

PATH GOES DOWN WOODED BANK TO MILL

Burneside Hall

CO-OP, ATM & PHONE

BURNESIDE

TO LAKELAND HILLS B&B, 100M

SPRINT BRIDGE

FLOW MEASUREMENT STATION

DON'T MISS GAP IN WALL ON YOUR LEFT

DUCKBOARDS

FAST ROAD & NO PAVEMENTS - TAKE CARE

BROKEN STILE IN WALL

BOWSTON

PAPER FACTORY

RIVER KENT

STEPS UP TO BRIDGE

KENT CLOSE

SMALL WASTEWATER PUMPING STATION

PHONE

SAILBLADES

DALES WAY SIGNPOST TO STAVELEY

CHURCH, TOILETS & POST OFFICE

RAILWAY STATION

BUS STOP

Jolly Fryer

Jolly Anglers

¼ mile

0

500m

0

APPROX SCALE

★ trailblazer

Northern Rail's Oxenholme Lake District to Windermere **train** service calls here; from Burneside it's four minutes to Kendal, or travelling in the other direction it's six minutes to Staveley and 12 to Windermere; for further details see box p45. **Bus** No 45 (see pp47-50) runs regularly between Burneside and Kendal (Mon-Sat).

For accommodation, there is actually a **campsite** at the lovely – if knackered – *Burneside Hall* (☎ 01539 722017; 🐾), a farmhouse on the way into the village that has been built beside an old 14th-century *pele* tower. (A pele or peel tower was a fortified watchtower built in the borderlands between England and Scotland; fires would be lit at the top of the tower at the first sign of any approaching danger to warn locals and summon defences.) Camping costs around £3pp and well-behaved dogs are allowed, though this is a working farm. While facilities are basic they do have an outside toilet and a hot and cold tap.

If, on the other hand, you want solid walls around you and something stronger than canvas over your head, the *Jolly Anglers* (☎ 01539 732552, 🖥 www.thejol lyanglersinn.com; 2T/1D en suite; ▬; 🐾 £10; WI-FI in the pub; B&B rates are £35pp, sgl occ £50), under new ownership, is the most convenient choice; it's around 10 minutes from the trail. **Food** (just simple pub grub for around £8-15) is served 6-8pm all week and from noon-3pm at weekends). A second option is the highly recommended *Lakeland Hills* (☎ 01539 722054, 🖥 lake landhills@tiscali.co.uk; 1T/1D en suite; ▬; WI-FI; Ⓛ; B&B costs £37.50pp, sgl occ £40), at 1 Churchill Court, run by a couple who are keen walkers themselves. They also provide lifts to and from the Gateway Inn, just inside the national park, which they suggest provides the best food around.

Back in Burneside, there's also a small chippy near the church, *Jolly Fryer* (Tue-Sat 11.30am-1.15pm, Tue, Wed & Sat 4.30-7pm, Thur to 7.30pm, Fri to 8pm).

KENDAL   [see map opposite]

It comes as something of a surprise to find that the market town of Kendal, a town so inextricably identified with the Lake District, actually lies outside the border of the national park. In all other ways, however, this place is quintessentially Cumbrian, from its sombre limestone buildings (which give the town its nickname of 'Auld Grey'), its glowering nearby hills, its friendly, no-nonsense residents and its, errm, 'changeable' weather. But don't be misled into thinking that Kendal is a gloomy place – indeed, not so long ago *The Sunday Times* was voting it the second best place to live in the UK, thanks to its 'superlative shopping, bags of community spirit and an enviable location'. Though your stop here may be brief, Kendal is small enough (the population is only 26,000) that you should have the chance to sample each of these aspects. See p14 for details of Kendal's festivals.

Services

Amongst the many services available in Kendal is the **tourist information centre** (☎ 01539 735891; 🖥 www.golakes.co.uk/kendal) in the heart of town at 48a Branthwaite Brow; the main **post office** (Mon-Fri 9am-5.30pm, Tue from 9.30am, Sat 9am-12.30pm) with **phone box** outside; the **chemists** such as Boots (Mon-Fri 8.30am-6pm, Sat to 5.30pm, Sun 10.30am-4.30pm), at 66 Stricklandgate; and the **trekking outlets** such as Tog24 (Mon-Sat 9.30am-5.30pm, Sun 11am-4pm) or Mountain Warehouse (Mon-Sat 9am-5.30pm, Sun 11am-4pm). There are several **ATMs** around Stricklandgate.

For **provisions** there's a couple of supermarkets within the environs of the town centre, including an M&S (Mon-Thur & Sat 8am-6pm, Sun 10am-4pm, Fri 8am-7pm) and a Booths (Mon-Sat 8am-8pm, Sun 9.30am-4pm), both a block west of Stricklandgate.

If your boots are struggling to last, The Key **Cobbler** (Mon-Sat 9am-5.15pm) is on the main square, Market Place, and if your dog's struggling too there's always Highgate **Vets** (Mon-Fri 8.30am-7.30pm, Sat 9am-12.30pm) at 173 Highgate.

Burneside Rd

Sonata B&B

To Balcony House B&B, 600m
& Kendal Camping &
Caravanning Club, 2.4km

Beezon Rd

Beezon Fields

Railway station

A6

A6

A684

Windermere Rd

A5284

Sandes Ave

Beezon Rd

Wildman St

Premier Inn

Pedro's

Déjà Vu

Maude St

Stricklandgate

To Bridge House B&B

Post Office

A6

★ trailblazer

River Kent

Public phone

McDonald's

M&S

Caffe Nero

Boots

The Key Cobbler

Relish

Stramongate

A65

Costa

Tourist Info

Famous 1657 Chocolate House

Booths

Tog24

The Globe

Mumbai

A65

Farrers Tearoom

Finkle's

TT's

Rainbow Tavern

Nevisport

Greggs

Marmaris

Kent St

Little Aynam

Pumpkins Bistro

Mountain Warehouse

A6

Pizzeria Italia

Allhallows La

Geno's Pizzeria

Bridge St

A65

Miles Thompson

0   50   100m

Fish Express

Master's House Tearoom

Kendal Hostel

Jintana

New Moon

Queen Katherine St

Silver Mountain

A6

Highgate Vets

A65

Kendal

Gillinggate

To Stonecross Manor,
¾ mile/1.2km

Transport

[See public transport map & table pp45-50]
Kendal is connected to Dales Way towns
Bowness, Burneside and Staveley by
Northern's **train** service between Preston
and Windermere.

For **bus** services, the S1 (Sat only)
runs to Sedbergh, Dent Village, Dent
Station and Cowgill, the W1 (Mon-Fri) and
W2 (Wed only) operate to Sedbergh and
Oxenholme, though the W2 also goes to
Dent. Stagecoach's 555, 599 and 755 buses
serve the major population centres in the
region; the 755 takes at least half an hour to
reach Bowness.

Where to stay

For **campers**, *Kendal Camping and
Caravanning Club* (☎ 01539 741363, 🖳
www.campingandcaravanningclub.co.uk;
WI-FI; 🐾; £6.45-10.95pp; Easter to the end
of Oct) is on Shap Rd about 1½ miles
(2.4km) to the north of the station. There's
nothing wrong with the place but there's a
strong case to be made for staying in
Burneside and camping at Burneside Hall –
it's a lot less hassle than catching the train
then walking to this campsite.

There's a **hostel** in Kendal and it's a
good one. The independent, family-run
Kendal Hostel (☎ 01539 724066, 🖳
.kendalhostel.com; 14 bedrooms with 2-14
beds in each; WI-FI; 🐾) is at 118-120
Highgate – ie the interesting end of the main
shopping street. Boasting a lounge with log
burner and TV, a self-catering kitchen and a
separate dining room, rates in the hostel are
usually around £20 per bed even if you
manage to get a private twin room for yourself and your travelling companion, and can
fall to £16 in the low season.

As for **B&Bs**, pretty close to the station at 65 Castle St is *Bridge House* (☎
01539 722041, 🖳 www.bridgehouse-ken
dal.co.uk; 1D/1T en suite, 1D private bathroom; 🛁; WI-FI; Ⓛ), a smart, listed building
with a lovely garden, a drying room and
reasonable rates (£40-45pp, sgl occ £45-
50), particularly for single occupancy.
Transfers for Dales Way walkers can also
be arranged. Convenient for the centre is
the award-winning *Sonata Guest House* (☎

01539 732290, 🖳 www.sonataguesthouse
.co.uk; 2D/1D or T/1T, en suite; 🛁; WI-FI),
another mid 19th-century property, situated
at 19 Burneside Rd, with rates around £41-
42.50pp or £50-60 single occupancy.

Most central of all, *Premier Inn
Kendal* (central reservations ☎ 0871 527
8562, 🖳 www.premierinn.com; 42D/50D
or T; all en suite; 🛁; WI-FI) is pretty much
identical to all the other establishments in
this chain. The tariff varies greatly depending on all sorts of factors but expect to pay
upwards from £39 **per room** – good value.

Moving away from the centre, and currently receiving great recommendations,
Balcony House (☎ 07528 360 339 or ☎
01539 731402, 🖳 www.balconyhouse.co
.uk; 2D/1T, en suite or with private facilities; WI-FI) is a lovely, super-smart B&B
though it is nearly a kilometre to the north
of the station (and thus away from town).
The tariff is £35-40pp (no single occupancy
rate during the summer).

Across town on Milnthorpe Road, **dog
owners** can stay with their best friend at
Stonecross Manor Hotel (☎ 01539
733559, 🖳 www.stonecrossmanor.co.uk;
30D or T, all en suite; 🛁; WI-FI; 🐾 £15 per
stay) comes highly recommended. It's a
smart stone place with all mod cons including swimming pool and spa. Rates in this
former girls' orphanage are £60-102.50pp
(sgl occ £110-195) including breakfast.
Unfortunately, it's over 1¼ miles (2km)
away from Kendal station, lying across
town on the southern side, so treat yourself
to a taxi from Oxenholme Station (which is
actually slightly closer).

Where to eat and drink

For those early starts there's dog-friendly
Caffe Nero (Mon-Sat 7.30am-6pm, Sun
9am-5pm), or dog-unfriendly *Costa* (Mon-
Sat 7am-6.30pm, Sun 8am-5.30pm) and a
branch of that burger behemoth,
McDonald's (Sun-Thur 6am-10pm, Fri &
Sat to 11pm), just up from the post office.

Considerably more memorable,
Farrer's (☎ 01539 731707; Mon-Sat 9am-
5.30pm) has been serving up a fantastic
array of the finest teas and coffees from the

same location since 1819. The shop itself is very handsome, all wood panelled and polished brass, they have WI-FI and they're dog-friendly too. They also serve food including a mixed meat platter (£7.95 for plate of roast ham, chicken and beef served with full salad, coleslaw and a roll), and I can personally vouch for the cheese scone, which was properly cheesy, and properly delicious.

Farrer's is just one of several cafés with a bit of history to them, including the *Famous 1657 Chocolate House* (☎ 01539-740702, 🖳 chocolatehouse1657.co.uk; Mon-Sat 10am-4.30pm), though in this case the history is largely about the 17th-century building rather than the shop itself, which has been in residence for only the past 30 years or so. Nevertheless for chocoholics it's an essential visit, with 16 speciality hot chocolates, including the Cortez – rum-flavoured chocolate finished with cream and rum fudge – pretty much the perfect warming pick-me-up on a soggy Kendal day. There's also *The Master's House Tearoom* (☎ 01539-720723, Tue-Sat 9.30am-4pm) at 80b Highgate, a tiny and traditional dog-friendly place housed in one of the oldest buildings in Kendal, and another great place for afternoon tea.

The vegetarian café *Waterside* (🖳 www.watersidekendal.co.uk; daily 8.30am-4pm, summer Thur-Sat till 10pm), just by the bridge over the Kent, was hit rather badly by the floods of winter 2015 but expects to open again in August 2016.

For food-on-the-go, *Relish* (☎ 01539 727279; Mon-Sat 8.15am-4pm) is a great little sandwich outlet with hot paninis from £3.50 (for brie and bacon) to £4 (medium rare beef and stilton).

Other cheap-eats in Kendal include the long-established *Finkle's* (☎ 01539 727325; Mon-Sat 9am-5pm, Sun 9am-3.30pm) where you can get the local take on shepherd's pie, Cumbrian shearman's pie, for £5.95; and *The Miles Thompson* (☎ 01539 815710; food served 8am-11pm), on Allhallows Lane, owned by the dog-unfriendly Wetherspoon's brand, which serves standard pub grub pretty much all the time they're open. The building used to

be the local baths, by the way, which were designed by the eponymous Mr Thompson. Across the way is the cheerful *Pumpkins Bistro* (☎ 01539 728722; Mon-Wed 9.30am-5pm, Thur-Sat 9.30am-8pm) with mains mostly around £7-8 including a delicious tagine (£7.50).

For the evenings, my favourite was a pub, *The Globe* (☎ 01539 721852; food served noon-9pm), partly because the landlord was very helpful and friendly to both me and the dog, but mainly because the food was inexpensive, the portions large and the quality very, very high. Try the lamb Henry (slow-cooked lamb on the bone marinated with mint), an absolute steal at £10.50.

On Highgate *New Moon* (☎ 01539 729254, 🖳 www.newmoonrestaurant.co .uk; Tue-Sat 11.30am-2.15pm & 6-9.15pm) serves local, 'British' dishes though with some unusual twists including hake fillet, sautéed potatoes, pea purée, shallots and a smoked bacon cream sauce (£13.75).

At the other end of the main shopping thoroughfare, at 124 Stricklandgate, *Déjà Vu* (☎ 01539 724843, 🖳 www.dejavukendal.com; daily from 5.30pm, also Wed-Sat noon-2pm) is a bistro with some very tasty fare including a lovely bouillabaise (£13.95). Next door, *Pedro's* (☎ 01539 722332; daily noon-10pm), ostensibly a tapas place (dishes £3-8) though one that, in their own words, offers much bigger portions than your average tapas place. Burgers (£8) and pizzas (from £6) are also on the menu in this friendly, happy establishment – and they do a mean cocktail too…

For takeaways you have several choices including: the pizzeria *Geno's* (daily 4pm to late), on Allhallows Lane; the kebab house *Marmaris* (☎ 01539-734443; daily 4pm to late), on Kent St; *Jintana* (☎ 01539 723123, 🖳 www.jintanathaicuisine.com; Tue 5-10pm, Wed-Sun noon-2.30pm & 5-10pm, Fri to 10.30pm); *Silver Mountain Chinese* (☎ 01539 729911; Tue-Thur & Sun 5-11.30pm, Fri & Sat 5pm-midnight); and the chippy, *Fish Express* (Mon-Thur 11.30am-7.30pm, Fri & Sat to 8pm), the last three all located on Highgate.

STAGE 6: BURNESIDE TO BOWNESS-ON-WINDERMERE
MAPS 32-36

And so you come to the final stage on the walk, an undaunting **9½-miler (15.4km; 3hrs 35 mins)** with glorious views back to the rolling Howgills and ahead to the sharper crags of the Lake District. This can, of course, be done in a busy morning but it seems a shame to hurry through to the end, so it's worth taking a short diversion for lunch into Staveley, where there's a good choice of eateries for such a small place.

The perceptive walker will notice how this ultimate stage seems somehow out of character with much of what's gone before. The landscape is now craggier and more 'pointed', particularly when juxtaposed with the smooth-topped Howgills. When one compares the landscape and buildings now with the beginning of the walk, when you were atop the Askrigg Block (see box p140), the change is startling: even the grass is different here, the soil more acid meaning the rougher, browner lakeland pasture thrives. It's a sign that the end is near, and your time on the Dales Way is almost over. So don't be in too much of a hurry to get this last leg completed; wherever you may be heading to afterwards, I'd be very surprised if it's more dramatic, or more beautiful!

The route

For most people, of course, the day begins with a train back from Kendal to Burneside and a walk through the village back to the Dales Way. Once on the trail the going is easy as you stroll through fields of livestock by the River Kent, a waterway you follow via **Bowston** and the residential development at **Cowan Head**, across the boundary of the **Lake District National Park** and on to Staveley.

STAVELEY   [see map p162]

Staveley is another one of those places – like Buckden, Dent, Sedbergh et al – that the Dales Way doesn't *quite* visit (it merely brushes against it as much as anything) but which is nevertheless very much part of the trail. It's a shame to miss the place, if only because it has several good eateries and as such is an ideal spot for a late lunch before the final amble to Bowness.

There are a few amenities here that you may want to take advantage of too. You can pick up **provisions** in the Bee Hive (Mon-Fri 7am-4.45pm, Sat 7am-1.30pm, Sun 9am-noon), which also houses the village **post office** and an **ATM** (£1 charge), while just up the street is a **pharmacy** (Mon-Fri 9am-6pm, Sat 9am-12.30pm).

Staveley is a stop on some of Northern's **train** services (see box p45) between Preston and Windermere.

For **buses**, the 555 calls here on its way between Kendal and Lancaster; for details see pp47-50.

For **accommodation**, the 400-year-old farmhouse known as *Li'le Hullets* (off Map 33; ☎ 01539 821148, ⌨ www.lilehullets .co.uk; 1D/1T en suite, 1D in attic with private bathroom; ✆; WI-FI; 🐾; Ⓛ) is a great choice. The restoration of the property has been sympathetic, so that many of the original features that make this place so charming are still present, including the oak-beamed lounge, oak staircases and even a recently discovered bread oven. The name, incidentally, means tiny owl in the old Westmoreland dialect. The rates are exceptional given the charm of this place, with the tariff including breakfast set at £35pp (£50 sgl occ), or £30pp (£40 sgl occ) in the smaller double room in the attic. The only

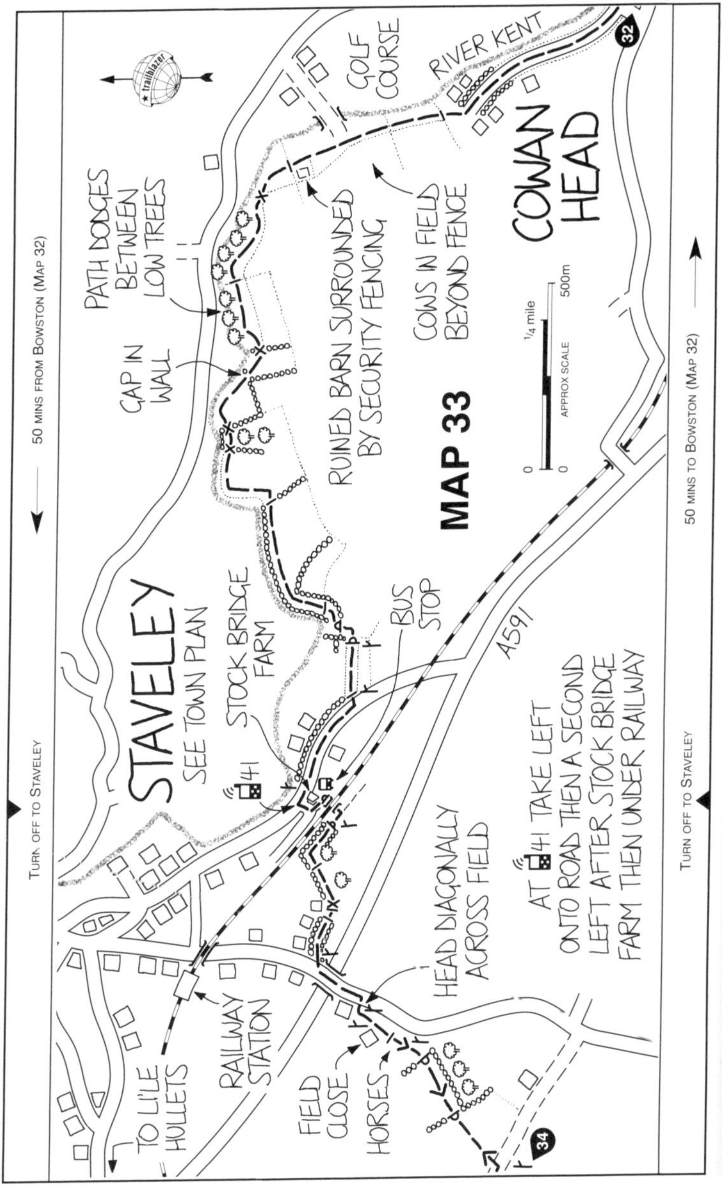

MAP 33

STAVELEY
SEE TOWN PLAN

COWAN HEAD

GOLF COURSE

RIVER KENT

PATH DODGES BETWEEN LOW TREES

GAP IN WALL

RUINED BARN SURROUNDED BY SECURITY FENCING

COWS IN FIELD BEYOND FENCE

STOCK BRIDGE FARM

BUS STOP

AT ☐41 TAKE LEFT ONTO ROAD THEN A SECOND LEFT AFTER STOCK BRIDGE FARM THEN UNDER RAILWAY

HEAD DIAGONALLY ACROSS FIELD

RAILWAY STATION

TO L'ILE HULLETS

FIELD CLOSE HORSES

A591

APPROX SCALE

0   ¼ mile

0   500m

50 MINS FROM BOWSTON (MAP 32)

50 MINS TO BOWSTON (MAP 32)

TURN OFF TO STAVELEY

TURN OFF TO STAVELEY

32

34

problem is that it's about a mile from the path: head up Kendal Rd and its continuation, Main St, to the centre of the village, then follow this thoroughfare as it bends left (opposite the chippy) and becomes Windermere Rd, which in turn eventually becomes Danes Rd. Seed Howe is on your right, with Li'le Hullets at No 3.

Much nearer to the path, and with a reputation for good pub grub, is the curiously named *Eagle and Child* (☎ 01539 821320, 💻 www.eaglechildinn.co.uk; 3D/3T, all en suite; 🛥; WI-FI; B&B £42.50-55pp; sgl occ £65-85). The name, incidentally, comes from an old tale about a local aristocrat, Sir Thomas Latham, who fathered a longed-for son by a servant girl (his wife having given him only daughters). To introduce the boy into the family, Sir Thomas deposited the child beneath a tree where an eagle was nesting. His wife, strolling past the tree, discovered the boy and, assuming the eagle had dropped the child, took him back home and adopted him as her own, much as Sir Thomas had planned. To this day the Latham family crest has an eagle and a child on it.

Where to eat and drink
While your feet may not thank you for forcing them to walk the extra few minutes into Staveley, your stomach certainly will as there is a surprising range of eating places for such a small place.

For lunch, I think you should continue up Main St to *Eclec* (☎ 01539 821393, 💻 staveleyantiques.co.uk; Mon-Sat 9am-5pm). Here, tucked away in the back of a home furnishings/antiques store, is a very fine café with a great selection of homemade dishes including the Eclec dhal, a lovely and very filling lentil dish.

The other options lie, rather unpromisingly, on a commercial estate behind here. *Wilf's* (☎ 01539 822329, 💻 www.wilfs-cafe.co.uk; daily 9am-5pm) is a hugely popular place, not surprising really given their tasty, hearty food including the big meaty breakfast (£6.90), with the veggie option the same price. The main draw on the estate, however, is *Hawkshead Brewery & Beer Hall* (☎ 01539 825260, 💻

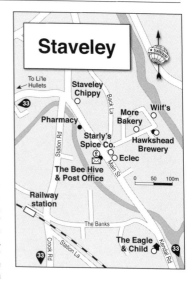

www.hawksheadbrewery.co.uk; food Mon-Thur noon-3pm, Fri & Sat noon-8.30pm, Sun noon-6pm), a modern glass affair with a large menu, much of it designed to accompany their range of beers; mains are £7-12 and there are also at least a dozen tapas dishes including maple-glazed pork belly and apple sauce and sticky BBQ babyback ribs.

Next door is the swish *More Bakery* (☎ 01539 822297, 💻 www.moreartisan .co.uk; Mon-Fri 7.30am-5pm, Sat & Sun to 5.30pm) with hot sarnis from £2.95 (for a basic bacon sandwich) up to £4.95 (for a bacon & chicken club sandwich).

For evening options, fine pub grub can be had at the *Eagle and Child* (see Where to stay; food daily noon-2.30pm & 6-9pm), including slow-roasted lamb shank served on creamy mash with a red wine, redcurrant and thyme jus for £13.95. Alternatively, *Starly's Spice Co* (☎ 01539 821807, 💻 www.starlys.co.uk; Thur 6.30pm to late, Fri & Sat from 6pm) is an Indian Bistro with a menu made deliberately small to allow them to cook as much as possible from fresh; mains are all a tenner or less, the most expensive being Kashmiri beef,

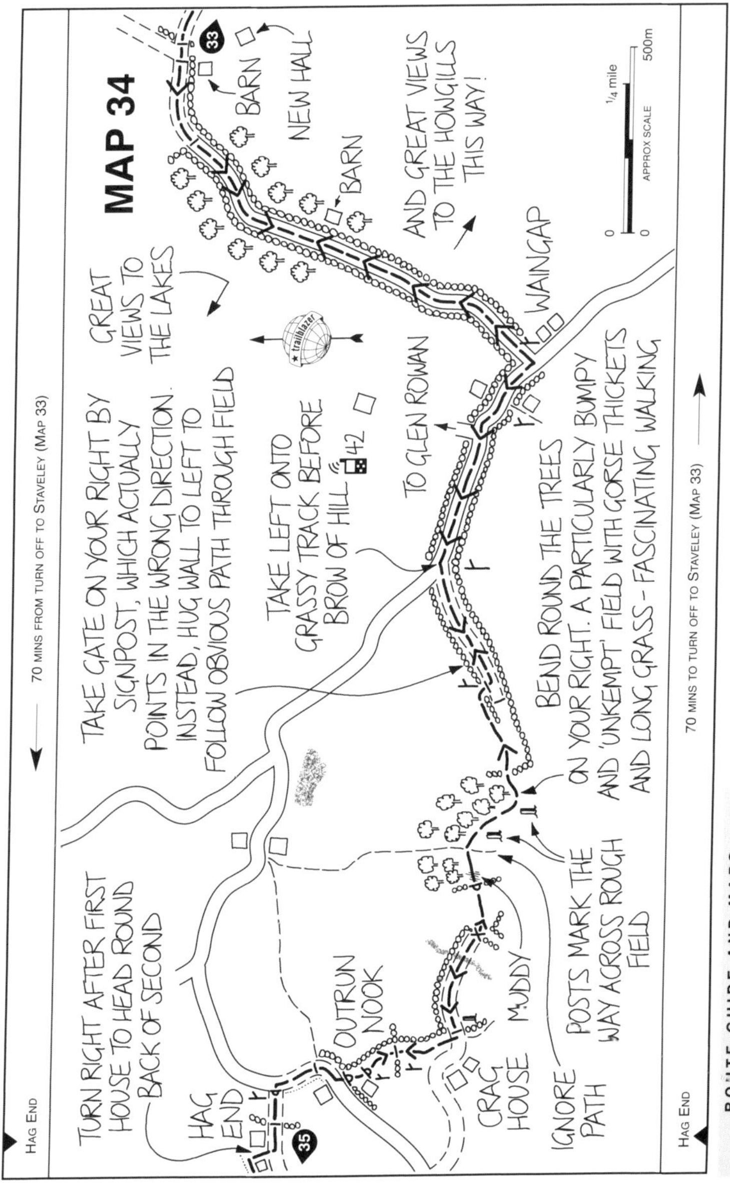
MAP 34
70 MINS FROM TURN OFF TO STAVELEY (MAP 33)
HAG END
TURN RIGHT AFTER FIRST HOUSE TO HEAD ROUND BACK OF SECOND
HAG END
35
OUTRUN NOOK
CRAG HOUSE
IGNORE PATH
MUDDY
POSTS MARK THE WAY ACROSS ROUGH FIELD
BEND ROUND THE TREES ON YOUR RIGHT. A PARTICULARLY BUMPY AND 'UNKEMPT' FIELD WITH GORSE THICKETS AND LONG GRASS - FASCINATING WALKING
TAKE GATE ON YOUR RIGHT BY SIGNPOST, WHICH ACTUALLY POINTS IN THE WRONG DIRECTION. INSTEAD, HUG WALL TO LEFT TO FOLLOW OBVIOUS PATH THROUGH FIELD
TAKE LEFT ONTO GRASSY TRACK BEFORE BROW OF HILL
42
TO GLEN ROWAN
GREAT VIEWS TO THE LAKES
trailblazer
WAINGAP
AND GREAT VIEWS TO THE HOWGILLS THIS WAY!
BARN
BARN
NEW HALL
33
0 1/4 mile
0 500m
APPROX SCALE
70 MINS TO TURN OFF TO STAVELEY (MAP 33)
HAG END

cooked for seven hours in a vinegar and garlic sauce. They accept cash only and note that this is a BYO place, so don't forget to bring the beer.

For takeaway, near the centre of the village is *Staveley Chippy* (☎ 01539 821457; Tue & Wed 5-8pm, Thur, Fri & Sat 11.30am-1pm & 5-8pm).

With Staveley visited and the A591 safely crossed, things start to get a little more interesting, particularly beyond **New Hall** where the path climbs steeply to afford some great views south-east to the Howgill Fells and the western edge of Dales, as well as **Cross Fell** on the northern Pennines (at 893m, the highest point in England outside of the Lakes), and, of course, to your left, the Lakeland Fells. More great views follow after the next climb as you finally leave the tarmac to enter a series of wild fields, the air heavy with the coconut-scent of the gorse bushes that grow thickly here. The farmhouses of Crag

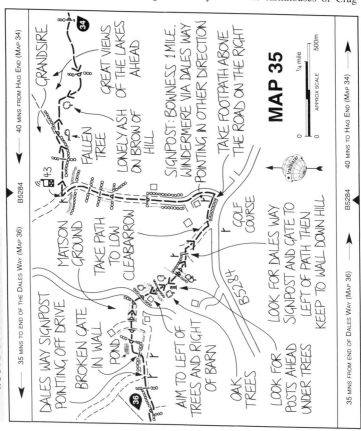

House, Outrun Nook and **Hag End** help you to count off the yards. The end feels close now and the view from the minor hill of **Grandsire** confirms this – a vista that on a good day encompasses many of the *grand-dames* of the Lakes, with Crinkle Crags, Bowfell, Langdale Pikes, School Knott and even the grandest of them all, Scafell Pike, appearing through the haze. From here it's a bit of a messy end, with plenty of small fields to march through and even a bit of road walking before the final drop to the finish.

The end – just like the beginning all those miles ago – is marked by a simple stone bench where you can sit, congratulate your companions, reflect on your expedition – and steel yourself for the hurly-burly below.

BOWNESS-ON-WINDERMERE
[see Map 36, p167]

No matter how much you think you've missed civilisation, the reality, when you finally reach it again at the very end of your trek, is a bit of a shock – and not, for most walkers, a particularly pleasant one. For the majority of Dales Way walkers find Bowness just too noisy, too crowded – and just too 'touristy'. And isn't it strange, and not a little depressing, to be back in a place where people don't bid you a 'good morning' as you walk by?

What brings the masses here are Bowness's historic connections with Beatrix Potter (including the town's number one attraction, the large **World of Beatrix Potter** (☎ 0844-5041233, 💻 www .hop-skip-jump.com; daily 10am-4.30pm). The town also has associations with the Romantic poets of the 18th and 19th centuries (though some may say you won't find a less romantic spot on the entire walk than Bowness). The wonders of Wharfedale, pretty little Dent and charming Sedbergh all seem light years away now. Perhaps that's why Colin Speakman, who created the Dales Way, chose to end the walk *above* the town rather than in it, so you can still enjoy Bowness's main appeal – the views it offers of gorgeous Windermere – without actually having to throw yourself into the maelstrom below.

But perhaps I'm being a little unfair, for I'm sure the vast majority of visitors to Bowness have a lovely time. And it does offer pretty much everything a walker could want, including restaurants and cafés galore, over 200 B&Bs, hotels and other accommodation, a large and helpful information centre – plus, most importantly, frequent transport connections.

So all that remains is to perform whatever ritual you find necessary to mark the end of your odyssey: dip one foot in the lake, maybe, collect a certificate from the outdoor outfitters Hawkshead – or just get roaringly drunk in the Hole in t'Wall (see Where to eat). Oh, and congratulations on finishing the Dales Way – wasn't that a beautiful journey!

Services

Down by the lake, the **Tourist Information Centre** (daily 9.30am-5.30pm late Mar to late Oct, daily 10.30am-4.30pm late Oct to late Mar) has free WI-FI and internet, sells maps and books and has a *café*. Up the hill on St Martin's Parade, a little back street, is the **post office** (Mon-Fri 9am-5.30pm, Sat 9am-12.30pm). On the main drag there are a couple of **supermarkets**: Co-op (daily 7am-10pm) and, back down the hill, Tesco (daily 6am-11pm). There's an **ATM** at the Co-op and a **payphone** opposite.

If you're starting your trek in Bowness or planning on doing some further walking in the Lake District, there are a few **trekking outfitters** including Mountain Warehouse (Mon-Sat 9am-6.30pm, winter to 5.30pm, Sun 9am-5pm), Trespass (Mon-Sat 9am-5.30pm, Sun 10am-5pm; to 6pm in summer, to 4pm after October) and Hawkshead (Mon-Fri 8am-8pm). From Hawkshead you can also pick up your **Dales Way Certificate**.

Transport

[See public transport map & table pp45-50]
The main **bus** stop is on the lakeshore, just before the tourist information centre. Stagecoach's 599 service links Bowness with its Siamese twin, Windermere (which, ironically, isn't actually on the lake but a mile and more up the hill), as well as those other Lakeland hotspots, Ambleside and Grasmere. Other services that call at Windermere Railway Station are the No 6, 508 & 755. **Windermere Lake Cruises** (see p50) offer cruises on the lake with 'steamers' heading to Brockhole, Lakeside and Waterhead (for Ambleside), but also a Cross Lakes Shuttle (May-Oct approx 10/day; £2.90; 🐕 free) from Bowness to Ferry House. Mountain Goat provides a bus connection from Ferry House to Hawkshead.

There are several **taxi** firms, including Austwick Taxis (☎ 015242 51364) and Lakeside & Windermere Taxis (☎ 015394 88888), who have an 8-seater vehicle and claim to be the cheapest in the area.

Where to stay

The nearest **campsite** situated on the eastern shore of Lake Windermere is *Braithwaite Fold* (off Map 36; ☎ 015394 42177; 🖥 www.campingandcaravanning club.co.uk; 🐕 must be kept on leads); there is a complicated pricing structure but walkers are charged from £7.10pp.

The closest **hostel** to the end of the walk is the secure, clean and friendly *Lake District Backpackers* (☎ 015394 46374, 🖥 www.lakedistrictbackpackers.co.uk; 1 x 6-bed/2 x 4-bed/2Tr; WI-FI); it's a mile up the hill in Windermere on the High St. A bed here is £16.50 in a dorm, or it's from £19.50pp in a private room – excellent value.

According to the tourist office there are around 280+ **hotels and B&Bs** in the immediate vicinity of Bowness and its neighbour Windermere. As such, this is just a tiny selection, largely made up of the hotels most popular with Dales Way walkers. Note that, at **virtually all the accommodation in Bowness, there is a two-night minimum stay at weekends**.

Fairfield (☎ 015394 46565, 🖥 www .the-fairfield.co.uk; 8D, en suite; ➽; 🐕 £10; WI-FI) lies closest to the path, halfway down Brantfell Rd. They offer parking for the duration of the walk – and for an extra charge will even get your car cleaned and valeted for your return! B&B costs £44.50 to £47pp, single occupancy is the full room rate at weekends, around £20 less than this at other times.

Continuing down the hill, *The Royal Oak* (☎ 015394 43970, 🖥 www.royaloak-windermere.co.uk; 8D en suite/2D with shared bathroom; ➽; WI-FI) proudly proclaims itself as 'the official finishing pub for the Dalesway (sic)' thanks to an endorsement by a writer of an old guidebook; and with a location at the bottom of Brantfell Rd, it's hard to argue with that. B&B costs £37.50pp-55pp; single occupancy is £50.

There's a whole string of B&Bs stretching south from the centre of town along the A5074, aka Kendal Rd, the lofty vantage point allowing views of the lake from any of them. One such is *Dene House* (☎ 015394 48236, 🖥 www.denehouse-guesthouse.co.uk; 1S/2D or T/4D all with private facilities; ➽; WI-FI) is one of the few B&Bs in the area with a single room (and the single is the only room that has access to a bath, in its own private – but not en suite – bathroom); rates are £48-55pp (sgl £56-9). Heading north back into the centre, *May Cottage* (☎ 015394 46478, 🖥 www .maycottagebowness.co.uk; 1D/1D or T/ 1Qd, all en suite; ➽; WI-FI). Rates are around £40pp (sgl occ £45-65).

Virtually opposite are the terraced gardens of *Nagoya Country House* (☎ 015394 44356, 🖥 www.nagoyabownessbandb.co .uk; 3D, all en suite; WI-FI) – though its address is actually on Brackenfield. With well-appointed rooms and a lovely patio overlooking the lake, it's a decent option and rates are fair by Bowness's standards at £35-45pp (sgl occ £60). Back towards the centre, homely *Virginia Cottage* (☎ 015394 44891, 🖥 www.virginia-cottage.co.uk; 11D, all en suite; ➽; WI-FI; 🐕 £10) is one of the few hotels in the town centre that

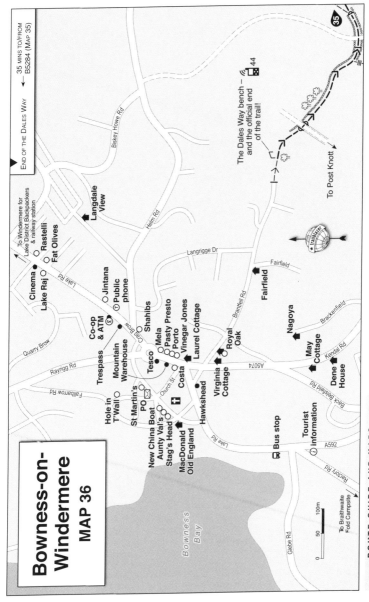

Bowness-on-Windermere
MAP 36

35 MINS TO/FROM B5284 (MAP 35)

END OF THE DALES WAY

To Windermere for
Lake District Backpackers
& railway station

Biskey Howe Rd

The Dales Way bench –
and the official end
of the trail!

44

To Post Knott

Langdale View

Helm Rd

Langrigge Dr

Fairfield

Fairfield

Cinema
Lake Raj

Rastelli
Fat Olives

Lake Rd

Jintana

Public phone

Crag Brow

Shahibs

Mela
Pasty Presto
Porto
Vinegar Jones

Laurel Cottage

Brantfell Rd

Brackenfield

Nagoya

May Cottage

Kendal Rd

Dene House

Quarry Brow

Co-op & ATM

Rayrigg Rd

Trespass
Mountain Warehouse

Tesco

Costa

Royal Oak

Virginia Cottage

A5074

Back Belsfield Rd

Fallbarrow Rd

Hole in T'Wall
St Martin's
PO

Church St

Hawkshead

New China Boat
Aunty Val's
Stag's Head
MacDonald
Old England

Lake Rd

Bus stop

Tourist information

A592

Rectory Rd

Bowness Bay

Glebe Rd

To Braithwaite
Fold Campsite

0   50   100m

ROUTE GUIDE AND MAPS

allows dogs (though not large ones). It's a long-established place, the building (originally two cottages) having been here for over 150 years and the business running for over 45 years. Rates start at £40pp for the 'economy double', rising to around £62.50pp for the suite with a four-poster bed; single occupancy is about £10 off the full room price.

Regularly receiving rave reviews, **Langdale View** (☎ 015394 44076, 🖳 www .langdaleview.co.uk; 4D/1D or T, all en suite; WI-FI) is one of the older properties in Bowness, having been built in the mid 19th century on Craig Walk, about 500m from the lakeshore. Rates are £47-54pp, single occupancy £73-82.

Finally, **MacDonald Old England Hotel** (☎ 0344 879 9144, 🖳 www.macdon aldhotels.co.uk; 106 rooms; ☛; WI-FI) with its smart rooms overlooking the lakeshore and uniformed staff bustling around the lobby, is perhaps the most up-market place in town, and the tariff of £69.50-140pp (sgl occ £104-280) for B&B refects this.

Where to eat and drink
There are a lot of mouths to feed in the high season in Bowness, and as a consequence a lot of cafés and restaurants to cater for them. The following, therefore, is but the briefest of overviews. My favourite **café** is **St Martin's Tearoom** (☎ 015394 442799; daily 10am-5pm), by the post office, mainly because it has WI-FI, is dog friendly, serves a range of speciality teas, is a great place to hide away from the hubbub outside – and does a cracking afternoon tea for £4.95. If you want something more familiar, there's a large **Costa** (Mon-Sat 7am-6pm, Sun 8am-6pm) nearby. Opposite, **Pasty Presto** (daily 8.30am-6.30pm, up to 8.30pm in summer) is open early and a great place to stock up if you're just starting out on your journey and want something to take with you, with their travelling beef empanada pasty just £2.95 to take away.

Pubs that do food include **The Royal Oak** (see p166; food daily 11am-9.30pm), with mains from £9.50 including a Cumberland sausage served in a giant Yorkshire pudding (for a taste of both coun-

ties) and rich onion gravy with mash and veg for £9.50; and **Hole in t'Wall** (☎ 015394 43488, 🖳 www.holeintwall.co.uk; food served Mon-Thur noon-2.30pm & 6-8.30pm, Sat noon-8pm, Sun noon-5pm). The pub is actually officially called the New Hall Inn but earned its nickname centuries ago when a hole was knocked through one of the walls so the neighbouring blacksmith could be served beer while working at the furnace. Built way back in 1612, it's a little squashed inside and can get a little rowdy too, but it's the most characterful place in town and my favourite spot.

Takeaways include several Chinese establishments, the best perhaps being **New China Boat** (☎ 015394 46326; Tue-Sun noon-2pm, daily 5-11pm), the chippy **Vinegar Jones** (☎ 015394 44846; daily noon-4pm & 4.45-8.30pm), with your standard fish & chips for £5.95; and **Jintana Thai** (☎ 015394 45002; daily noon-2.30pm & 5-10pm), sister branch of the one in Kendal. There are also several good Indian restaurants, including **Shahib's** (☎ 015394 43944; 12.15-2.15pm, Sun-Thur 5.15-11.15pm, Fri & Sat 5.15pm-12.15am), down the bottom of the Crag by the roundabout; **Mela** (☎ 015394 45781; daily 5.30-11.30pm); and up the hill near the cinema, **Lake Raj** (☎ 015394 45900) with mains £6.95-12.95. Also by the cinema is **Fat Olives Brasserie** (☎ 015394 47447, 🖳 www.fatolives.com; daily from 4pm), an English-Mediterranean affair with a good collection of sharing plates (eg vegetarian tapas plate for £10.25); and **Rastelli** (☎ 015394 44227, 🖳 www.raste.co.uk; Mon & Wed, Thur & Sat 5.30-9pm, Fri to 9.15pm, Sun to 9.30pm), an Italian place with pizzas from £7.50.

For a slap-up celebration, however, the best restaurant in town is widely regarded to be **Porto** (☎ 015394 48242, 🖳 www.porto-restaurant.co.uk; Wed-Mon noon-2pm, & 6pm to late), on pedestrianised Ash St; it serves what it describes as modern British fare, including dishes such as poached smoked haddock, Cullen skink (a Scottish fish soup), king scallops, bacon crisps and creamed potatoes for £18.95.

APPENDIX A: GPS WAYPOINTS*

MAP	REF	GPS WAYPOINTS	DESCRIPTION
1	01	30 U 576772 5976258	Old Bridge at Ilkley, start of trail
2	02	30 U 573871 5977822	Join road in Addingham after church
3	03	30 U 573101 5979864	Gate near Quaker Farfield Meeting House
3	04	30 U 573010 5982227	Footbridge by Bolton Abbey
4	05	30 U 573256 5983390	Cavendish Pavilion
5	06	30 U 571889 5984476	The Strid
5	07	30 U 571166 5984895	Barden Bridge
6	08	30 U 570110 5988074	Footpath to Appletreewick
7	09	30 U 568611 5989207	Burnsall Bridge
7	10	30 U 567891 5990358	Hebden Suspension Bridge
8	11	30 U 565481 5991344	Bridge with views of weir
9	12	30 U 564783 5995246	Limekiln
10	13	30 U 564135 5996639	Gated stile by Conistone Pie
11	14	30 U 562686 5999438	Turn off road thro' gate by K'well ⅝ mile sign
11	15	30 U 562246 6000216	Kettlewell maypole
12	16	30 U 560302 6002386	Dales Way signpost
13	17	30 U 559112 6005225	Buckden Bridge
14	18	30 U 557825 6006096	Hubberholme Church
15	19	30 U 554364 6007554	Bridge at Deepdale
16	20	30 U 552491 6008022	Bridge at Beckermonds
16	21	30 U 551264 6009956	Nethergill Eco Farm
17	22	30 U 549817 6010256	Swarthghyll Farm
18	23	30 U 547534 6009914	Cam Houses
18a	23a	30 U 547738 6011031	Cold Keld Gate
18a	23b	30 U 546390 6010913	Gavel Gap
18b	23c	30 U 544569 6011240	Onto Road at Newby Head
18c	23d	30 U 544251 6013823	Galloway Gate; junction at Arten Gill
18	24	30 U 546423 6009422	Join Cam High Road/high point of trek
19	25	30 U 543446 6007900	Far Gearstones
20	26	30 U 542806 6012063	Dent Head Viaduct
21	27	30 U 542122 6013562	Stone House
21	28	30 U 541405 6014335	Bridge at Lea Yeat
22	29	30 U 538242 6013787	Nelly Bridge
23	30	30 U 535748 6014725	Church Bridge/turn-off to Dent
24	31	30 U 533141 6016084	Join road near Dent Fault!
25	32	30 U 531681 6016860	Gate before Brackensgill Bridge
26	33	30 IJ 529263 6018405	Gate – view of old railway bridge
27	34	30 U 528030 6020490	Lune Viaduct
28	35	30 U 526932 6023678	Onto road before Crook of Lune Bridge
29	36	30 U 524861 6023233	Across M6 motorway
30	37	30 U 520737 6024355	Gate off track
31	38	30 U 519533 6024522	White house after pylon
32	39	30 U 515727 6023210	Turn-off to Burneside
32	40	30 U 514598 6023997	Turn off road at Bowston
33	41	30 U 512216 6025039	Turn-off to Staveley
34	42	30 U 509773 6023777	Turn-off road onto grassy farm track
35	43	30 U 507093 6024249	Sharp left turn by signpost
Bowness	44	30 U 505618 6023844	Finish!

*downloadable from ⌨ **www.trailblazer-guides.com**

APPENDIX B: WALKING WITH A DOG

THE DALES WAY WITH A DOG

Many are the rewards that await those prepared to make the extra effort required to bring their best friend along the trail. You shouldn't underestimate the amount of work involved, though. Indeed, just about every decision you make will be influenced by the fact that you've got a dog: how you plan to travel to the start of the trail, where you're going to stay, how far you're going to walk each day, where you're going to rest and where you're going to eat in the evening etc.

If you're also sure your dog can cope with (and will enjoy) walking 12 miles or more a day for several days in a row, you need to start preparing accordingly. Extra thought also needs to go into your itinerary. The best starting point is to study the town and village facilities table on p32 (and the advice below), and plan where to stop and where to buy food.

Looking after your dog

To begin with, you need to make sure that your own dog is fully **inoculated** against the usual doggy illnesses, and also up to date with regard to **worm pills** (eg Drontal) and **flea preventatives** such as Frontline – they are, after all, following in the pawprints of many a dog before them, some of whom may well have left fleas or other parasites on the trail that now lie in wait for their next meal to arrive.

Pet insurance is also a very good idea; if you've already got insurance, do check that it will cover a trip such as this.

On the subject of looking after your dog's health, perhaps the most important implement you can take with you is the **plastic tick remover**, available from vets for a couple of quid. These removers, while fiddly, help you to remove the tick safely (ie without leaving its head behind buried under the dog's skin).

Being in unfamiliar territory also makes it more likely that you and your dog could become separated. For this reason, make sure your dog has a **tag with your contact details on it** (a mobile phone number would be best if you are carrying one with you); the fact that now all dogs in the UK have to be **microchipped** provides further security.

When to keep your dog on a lead

● **When crossing farmland**, particularly in the **lambing season** (around May) when your dog can scare the sheep, causing them to lose their young. Farmers are allowed by law to shoot at and kill any dogs that they consider are worrying their sheep. During lambing, most farmers would prefer it if you didn't bring your dog at all.

The exception to the dogs on leads rule is if your dog is being attacked by cows. A few years ago there were three deaths in the UK caused by walkers being trampled as they tried to rescue their dogs from the attentions of cattle. The advice in this instance is to let go of the lead, head speedily to a position of safety (usually the other side of the field gate or stile) and call your dog to you.

● **Around ground-nesting birds** It's important to keep your dog under control when crossing an area where certain species of birds nest on the ground. Most dogs love foraging around in the woods but make sure you have permission to do so; some woods are used as 'nurseries' for game birds and dogs are only allowed through them if they are on a lead.

● **On mountain tops** It's a sad fact that, every year, a few dogs lose their lives falling over the edge of steep slopes.

What to pack
You've probably already got a good idea of what to bring to keep your dog alive and happy, but the following is a checklist:

● **Food/water bowl** Foldable cloth bowls are popular with walkers, being light and taking up little room in the rucksack. You can get also get a water-bottle-and-bowl combination, where the bottle folds into a 'trough' from which the dog can drink.
● **Lead and collar** An extendable one is probably preferable for this sort of trip. Make sure both lead and collar are in good condition – you don't want either to snap on the trail, or you may end up carrying your dog through sheep fields until a replacement can be found.
● **Medication** You'll know if you need to bring any lotions or potions.
● **Bedding** A simple blanket may suffice, or you can opt for something more elaborate if you aren't carrying your own luggage.
● **Poo bags** Essential.
● **Hygiene wipes** For cleaning your dog after it's rolled in stuff.
● **A favourite toy** Helps prevent your dog from pining for the entire walk.
● **Food/water** Remember to bring treats as well as regular food to keep up the mutt's morale. That said, if your dog is anything like mine the chances are they'll spend most of the walk dining on rabbit droppings and sheep poo anyway.
● **Corkscrew stake** Available from camping or pet shops, this will help you to keep your dog secure in one place while you set up camp/doze.
● **Tick remover** See opposite.
● **Raingear** It can rain!
● **Old towels** For drying your dog.

When it comes to packing, I always leave an exterior pocket of my rucksack empty so I can put used poo bags in there (for deposit at the first bin). I always like to keep all the dog's kit together and separate from the other luggage (usually inside a plastic bag inside my rucksack). I have also seen several dogs sporting their own 'doggy rucksack', so they can carry their own food, water, poo etc – which certainly reduces the burden on their owner!

Cleaning up after your dog
It is extremely important that dog owners behave in a responsible way when walking the path. Dog excrement should be cleaned up. In towns, villages and fields where animals graze or which will be cut for silage, hay etc, you need to pick up and bag the excrement.

Staying with your dog
In this guide I have used the symbol 🐕 to denote where a **hotel, pub, or B&B** welcomes dogs. However, this always needs to be arranged in advance – many places have only one or two rooms suitable for people with dogs. In some cases dogs need to sleep in a separate building. Some places make an additional charge (usually per night but occasionally per stay) while others may require a deposit which is refundable if the dog doesn't make a mess.

Hostels (both YHA and independent) do not permit them unless they are an assistance (guide) dog.

Smaller **campsites** tend to accept dogs, but some of the larger holiday parks do not; look for the 🐕 symbol in the text.

When it comes to **eating**, most landlords allow dogs in at least a section of their pubs, though few cafés/restaurants do. Make sure you always ask first and ensure your dog doesn't run around the pub but is secured to your table or a radiator.

INDEX

Page references in **bold** type refer to maps

TRAILBLAZER TITLE LIST

Adventure Cycle-Touring Handbook
Adventure Motorcycling Handbook
Australia by Rail
Azerbaijan
Coast to Coast (British Walking Guide)
Cornwall Coast Path (British Walking Guide)
Corsica Trekking – GR20
Cotswold Way (British Walking Guide)
The Cyclist's Anthology
Dales Way (British Walking Guide)
Dorset & Sth Devon Coast Path (British Walking Gde)
Exmoor & Nth Devon Coast Path (British Walking Gde)
Great Glen Way (British Walking Guide) – due early 2017
Hadrian's Wall Path (British Walking Guide)
Himalaya by Bike – a route and planning guide
Inca Trail, Cusco & Machu Picchu
Japan by Rail
Kilimanjaro – the trekking guide (includes Mt Meru)
Moroccan Atlas – The Trekking Guide
Morocco Overland (4WD/motorcycle/mountainbike)
Nepal Trekking & The Great Himalaya Trail
New Zealand – The Great Walks
Offa's Dyke Path (British Walking Guide)
Overlanders' Handbook – worldwide driving guide
Peddars Way & Norfolk Coast Path (British Walking Gde)
Pembrokeshire Coast Path (British Walking Guide)
Pennine Way (British Walking Guide)
Peru's Cordilleras Blanca & Huayhuash – Hiking/Biking
The Railway Anthology
The Ridgeway (British Walking Guide)
Sahara Overland – a route and planning guide
Scottish Highlands – The Hillwalking Guide
Siberian BAM Guide – rail, rivers & road
The Silk Roads – a route and planning guide
Sinai – the trekking guide
South Downs Way (British Walking Guide)
Thames Path (British Walking Guide)
Tour du Mont Blanc
Trans-Canada Rail Guide
Trans-Siberian Handbook
Trekking in the Everest Region
The Walker's Anthology
The Walker's Anthology – further tales (due Aug 2016)
The Walker's Haute Route – Mont Blanc to Matterhorn
West Highland Way (British Walking Guide)

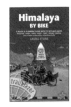

For more information about Trailblazer and our
expanding range of guides, for guidebook updates or
for credit card mail order sales visit our website:

www.trailblazer-guides.com

TRAILBLAZER'S LONG-DISTANCE PATH (LDP) WALKING GUIDES

We've applied to destinations which are closer to home Trailblazer's proven formula for publishing definitive practical route guides for adventurous travellers. Britain's network of long-distance trails enables the walker to explore some of the finest landscapes in the country's best walking areas. These are guides that are user-friendly, practical, informative and environmentally sensitive.

● **Unique mapping features** In many walking guidebooks the reader has to read a route description then try to relate it to the map. Our guides are much easier to use because walking directions, tricky junctions, places to stay and eat, points of interest and walking times are all written onto the maps themselves in the places to which they apply. With their uncluttered clarity, these are not general-purpose maps but fully edited maps drawn by walkers for walkers.

● **Largest-scale walking maps** At a scale of just under 1:20,000 (8cm or 3^1/$_8$ inches to one mile) the maps in these guides are bigger than even the most detailed British walking maps currently available in the shops.

● **Not just a trail guide – includes where to stay, where to eat and public transport** Our guidebooks cover the complete walking experience, not just the route. Accommodation options for all budgets are provided (pubs, hotels, B&Bs, campsites, bunkhouses, hostels) as well as places to eat. Detailed public transport information for all access points to each trail means that there are itineraries for all walkers, for hiking the entire route as well as for day or weekend walks.

Coast to Coast *Henry Stedman*, 7th edition, £11.99
ISBN 978-1-905864-74-4, 268pp, 110 maps, 40 colour photos

Cornwall Coast Path (SW Coast Path Pt 2) *Stedman & Newton*, 5th edition, £11.99
ISBN 978-1-905864-71-3, 3526pp, 142 maps, 40 colour photos

Cotswold Way *Tricia & Bob Hayne* 3rd edition, £11.99
ISBN 978-1-905864-70-6, 204pp, 53 maps, 40 colour photos

Dales Way *Henry Stedman* 1st edition, £11.99
ISBN 978-1-905864-78-2, 176pp, 45 maps, 40 colour photos

Dorset & South Devon (SW Coast Path Pt 3) *Stedman & Newton*, £11.99
ISBN 978-1-905864-45-4, 336pp, 88 maps, 40 colour photos

Exmoor & North Devon (SW Coast Path Pt I) *Stedman & Newton*, £11.99
ISBN 978-1-905864-43-0, 192pp, 68 maps, 40 colour photos

Great Glen Way *Jim Manthorpe*, 1st edition, £11.99 – due early 2017
ISBN 978-1-905864-80-5, 192pp, 55 maps, 40 colour photos

Hadrian's Wall Path *Henry Stedman*, 4th edition, £11.99
ISBN 978-1-905864-58-4, 224pp, 60 maps, 40 colour photos

Offa's Dyke Path *Keith Carter*, 4th edition, £11.99
ISBN 978-1-905864-65-2, 240pp, 98 maps, 40 colour photos

Peddars Way & Norfolk Coast Path *Alexander Stewart*, £11.99
ISBN 978-1-905864-28-7, 192pp, 54 maps, 40 colour photos

Pembrokeshire Coast Path *Jim Manthorpe*, 4th edition, £11.99
ISBN 978-1-905864-51-5, 224pp, 96 maps, 40 colour photos

Pennine Way *Stuart Greig*, 4th edition, £11.99
ISBN 978-1-905864-61-4, 272pp, 138 maps, 40 colour photos

The Ridgeway *Nick Hill*, 3rd edition, £11.99
ISBN 978-1-905864-40-9, 192pp, 53 maps, 40 colour photos

South Downs Way *Jim Manthorpe*, 5th edition, £11.99
ISBN 978-1-905864-66-9, 192pp, 60 maps, 40 colour photos

Thames Path *Joel Newton*, 1st edition, £11.99
ISBN 978-1-905864-64-5, 256pp, 99 maps, 40 colour photos

West Highland Way *Charlie Loram*, 6th edition, £11.99
ISBN 978-1-905864-76-8, 208pp, 60 maps, 40 colour photos

'The same
attention to detail
that
distinguishes
its other
guides has
been brought
to bear here'.
*THE
SUNDAY TIMES*

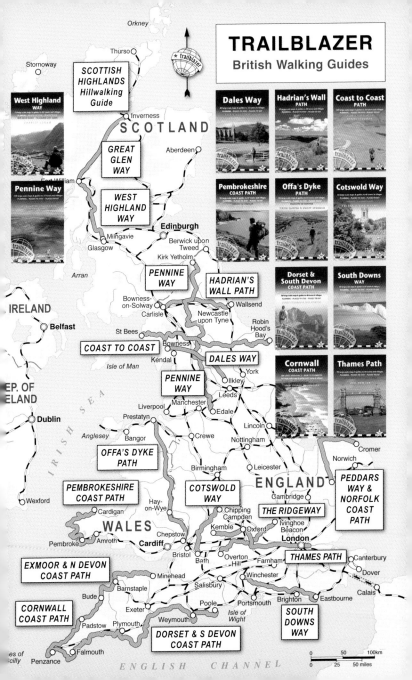

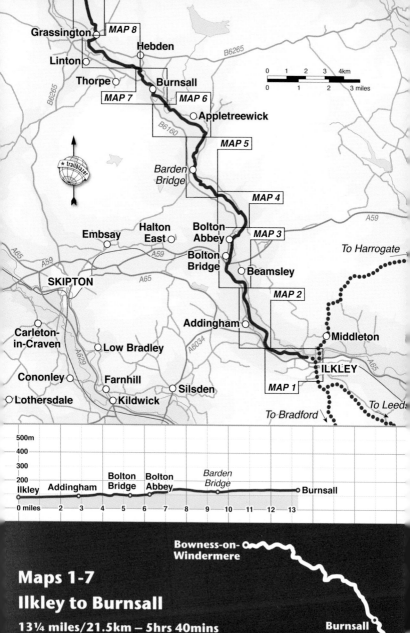

0   1   2   3   4km
0   1   2   3 miles

Grassington
Hebden
Linton
Thorpe
Burnsall
Appletreewick
Barden
Bridge
Embsay
Halton
East
Bolton
Abbey
Bolton
Bridge
Beamsley
SKIPTON
Carleton-
in-Craven
Low Bradley
Addingham
Middleton
Cononley
Farnhill
Silsden
Lothersdale
Kildwick
ILKLEY

To Harrogate
To Leeds
To Bradford

MAP 8
MAP 7
MAP 6
MAP 5
MAP 4
MAP 3
MAP 2
MAP 1

trailblazer

500m
400
300
200
Ilkley   Addingham   Bolton Bridge   Bolton Abbey   Barden Bridge   Burnsall
0 miles   2   3   4   5   6   7   8   9   10   11   12   13

Bowness-on-
Windermere

Burnsall

Ilk

Maps 1-7
Ilkley to Burnsall

13¼ miles/21.5km – 5hrs 40mins

NOTE: Add 20-30% to these times to allow for stops

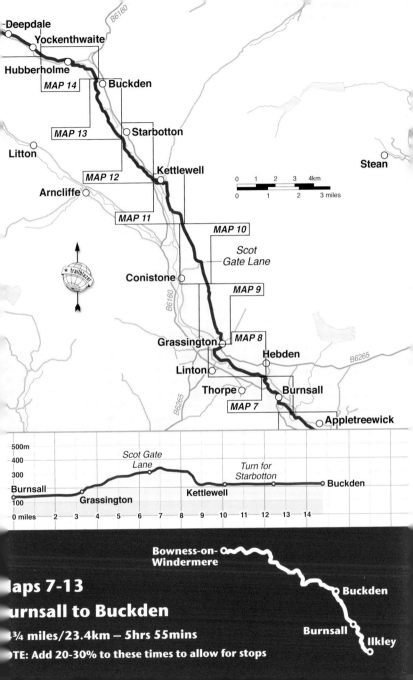

Deepdale

Yockenthwaite

Hubberholme

MAP 14

Buckden

MAP 13

Starbotton

Litton

MAP 12

Arncliffe

Kettlewell

MAP 11

Stean

0 1 2 3 4km
0 1 2 3 miles

MAP 10

Scot Gate Lane

Conistone

MAP 9

Grassington

MAP 8

Hebden

Linton

Thorpe

Burnsall

MAP 7

Appletreewick

500m
400
300
200
100

Scot Gate Lane

Turn for Starbotton

Burnsall

Grassington

Kettlewell

Buckden

0 miles 2 3 4 5 6 7 8 9 10 11 12 13 14

Bowness-on-Windermere

Buckden

Burnsall

Ilkley

Maps 7-13
Burnsall to Buckden

14¾ miles/23.4km – 5hrs 55mins

NOTE: Add 20-30% to these times to allow for stops

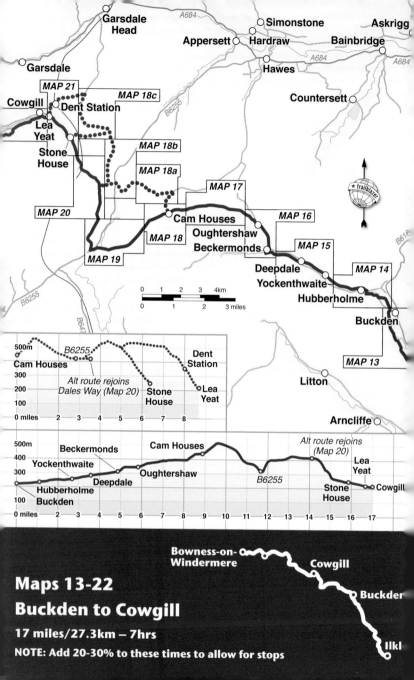

Maps 13-22
Buckden to Cowgill

17 miles/27.3km – 7hrs

NOTE: Add 20-30% to these times to allow for stops

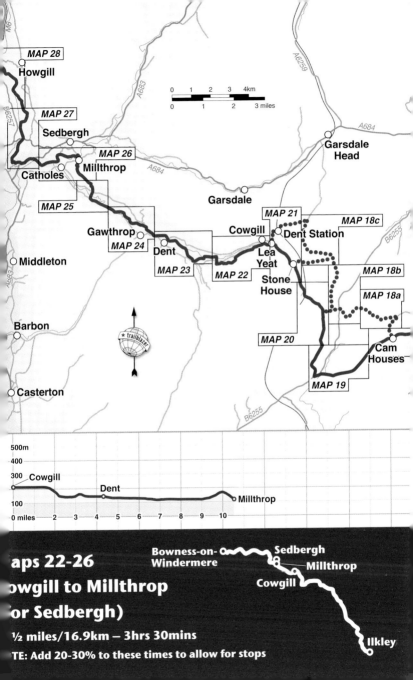

MAP 28
Howgill

MAP 27
Sedbergh

MAP 26
Millthrop

Catholes

MAP 25

Gawthrop

MAP 24
Dent

Middleton

MAP 23

MAP 22

Barbon

Casterton

Garsdale
Head

Garsdale

MAP 21
Cowgill
Dent Station

MAP 18c

Lea
Yeat

Stone
House

MAP 18b

MAP 18a

MAP 20

Cam
Houses

MAP 19

500m
400
300 Cowgill
        Dent
100   Millthrop
0 miles   2   3   4   5   6   7   8   9   10

Bowness-on-   Sedbergh
Windermere   Millthrop
                  Cowgill

aps 22-26

owgill to Millthrop

or Sedbergh)

½ miles/16.9km – 3hrs 30mins

TE: Add 20-30% to these times to allow for stops

Ilkley

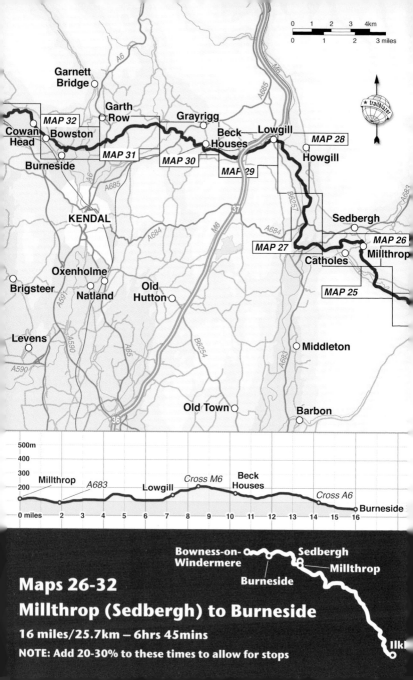

Garnett
Bridge ○

A6

M6

A685

A591

*Garth
Row ○

Grayrigg ○

Beck
Houses

Lowgill ○

MAP 28

Howgill ○

MAP 32
Cowan
Head ○
Bowston ○

MAP 31

MAP 30

MAP 29

B6257

Burneside ○

A6

A685

A684

M6

37

A684

Sedbergh ○

A683

KENDAL

A684

M6

MAP 27

Catholes ○

MAP 26
Millthrop ○

MAP 25

Oxenholme ○

Natland ○

Old
Hutton ○

Brigsteer ○

A591

A65

B6254

A683

Levens ○

A590

Middleton ○

Old Town ○

Barbon ○

36

0   1   2   3   4km
0   1   2   3 miles

★ trailblazer

500m
400
300
200

Millthrop   A683   Cross M6   Beck
                                                          Houses

Lowgill   Cross A6

                                                          Burneside

0 miles   2   3   4   5   6   7   8   9   10   11   12   13   14   15   16

Bowness-on-
Windermere ○——○

Sedbergh ○

Burneside ○

Millthrop ○

Ilkl

Maps 26-32
Millthrop (Sedbergh) to Burneside
16 miles/25.7km – 6hrs 45mins
NOTE: Add 20-30% to these times to allow for stops

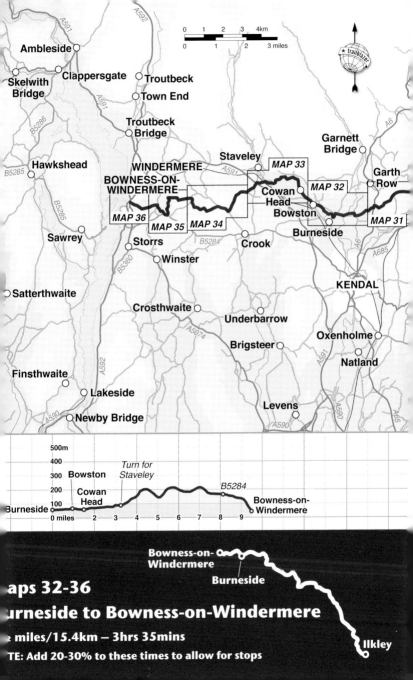

Maps 32-36

Burneside to Bowness-on-Windermere

9 miles/15.4km – 3hrs 35mins

NOTE: Add 20-30% to these times to allow for stops

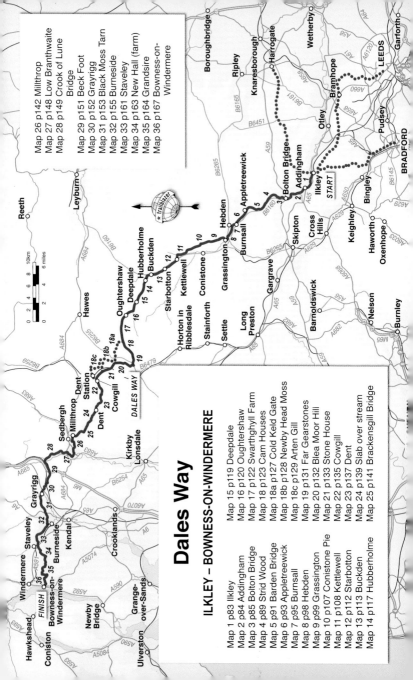

Dales Way

ILKLEY – BOWNESS-ON-WINDERMERE